OUR HOME

Memories of living and growing up in

The American Legion Children's Home

82 Years of Serving Children of Oklahoma Veterans

Barbra Mahorney Alusi

Candes,
Thank you for your love
and support.
Barbra Mahorney Alusi

Booklogix Publishing Services, Inc.
Alpharetta, Georgia.

Printed in the United States of America

ISBN 978-1-61005-007-4

If you would like to make a gift to the American Legion Children's Home, please call 866-941-0110 or visit the website www.americanlegionchildrenshome.org.

No donation is too large or too small.

A Special Thank You to all Veterans

In special memory of our American Legion Home School boys
who gave their lives in World War II for God and Country

Rubin Gooch ~ Alvia Minor ~ Porter Masters ~ Carl Reynolds ~ Elvis Reynolds

To Honor the Memory of

My good friend, Henry Duane Odom, from the Ponca Military Academy,
whom I met at the Church of Christ in Ponca City, Oklahoma.
He was a wonderful Christian from Eldorado, Oklahoma
who joined the United States Marines.
Born August 27, 1946, he died March 4, 1966 at age 19, a ground
casualty in Vietnam.
He gave his all.

The Printing of this Book Was Made Possible by a Grant from The American Legion Child Welfare

Program

American Legion Children's Home Grant Update

2008 marks our 80th year of service to children and our generous gift from the American Legion Child Welfare Foundation; we will be launching a campaign specifically designed to expand our ability to provide for more veterans' children. Currently, our Website is "under construction." Our Video/Commercial production is scheduled for early May and the writers are already busy creating a script. The remainder of the publisher's stock for the book written by our alumnus, Barbara Alusi, is on order. Our goal is to have the video and commercial completed before the American Legion National Convention so that we may show it at our booth. We are ecstatic to tell others about the amazing history and service which the American Legion has done for the past 8 decades and we look forward to continuing, enhancing and expanding this grand tradition as a sacred obligation to enable the wholesome growth and development of children.

In Loving Memory of

Mrs. Geneva Mayhue

Mr. & Mrs. Earl N. Summers

Lt. Col. T. L. Rider
First Graduate of
American Legion Children's Home

Special Dedication

*Goes to my loving husband, Thana, who has given me
the love and support to do these projects.
To my sons Safie, Demetrius, and Lee.
To my beautiful granddaughters Kai, Gillian, and Darby.
To April and Diane.*

*Barbra Alusi's Granddaughter
Kai Maisun Alusi*

*Barbra with her Granddaughters
Darby and Gillian*

Images by Rainy

Preface

During the time I spent arranging our first reunion of the Alumni of the American Legion Home School, now known as American Legion Children's Home, in August of 1983, I began to feel a strong bond between all of the graduates and ex-students. When we tried to share our past, I realized there were no records or pictures available to show that our lives at the Home had been a reality.

I began to work hard to research the history of the Home and to piece together information from individuals, newspaper articles and pictures that would tell a story that everyone who had lived or worked there could treasure. The task was not easy, but with persistence, the help of many kind and patient people (including my husband and children), lots of prayers and God's help, I knew it would be done.

I believe God gave me the courage to follow through with this project, and the opportunity to thank the American Legion and all the people who made it possible for me and many other children to have had such a marvelous place to live - a place we could all call "My Home."

It is now 2010, twenty-four years after the first printing of this story of the lives of the children who grew up in the American Legion Children's Home. We have all raised our families, lived our lives and matured to become "Senior" citizens. The world is a different place, but the memories of the years at the Home are still there. Some of those memories have become more precious as time passes.

I felt the urging by God the beginning of this year to revise the first book about the Home and to try and add more pictures and stories that weren't in the first book. Since the revision was begun the Home has experienced changes in their arrangement to accept funding and children placed by the State of Oklahoma. A law, which has laid dormant and unused, is threatening the future of the Home. Through God's perfect timing I hope this revision will allow the Home to spread the word about what a wonderful home this has been to so many of us and raise awareness and funding to keep this Home, the only one of its kind in America, open and serving children.

It has been my goal to preserve the stories, pictures and memories of even more alumni. There are many who are no longer here to share, but they are still a part of the story.

As always, this revision is a work of love from the heart with all proceeds going back to the Home. I am praying that my interpretation of God's will concerning this project is correct and His love is able to shine through.

Barbra Mahorney Alusi

Acknowledgements

Special recognition and thank you to the following organizations and individuals:

The Oklahoma American Legion
Ponca City American Legion
Stillwater American Legion and Auxiliary
National American Legion

The Ponca City News for keeping our history in print all of these years and for allowing me to use them in this book, without you we would have no written history or some of the great photos.

The Oklahoman for articles used in this book.

Carol Shultz Yocum for her loving support and editing.

Sallie Mahorney Bush for always loving me as only a big sister would and always saying I know you can.

Alice Grisso Coffman for her wonderful stories and willingness to share.
Lawrence Gregory for input of stories and loving support.

Bill Bailey for doing the genealogy of our alumni, staff, and Legion board members.

And my Home School sisters:
Diann Cowling, Sandy Brissel Jackson, Nancy Curnutte Butler, Linda Stewart Dundee, Susan Summers Marks, Rita Childers Hartzog, Mary Childers Bolding, Verda Evans Sisney, Grace Wilson Stroud, Darlene Wilson Tanner, Sherry Brissel Bean, Judya Mingus Garrison, Donna Willeford Haffner, Carol Stewart Free, Janice Franklin Neely, Glenda Grisso Barber.

Those Home School sisters who were with me in spirit as I tell our story, Beverly Wheeler Feathers, Donna Cowling Ellis, Linda Avon (Appleman) Thompson, Charlene Wilson Knight. Lavonne Lanter MacDonald.

Table of Contents

Introduction   xvii

Chapter One – How It Began   1

Chapter Two – A Gala Event   9

Chapter Three – T. L. Rider   35

Chapter Four – 'Santa Claus Plans Big Doings'   43

Chapter Five – More Billets and Improvements   59

Chapter Six – The ALCH Committee   75

Chapter Seven – How It was In the Beginning   87

Chapter Eight – House Parents   99

Chapter Nine – Sponsors   103

Chapter Ten – Biographies   107

Chapter Eleven – Scholarship Funds   131

Chapter Twelve – Busy Days at the Home School   135

Chapter Thirteen – Memories   139

Chapter Fourteen – Girls State   203

Chapter Fifteen – Norval Bryson   207

Chapter Sixteen – 1940's   209

Chapter Seventeen – 1950's   217

Chapter Eighteen – 1960's   227

Chapter Nineteen – Activities at the Home School   239

Chapter Twenty – Where are they Today?   253

From The Author – Mrs. Barbra Mahorney Alusi   259

Introduction

WRITTEN BY LAWRENCE GREGORY TO BARBRA MAHORNEY ALUSI

July 28, 2010

Barbra, you are loved and respected by so many of us even though some of us have never met you face to face; my message to you is the truth. Sometimes greatness is thrust upon one. Remember the story of "Moses." You and you alone started what could be referred to as a beautiful work of art, a "Tapestry of Human Lives" or "A Modern Joseph's Coat." By piecing together the history of the American Legion Children's Home, each of us alumni represents a patch on the coat that is used to complete this wonderful historical record, of man's struggle to become a part of an on-going thing we refer to as LIFE.

HISTORY

God certainly had a variety of individual materials to work with in this project. Each of us alumni has gone our own various ways and now contributes to this project as a whole. I am thrilled that this story is finally coming together. With the addition of each new alumnus we find, we are able to see how God in his wisdom was able to mold each of us into wonderful colorful patches (using people) for this Tapestry. This project is far from complete for new pieces are being added from time to time, and hopefully even more will be found and added.

All in all, there seems to be a ribbon of truth that is woven throughout this tapestry that seems to surface from time to time. That ribbon could be called the ribbon of love and admiration that we have for each other, and it seems to entwine itself in each of us regardless of the time we were part of the Home School experience. Our brief time at the Home allowed each of us to form lifetime bonds with each other that are only memories now, but when recalled, are as vivid as the time they took place. As I get older those memories are all I have left. Thank God for that place (the American Legion Home School), the place we all called Home and for all the brothers and sisters that made our lives while there worthwhile.

I for one, will never forget the wonderful friendships that were formed during those difficult times in our fragile youth... God Bless Each and Every One of You my alumni brothers and sisters.

Lawrence class of '56'

FROM THE DESK OF BILL ALEXANDER, EXECUTIVE DIRECTOR OF THE AMERICAN LEGION CHILDREN'S HOME

June 23, 2010

After 8 decades of service to our nation's heroes and approximately 8,000 of their children, grandchildren and siblings – after surviving the Great Depression – the one and ONLY American Legion Children's Home continues in the mission set forth by the WWI Veterans in 1928. This one-of-a-kind home still sits atop the highest hill in the city overlooking 100 acres of plush pasture and dense tree lines – right next to Lake Ponca. Meanwhile, staying true to its original mission, the ALCH is doing its part to ensure that these children will not go without the warm and loving home they deserve.

This legacy continues today as American Legion Posts, Units, Sons or Riders sponsor each child at the Home. The children are also encouraged to participate in veteran appreciation activities such as Veterans Day parades, the Homecoming festivities for the 45th Infantry Division, the flag raising ceremony on the 4th of July, and in on-site Americanism classes.

Currently, the Home includes 4 dormitories, lived in by 62 boys and girls from the ages of 11 – 18. Each dorm includes a study/game room, kitchenette and a large living area. It provides an on-campus school with Public School teachers, including art class and gym class in our recreation center, a game room, weight room, a baseball field, playground, barn and a pond for fishing.

ALCH welcomes visitors, as we love to show our beautiful campus. As well, the Home reflects the willingness of veterans and community leaders to step in and help children and their families in times of crisis.

Writer Pearl S. Buck once said, "If the American way of life fails the child, it fails us all." This unique American Legion Children's Home is determined not to fail the children.

For more information about the American Legion Children's Home, visit our website www.americanlegionchildrenshome.org.

EFFORT CONTINUING TO OFFSET LIMIT AT ALCH

By Beverly Bryant ~ News Staff Writer
Ponca City News ~ June 2010

The American Legion Children's Home "keeps taking three steps forward and two steps back" when it comes to dealing with a federal rule which limits the number of residents in a children's home to 16, Executive Director Bill Alexander said today.

Alexander said in May the rule has gone unnoticed since it went into effect in 1988, but the Oklahoma Department of Human Services had notified him it planned to enforce the rule and gave him time to develop a plan to meet the requirements.

"We are looking at several options to get the rule changed or to comply with it," Alexander said today.

"Our first option is to get an exemption from the rule," he said. "It's like the rule that you can't park a motor vehicle in front of a store in spaces reserved for horses, it's obsolete."

Alexander said he is not sure if the rule will ever be enforced. He has a meeting scheduled July 21 with state Sen. David Myers, U.S. Sen. Tom Coburn, U.S. Sen. Jim Inhofe, U.S. Rep. Frank Lucas, Department of Human Services Director Howard Hendrick and Oklahoma Health Care Authority Executive Director Mike Fogarty. "The meeting is to help us decide which route is the best for us to take," Alexander said. He said other states also are dealing with this issue restricting the number of children in group homes to 16.

"It's a bad rule and needs to be changed, but because it is tied to so many other issues, it probably will not be changed," Alexander said. "We need to have them tell us it's not going to be enforced."

Alexander said he recently returned from Beaumont, Texas, where he spoke to the Texas State Association of the American Legion, and Alexandria, La., where he spoke with the Louisiana Association. He said both groups have offered their support of the Children's Home. "We're getting the word out, but we don't know how to tell people to help us at this point," he said.

"We'll know more after our meeting July 21." Meanwhile, he said the home continues to look for additional funding sources to lessen the home's reliance on state and federal funding.

The American Legion

For God and country

★ NATIONAL HEADQUARTERS ★ P.O. BOX 1055 ★ INDIANAPOLIS, IN 46206-1055
★ (317) 630-1253 ★ Fax (317) 630-1368
Web Site: www.legion.org

**OFFICE OF THE
NATIONAL COMMANDER**

May 10, 2010

Mrs. Barbra Mahorney Alusi

Dear Mrs. Alusi:

The American Legion has been a staunch supporter of the children of our nation since its founding in 1919. Our commitment to youth is one of the Four Pillars of our organization.

Every generation of veterans knows that the key to the future of a free and prosperous country is held by the children of today. We have always supported strong values, assistance for children in need and activities that promote their healthy and wholesome development.

The American Legion Children's Home in Ponca City epitomizes that commitment. Since its founding in 1928, more than 8,000 young Americans have become members of that very special family that instilled in them the values of self worth, citizenship, honor and patriotism as they became young adults. During my visit, I had the pleasure of attending a moving awards ceremony and received a tour of the facility from a group of very special young people. It is clear to me that the commitment to these outstanding youth is being accomplished with enthusiasm, pride and professionalism.

On behalf of the 2.5 million military veterans who proudly call themselves American Legionnaires, I salute all those who have served in the past, and who work today, to ensure that The American Legion Children's Home continues its proud legacy of service to our nation's most precious resource – America's youth.

To each alumnus of ALCH, we are proud that you are – and will always be – a member of The American Legion family.

It is comforting to know that the American Legion Children's Home is there in Ponca City, always ready to carry out the promise that the founders of The American Legion made in 1919 – "A square deal for every child."

For God and country,

Clarence E. Hill

Clarence E. Hill
National Commander

The American Legion

OFFICE OF THE
NATIONAL ADJUTANT

★ NATIONAL HEADQUARTERS ★ P.O. BOX 1055 ★ INDIANAPOLIS, INDIANA 46206 ★
(317) 630-1200 ★ FAX (317) 630-1223 ★

May 6, 2010

Barbra Mahorney Alusi

Dear Mrs. Alusi:

The story you've shared of your years living at The American Legion Children's Home in Ponca City, Oklahoma, and the experience having such a meaningful impact it made on your life is indeed inspirational.

From the inception of The American Legion, children have been focal point of our work. Our Children & Youth Commission has three main objectives: to strengthen families; to support quality organizations that provide services to young people; and to maintain a well rounded program that meets the physical, intellectual, emotional and spiritual needs of young people. The Children's Home accomplishes that still today.

Permission is granted to use the name and emblem of The American Legion as part of the reprinting of the book on the history of The American Legion's Children's Home.

The National Commander and I applaud your efforts and wish you all the best in the new release of the book that shares a story of hope of a life changed.

Sincerely,

DANIEL S. WHEELER
National Adjutant

The Oklahoma American Legion Endowment Fund Corporation

It was on September 21, 1925 that the Oklahoma American Legion Endowment Fund Corporation was created. The need for rehabilitation work among the children of veterans of World War I became critical in Oklahoma and throughout the nation. Legionnaires realized that they must live up to the principle "Veterans assisting Veterans unable to help themselves."

The original money placed in the Fund came from contributions made by various American Legion Posts, Auxiliary Units, individual Legionnaires and Auxiliary members. From time to time additions have been made to improve the facilities.

The investment and management of the funds are under the control of a Board of Directors of nine members of the American Legion. The members have varied terms, with the Department Commander of the American Legion appointing three members each year. This method of selection makes the Board entirely free of undue influences from any group or individual. Its investments are made in accordance with the Board's judgment as to what are sound investments.

Provisions contained in the charter make the fund untouchable except for reinvestment. Only the increment may be spent. This is done by annually transferring the earnings to the American Legion Children's Home.

The need is still great, and the methods of handling the funds guarantee that the benefits of all contributions will go to help the children of men who helped defend this nation in its hour of need.

Chapter One

How It Began

In 1925 the National American Legion became concerned about the needy children of veterans of the World War. A plan was made to conduct a drive to raise $5,000,000 to provide help for these children. A quota of $75,000 was assigned to the state of Oklahoma. The story of how that money was collected in "ten hectic days" was told by Wesley I. Nunn, a long-time Legionnaire and former resident of Ponca City. This is his story:

"The Executive Committee of the Department of Oklahoma decided to have a prominent civilian leader as the chairman of the drive, and to have both a civilian leader and a veteran leader in each of the seventy-seven Counties. They decided to invite E.W. Marland, the State Commander, to be the chairman for the State. The Department Commander, Jim Hatcher of Chickasha, telephoned me to discuss how to approach him. I told him E.W. was at the Plaza Hotel in New York and helped him prepare a telegram of invitation. A couple of hours later, Jim phoned me again and read a telegram from Mr. Marland, which, in effect, said that he could not accept as he was out of the state a great deal of time and would not take on such a responsibility without being in a position to handle it properly.

Jim asked me what to do, "Give up or try again?" I told him to wire E.W. that the Legion had talked it all over with me, and I said that if Mr. Marland would accept the responsibility, I would guarantee to do everything necessary. This time E.W. accepted. So Jim, and his associates, and I began working out detailed plans to go after the seventy-five thousand dollars allotted for Oklahoma.

But, we were reckoning without the vision, foresight and generosity of Ponca City's outstanding citizens! When E.W. returned to Ponca City, he sent for me to discuss the drive. He asked me, "Wes, how many soldiers did Oklahoma have in the war?" "Ninety Thousand," I answered. Then he asked, "How many old soldiers are in the home in Ardmore?" "About Two Hundred," I told him.

Then the plan that E.W. had evolved in New York, after the exchange of telegrams, was revealed.

"Wes," he said, "when the Civil War was over, sixty years later, two hundred soldiers are in the home at Ardmore. With ninety thousand Oklahomans in the World War, think of the need for homes for old soldiers forty, fifty, sixty years from now!!! In the meantime there are probably many needy children of Oklahoma soldiers who were killed or incapacitated. So, why not NOW establish a home school for them which in the future years can be used as an old soldiers' home?"

As I struggled with his partly revealed idea, he went on, "Instead of just seventy-five thousand dollars for the National Legion, why not raise one hundred fifty thousand dollars, send the National their seventy-five thousand dollars and start our own home school with the other seventy-five thousand dollars. I will donate to the Legion of the state for the purpose one hundred twenty acres of valuable land, on a hill just beyond the Quadasita Club, and I will pay fifteen thousand dollars for the first billet. Also, I will see that Bill McFadden builds another billet at the same time.

I was thrilled, and without revealing the idea, telephoned Jim Hatcher to come to Ponca City at once for a meeting with Mr. Marland. Jim was thrilled too, and so were all the members of the committee.

We set a statewide goal of two hundred fifty thousand dollars and featured the Marland plan in the drive. I had a second desk and telephone installed in my office in the Marland Building for Jim Hatcher, the State Commander, and he and I jointly ran the drive from there – ten hectic days!! When it was all over we had nearly one hundred sixty thousand dollars cash. Seventy-five thousand dollars was sent to the National at Indianapolis, and plans were started for the Oklahoma project. Mr. Marland's sister, Mrs. Rittenhouse, conducted a survey that indicated that there were about five hundred children who might qualify.

Dr. McGregor of Mangum, a dedicated Legionnaire, and I together visited Mooseheart in Illinois for ideas – and reported back that the initial billets would cost – not fifteen thousand dollars but thirty-five thousand dollars each. Neither Mr. Marland nor Mr. McFadden batted an eye.

Everything took time, but on June 17, 1928 the American Legion Children's Home was officially opened in Ponca City with the Marland and McFadden billets, a capable staff of four, headed by Miss Jolly, a graduate of Orange Memorial Hospital and a nurse overseas during the World War. There was room then for only sixty kids.

After a couple of months of operation, E.W. asked me how much it cost each day for food for the boys, girls and the staff. As I now recall, it was about fifty-four cents.

He said "With ninety thousand veterans in Oklahoma, some of them are in the State Legislature; the Legislature could not refuse to pay the per diem cost for food, so the Legion should lose no time in making the request."

When I passed this thought on, the Legion acted promptly and so did the Legislature – both very favorably!

That is the "inside story" of why there is an American Legion Home School in Oklahoma – Ponca City! It is not important whether the facilities are used for "old soldiers" or for the needy children of soldiers. It is evident that the need for, the value of, the American Legion Children's Home will continue to increase!"

The Oklahoma City Legionnaire ~ May 1971

LEGION GOING FORWARD WITH ITS PLANS FOR CHILDREN'S HOME HERE

Ponca City News Sunday ~ January 8, 1928

STATE ORGANIZATION ASSISTED BY MRS. RITTENHOUSE AND MISS JOLLY IN PROMOTING PROGRAM FOR INSTITUTION TO BE LOCATED IN PONCA

Present indications are that the first two units of the "American Legion Home School," by which name the state Legion children's home here is to be known, will be completed and ready for occupancy by April 1 of this year. This is in accord with a recent announcement to Legion officials by Mrs. I. M. Rittenhouse of this city, "who is in charge of the state survey to ascertain the number of Legion children who will expect to be or who should be occupants of the home. It is anticipated that there are several hundred. The first two units will care for forty. It is known that the Officials desire that the first forty shall include the most deserving, or rather those who because of conditions should be taken care of first.

The site for the home, which eventually will be made up of numerous units is on a 100 acre tract, lying just east of the Marland game preserve here, and donated about two years ago by E.W. Marland, oil man of this city, to the State American Legion. State officials met here early in October; last announcement was made by William H. McFadden, Senior Vice President of the Marland Oil Company, that he would subscribe the necessary amount for the second unit's cost; if these two units that are to be constructed and completed by April 1.

OF SPANISH STYLE

The first unit, upon which work was started today, will be a Spanish style building of stucco and tile, similar to the Marland educational unit now under construction, and carrying out the general design of several Ponca City public and private buildings. It will provide "billet" quarters for 20 boys, in addition to dining hall, social and recreational rooms and quarters for the Housemother and other employees.

Mrs. I. M. Rittenhouse, sister of Mr. Marland, is working now upon a survey which she is helping the legion to conduct, to determine children who shall be admitted to the home when it begins functioning.

MRS. RITTENHOUSE

It was the time that announcement was made that Mrs. Rittenhouse, the sister of Mr. Marland, had agreed to work with the Legion in making a survey of the State to find needy children of ex-service men, and to aid in the administration of the home.

Mrs. Rittenhouse recently moved her residence from New York to Ponca City. She has had wide experience in child welfare work, and since coming to Ponca City a few months ago, has been very active both locally and throughout the State.

Mrs. Rittenhouse is making a comprehensive survey of Oklahoma to find the needy children of ex-service men, and determine which of the cases most worthy of the first two units are. It is estimated from only preliminary surveys that there are at least several hundred children in need of assistance.

It is expected that a list of the most worthy will be ready by the time the buildings are completed on April 1, and that the Home can begin functioning as soon as the doors are thrown open. Entire facilities of the State Legion have been offered to aid Mrs. Rittenhouse in the work.

TO COST $40,000 EACH

Each of the first two units is to cost approximately $30,000 without furnishings. Equipment and furnishings of all kinds; which also are to be furnished by the donors Mr. Marland and Mr. McFadden, are expected to bring the total cost of each unit to more than $40,000.

The buildings will be located to form part of an oval arrangement such as that on the campus of the University of Oklahoma at Norman. Future plans call for an Administration Building and other units as required. The site overlooks Ponca City and the Arkansas valley, and is declared by Legion officials to be a location of remarkable beauty.

Just to the east are the sites of the educational and recreational activities, which the Marland Oil Company is providing at a cost of three quarters of a million dollars. The grounds of the Rock Cliff Country club and of the modern Boy Scouts camping site will be provided by I. H. Wentz, the oil man.

Mrs. Rittenhouse is chairman of child welfare work for the state, and also from New Jersey. Mrs. Rittenhouse came to Ponca City during the past year following the death of her sister Miss Charlotte Marland. She took over the latter's home and then secured Miss Jolly's services as an Assistant. Both have been active recently in the organization and promotion of the State League of Women Voters.

MARLAND UNIT OF LEGION HOME AWARDED ON CONTRACT TO TULSA FIRM, WORK GETS UNDER WAY

Ponca City News ~ Thursday ~ February 2, 1928

IS FIRST OF EXTENSIVE PLANT SOON TO BE PLACED UNDER WAY HERE McFADDEN WILL BUILD SECOND BUILDING

Losing no time after receiving a contract late Wednesday, the Shallenberger Construction Company of Tulsa this morning started building the first unit of the American Legion's Oklahoma Home for the needy children of ex-service men, east of the Marland game refuge.

The first unit in the statewide program, the gift of E. W. Marland, was left to the Shallenberger Company yesterday on contract, J. Duncan Forsythe, Architect of the Forsythe Corporation, announced. The contract price for the building was not given.

FIRST ON THE BIG PROGRAM

Beginning of work on the Marland unit marks the first step in a program which will eventually build a large home, caring for both boys and girls, and program announced last fall when the State Executive Committee of the Legion conferred with Mr. Marland, W. H. McFadden, then Senior Vice President of the Marland companies, and local legion officials. It was said at that the work on the Marland unit for boys and a second to be built by Mr. McFadden building are being prepared by Mr. Forsythe.

Work on the Administration Building and other units will go forward when the legion has raised a promised sum of money to put with the Marland and McFadden donations.

LEGION PLANS ADDITIONS TO HOME SCHOOL ADMINISTRATION UNIT IS UNDERSTOOD NEXT ON PROGRAM COSTS ABOUT $100,000 MAY ADD KINDERGARTEN AND HOSPITAL

Construction of an Administration Building, with possibly a small kindergarten and small hospital unit adjoining it on either side, probably will be the next move of the American Legion of Oklahoma for the Home School for the dependent children of World War veterans, located here.

George Davis, Department Commander; Frank A Douglass, past Department Commander and Ted Petit, Department Adjutant, held a conference Friday with local legion officers and members of the State Executive Committee, and plans for the new unit were taken under advisement.

E. W. Marland, who headed the recent state drive for funds with which to build and equip the Home School here, attended the conference.

The Administration Building is now definitely to be the next building planned, although the Home School also has need of more billets similar to the ones dedicated here this summer, to house the children for whom admittance to the home is sought.

THE J. DUNCAN FORSYTHE CORPORATION IS AT WORK ON PLANS FOR THE NEW BUILDING

Approximately the cost of the new unit; exclusive of the hospital and kindergarten buildings, is set at about $100,000. It is expected that at least two Oklahomans, who have indicated a willingness to cooperate with the Legion in its program for the school, may add the two smaller units when the building plans get underway.

Quarters for the Home School staff would be maintained in the Administration Building, under present plans.

It has been indicated unofficially that the Legion plans to build the various units of the home, and will ask the State for some appropriation toward maintaining it once the project nears completion.

A CENSUS OF THE CHILDREN STARTING FROM THE BEGINNING

June 24, 1928   40 (20 girls 20 boys)
        1930   56
        1935   103

In 1935 was the first time that all kids went to public schools - out of the 103 kids, 73 went to Roosevelt grade school. 24 went to Junior High.
6 went to Senior High school.

May 2 1938   102
June 14 1942   117
February 1948   115
March 7 1965   105

These numbers are validated from the news articles.

Chapter Two

A Gala Event

E. W. MARLAND

There was a lot of excitement in Ponca City in the early part of 1928. Many people were getting ready for a gala opening of the American Legion Home School. They were expecting thousands of very important people from all over the United States as well as the state of Oklahoma.

Perhaps the most important was a man from Ponca City. E.W. Marland, President of the Marland Oil Company, had been chairman of a drive for money that would help needy children all over the United States – children of disabled or deceased veterans of wartime service. Mr. Marland encouraged the people of Oklahoma to create an endowment fund that would be used to support a home for the children of Veterans of Oklahoma. To get the drive started, he donated 120 acres of land to be used for the home, and gave enough money to build the first billet.

W. H. McFADDEN

Another key figure who was expected to be seen at the Grand Opening was W.H. McFadden, Vice President of the Marland Oil Company. He had followed the lead of Mr. Marland and had given enough money for a second billet. The buildings were to be located on a site at the edge of Ponca City, overlooking the Arkansas River Valley. They were to be ready for open house and dedication on June 17, 1928.

On February 1, 1928 a contract was signed by the Shallenberger Construction Company of Tulsa. The next day they started to build the first unit with plans that were made by Duncan Forsythe, an architect for the Forsythe Corporation. That building was to be the Marland Billet and was to have a Spanish style of stucco and tile, carrying out the general design of several public buildings in Ponca City. It was to provide "billet" quarters for 20 boys in addition to a dining hall, social and recreational rooms and quarters for the housemother and other employees. The second building was to be similar on the inside with slight differences in the outside design. The McFadden billet was to be quarters for 20 girls.

MRS. I. M. RITTENHOUSE

While construction was progressing, there was a lot of research to be done to find 40 children who would qualify to be the first residents of the Home. Mrs. I. M. Rittenhouse, sister of Mr. Marland, agreed to work with the Legion in making a survey of the state to find needy children of ex-servicemen and aid in the administration of the Home. The study showed that several hundred children were in need of assistance, but the big task would be to limit the list to the most worthy and no more than forty for the first two units that would be ready by April first.

MISS R. M. JOLLY

Mrs. Rittenhouse had recently moved her residence from New York to Ponca City. She had wide experience in child welfare work. Assisting Mrs. Rittenhouse in the survey for the Legion was Miss R.M. Jolly, a friend for many years. She had been a nurse in the English army during the World War. After the war was over she came to America and did child welfare work with Mrs. Rittenhouse in New York and New Jersey.

MISS RUTH DEWBERRY

It was decided that Miss Jolly would be the director in charge of the Home, and one of her helpers would be Miss Ruth Dewberry, who was a graduate of Barnard College and did post graduate work at Oxford University. She was to be in charge of kindergarten work. Also helping would be Mrs. Pearl Marks. All of the ladies had experience in child welfare work.

All was ready when the big day came for the dedication. Twenty thousand people were expected to attend. *The Ponca City News* pointed out that, "A crowd such perhaps never before assembled in the State to fund homes to children," and gave credit to two Ponca City men, "E.W. Marland and W.H. McFadden, whose foresight and generosity made it all possible."

FRANK P. DOUGLAS

Mr. Marland presented to Frank P. Douglas, Commander of the Oklahoma Department of the American Legion, the deed to the site and the two residences, which are on land that joins another part of the Marland Estate. The Legion commander accepted the property and then introduced W. J. Holloway, Lieutenant Governor of Oklahoma, who made a formal address about the significance of the occasion.

The program was broadcast over radio station WBBZ from the site of the two billets; and Jim Hatcher, former Commander presided.

JIM HATCHER

Mrs. W. R. Marlin of Pawnee, who was President of the Women's Auxiliary of the American Legion Department of Oklahoma, made an address in which she expressed pride in the Child Welfare Program of the Legion, and pledged the giving of a "mother's loving care to help administer the Home School, the auxiliary holding it," she said, "as a sacred trust."

The Enid National Guard Band gave a concert before the ceremonies began and again at the end of the service. Entertainment was furnished by members of the all-Indian post of the American Legion at White Eagle, in full regalia, and the Chilocco National Guard Troop composed of Indian boys directed traffic for the thousands of cars.

After the formal dedication, guests were invited to tour the new buildings. Both buildings were designed and furnished as comfortable homes for the children. The rooms were described as being large, sunshiny and cool, having plenty of room for children to play. A large porch across the east side of the Marland Billet also provided a cool play area for the children.

Throughout the billets the best of taste was used in selecting the furnishings and decorations. Warm browns, blues and greens were the predominant colors.

On the ground floor of the Marland Billet there was a large drawing room extending the entire length of the south side. That room had red and green leather upholstered furniture, with dark brown oak tables and parchment shaded lamps.

Off from the drawing room on the east was a dining room containing small green topped tables with brown oak chairs.

The kitchen was decorated in white with built-in cabinets all around the room. There was a large gas range and an electric icebox.

THE MARLAND BILLET IN 1932

There were two bedrooms downstairs, furnished in dark oak, with brilliant colored curtains and cream tinted walls. One room had three baby cribs. Upstairs there were four bedrooms. Each room was furnished with little individual beds, chifferobes, a dresser and small desks - all in dark oak. Three of the bedrooms were large enough to have five beds, while the room on the east had only three beds. The beds were covered with brilliantly pieced quilts which were made by various American Legion Auxiliary units of the State.

Several businesses had presented greetings of large baskets of flowers which decorated the rooms for that special day.

The forty children were there to meet the guests. They mixed in with the crowd, stopping to talk with anyone who would listen. One tow-headed youngster said he had moved in just the week before. "How do you like it here?" he was asked. His answer was direct, without hesitation. "Mister, they sure do feed good!"

THE McFADDEN BILLET IN 1932

The general feeling that day was that Marland had accomplished the results he wanted. He was determined it was to be a Home – not an Institution.

The aim of the American Legion was to provide and maintain for the children a comfortable and well ordered home life in suitable surroundings, sound moral and religious training, education in public schools, training in citizenship and love of their country.

OKLAHOMA HAS THOUSANDS AT SERVICES HERE

The Ponca City News ~ Monday ~ June 18, 1928

AMERICAN LEGION DEDICATES TWO BILLETS OF NEW HOME
MARLAND TENDERS DEED AND
COMMANDER DOUGLASS ACCEPTS PROPERTY

Oklahoma viewed the concrete symbols of the American Legion's child welfare work in this State here Sunday and called them good.

A crowd such as perhaps never before assembled in the state to do honor to children attended the dedication of the first two billets of the Legion Home School, and gave credit to two Ponca City men, E. W. Marland and W. H. McFadden, whose foresight and generosity have made possible the beginning of an estate which eventually will care for possibly several hundred children, the dependents of Oklahoma men who either were disabled or gave their lives in the World War.

Mr. Marland presented to Frank P. Douglas, Commander of the Oklahoma Department of the Legion, the deed to the site and the two residences, which are on land immediately adjoining other portions of the Marland estate. The Legion Commander accepted the property, paid his thanks and left W. J. Holloway, Lieutenant - Governor, the task of making the formal address outlining the significance of the occasion.

The program was carried out and broadcast over radio station WBBZ from the site of the two billets, northeast of town. Jim Hatcher, former Department Commander, presided.

Mr. Marland pointed out in his talk that there are now facilities to care for 40 children - 20 boys and the same number of girls and declared that "it is our duty, and it should be our pleasure, to be able to care for ten times that number two years from now."

"I have never found Oklahoma slow to respond to a cause of this kind," he said. "You folks who are here from over the State tell your home communities of these children; tell them, not what you heard from this platform, but what you saw. Your children may never need such a home as this but you don't know. We have two buildings for these children here today; let's have 20 such buildings two years from now."

PRAISES CHIEF AIDE

"When I first decided to build a building which would house 20 little boys," Mr. Marland continued, "I went to an old friend and said, I'd like to have you build one of these buildings, it's a home for 20 girls. It will cost, 'never mind what it costs, I'll build it,' Bill McFadden said, and today we have two of these buildings ready for the children." Mr. Marland declared that "Oklahoma needs more McFaddens" to carry on the Home School project which has been started here. He then presented to Douglas the deed to the site, and received the commander's expression of gratitude from the American Legion.

'Child Welfare Greatest Work,' declaring that "the greatest work of charity in Oklahoma today is the Child Welfare Program of the American Legion," Douglas thanked Mr. Marland and Mr. McFadden for their part in "making this wonderful dream come true. The legion members," he said, "have been earnest in our desire and prayerful in our hearts that such a project as a Home School could be carried out for children of men who saw service in the war."

"These kiddies are kiddies of soldiers of the World War. They had nothing to do with that conflict, but they must make a part of the sacrifice of that war. It would be the most unpatriotic thing in the world to leave them by the side of the road of life, alone; it would be the most unpatriotic thing in the world to leave a realization that their father's sacrifice was not appreciated," Douglas said.

He gave to the children the pledge that the American Legion is going to care for them until they are able to care for themselves.

IT'S UP TO THE STATE

Mr. McFadden was called upon, and declared that he and Wesley I. Nunn and others who have been active in pushing through the Home School projects to its present stage were the Lieutenants of Mr. Marland in the project.

"Mr. Marland furnished the inspiration, and nobody could refuse Mr. Marland when he becomes inspired," he said. "Everything that we have done has been to show our faith in him." His remarks drew prolonged applause. "God Almighty and nature have done so much for this state, and the people themselves so little, it is time for the residents of the State to begin to do their part," Mr. McFadden concluded.

AUXILIARY HEAD SPEAKS

Mrs. W. R. Martin of Pawnee, State President of the American Legion Auxiliary, expressed that organization's pride in the Child -Welfare Program of the Legion, and pledged the giving of "a mother's loving care" to help administer the Home School, the auxiliary holding it, she said, as "a sacred trust."

Unstinted praise to Mr. Marland and Mr. McFadden, and a hope that other wealthy men of Oklahoma would assist in the construction of further units of the Home School, were expressed by Holloway, Lieutenant Governor.

"When I was a boy, I longed for wealth. Mr. Marland has wealth, and I say that when any man's wealth is used for a good purpose such as this, that man is a good man."

Holloway declared that while "God had been good to E. W. Marland and W. H. McFadden, there are many other men in Oklahoma to whom God has been good, who don't realize fully the responsibilities of their citizenship. I only hope Ponca City, Kay County and the northern part of Oklahoma appreciate these men for their true worth, as do other communities of the State."

"The only way to appraise a situation of this kind is to bring it home to you. It matters not how humble the station of any of us, it is our duty to do all we can for these little fellows."

Holloway said that the Legion looks to E. W. Marland frequently for counsel and help and declared it had never been refused. "There are a hundred others in the State who enjoy immense wealth, but who are not willing to come forth and take leadership in a project of this kind," he declared.

Holloway expressed the hope that the day will come when all citizens, "wealthy or of more moderate circumstance, will come to recognize their duty to these angels on earth, and will be willing to discharge their part of their duty to the orphan or dependent child of the man who was willing to make the supreme sacrifice in France."

Rev. John A. Callan of Chickasha, Department Chaplain of the American Legion, opened with a prayer followed by the field services held Sunday morning at the site.

"Suffer little children to come unto me and forbid them not, for such is the kingdom of heaven, as spoken by the Lord so long ago, is still as applicable as in the Savior's day," he said.

"The greatest assets we have are our children, the men and women of tomorrow. Their value is immense, as our greatest values are determined by humanity. They have youth that is worth of the greatest development we can offer, and by the home school made possible here through the American Legion, a two-fold purpose is served, humanitarian and beneficent. It means much to the future that this is established."

"The children who will make their homes here are the children of dead or disabled soldiers. Their fathers stood between the flag and enemy bullets. They did not shirk their task and gladly made the greatest sacrifices possible for human beings to make; they laid down their lives for their Country."

"We recognize the children's right to enjoy the best life has to offer. We are here to offer what we can toward their welfare and happiness. We will stand by them, and it is in the name of the American Legion that we pledge ourselves to care for them."

The field service was followed by a song service by the assembly with music by the Enid National Guard band.

MANY SEND TELEGRAMS

The ceremony concluded with the exception of the benediction. Chairman Hatcher read several telegrams, sent to convey the best wishes of other legion officials and posts for the success of the dedication program.

These included a wire from Maywood, ILL post; one from Harold Janeway, former state adjutant.

"THEY SURE DO FEED GOOD" SAYS TOW-HEAD AT OPENING OF AMERICAN LEGION HOME

Ponca City News ~ Monday ~ June 18, 1928

He probably had never had a square meal of real food before in his life. He was a tow-headed urchin, one of the youngsters who moved last week into the American Legion Home School, formal opening and dedication of which was held here Sunday.

"How do you like it here," he was asked. His answer was direct, without hesitation, "Mister, they sure do feed good!"

Undoubtedly there were many others equally as impressed by the culinary capability of the Home School cooks as was our tow-headed friend. Through the glass door of the oven in the big range in the kitchen of the Marland billet could be seen a big roaster containing a chicken, browned to a King's taste. "Doesn't it look good?" was the usual comment.

"I thought Bill Holloway was an honest Lieutenant-Governor," commented W. H. McFadden "but he stole my hat." The comment was voiced after the program when, after searching for several minutes for his leghorn, he found only one hat on the speaker's platform, with the initials "W. K. H." - W. J. Holloway in the band. McFadden caught Holloway just as the latter entered E. W. Marland's car, preparing to leave the Home School, and 'swapped' hats with him.

Incidentally, friends of Holloway aver that it's a good thing he recovered his own hat, because he may be induced to throw it into the gubernatorial ring at the next election.

There was at least one of the young residents of the Home School who was not impressed by the ceremony of the dedication, and the thousands who visited the Marland billet. A tiny curly headed blond child she was and o-so sleepy. She pulled a chair up to a table in the center of the room, laid her head on the table and slept soundly while the throng of visitors milled around her.

One of the features of the program for Oklahoma newspapermen who were guests of the American Legion and of Miller brothers at a buffalo barbecue banquet Saturday night at the 101 Ranch were miniature terrapins, posting 50 cents each to make up the purse. Manager of the ranch, Bill Brooks was the judge.

DO THEY LIKE THEIR BENEFACTORS? WELL, LOOK HERE!

Ponca City News ~ Sunday ~ June 24, 1928

LEGION BILLETS BUILT A COMFORTABLE HOME FOR CHILD OCCUPANTS

SPACIOUS DINING AND LIVING ROOMS ADEQUATE KITCHEN AND BEDROOM FACILITIES ARE AMONG FEATURES OF HOME SCHOOL QUARTERS

The American Legion billets, formally dedicated last Sunday, are designed and furnished primarily as comfortable homes for children. From top to bottom in every small detail the comfort of the 40 children who are to make their homes in the billets has been taken into consideration.

The Marland billet was the first unit of the American Legion Home School to be completed. The McFadden billet, although a little different on the exterior is practically the same as the Marland billet on the interior.

Both buildings are of Spanish design, stucco and tile and are of fireproof construction. The rooms are large, sunshiny and cool, having plenty of room for the children to run and play. A large porch across the east side of the billet also offers a cool playground for the children.

Throughout the billets the best of taste has been used in selecting the furnishings and decorations. Warm brown, blues and greens predominate in the color schemes making the billets extremely cheerful and homelike.

LIVING ROOM LARGE

On the ground floor of the Marland billet there is a large drawing room extending practically the entire length of the south side of the building. The room is furnished in red and green leather upholstered furniture, with dark brown oak tables and parchment shaded lamps.

Off from the drawing room on the east is a dining room, containing small green topped tables with brown oak chairs.

The kitchen is decorated in white with built in cabinets surrounding the entire room. There is a large gas range and an electric ice box included in the equipment.

There are two bed rooms on the ground floor, both furnished in dark oak, with brilliant colored hangings and cream tinted walls. One room contains three cribs for babies.

UPSTAIRS IS ATTRACTIVE

On the upper floor there are four bedrooms for the orphans. Each room is furnished with little individual beds, chifferobes, one dresser and small desks. The furniture is all in dark oak.

Three of the bedrooms in the billet are large enough to accommodate five beds each, while one room on the east side only contains three beds. A number of the small beds were covered with brilliantly pieced quilts, furnished by various American Legion Auxiliary units of the state.

The bathroom is all furnished in white, with shower baths for the children. Floors throughout the place are stained a dark oak but are not polished.

CROWDS INSPECTED BILLETS

A continuous stream of people poured through the billets Sunday about 5 o'clock in the evening inspecting the rooms, which were decorated with large baskets of flowers donated by various firms here.

The 40 children living in the home seemed to enjoy the occasion of the dedication immensely. They darted here and there throughout the crowd stopping to talk to any of the guests who cared to enter into conversation. All sorts and types were represented from blond-haired chubby youngsters smiling continuously to quiet little persons with solemn dark brown eyes. A number went through the house absolutely undisturbed by the noise and confusion occasioned by the numerous visitors. One little girl sat on her bed and played with a doll throughout the entire afternoon.

SOME OF THE FIRST OCCUPANTS OF THE HOME SCHOOL AND THEIR BENEFACTORS IN 1928

FRONT ROW: PORTER MASTERS, HOLDING HIS LITTLE BROTHER, PAUL ~ ROBERT WILSON AND SISTER, JOSIE

SECOND ROW: LEON "JIGGY" RIDER ~ T. L. RIDER ~ PAUL JACKSON ~ SIDNEY MARKS ~ LELAND HARDER
JULIUS MARKS ~ LESTER GATTIS

BACK ROW: ELMER GATTIS ~ E.W. MARLAND ~ JUNIOR RIDER AND W. H. MCFADDEN HOLDING JOHNNY MARKS

MR. MARLAND AND SOME OF HIS LEGION CHILDREN IN 1928

BACK ROW: ELMER GATTIS ~ E. W. MARLAND HOLDING JOSIE WILSON AND PAUL MASTERS

FRONT ROW: JULIUS MARKS ~ ROBERT WILSON ~ SIDNEY MARKS ~ PAUL JACKSON ~ JUNIOR RIDER

PROGRAM DEDICATION AND FORMAL OPENING OF THE AMERICAN LEGION HOME SCHOOL

PROGRAM

* *

10:30 A. M.—Field Service, conducted by Rev. John A. Callan, of Chickasha, Department Chaplain of the American Legion. Song Service, with music by the Enid National Guard Band.

11 A. M. to 12 Noon—Marland Estate opened to all visitors. Ponca City Churches have arranged special services today, in observance of the American Legion Home School dedication, and all visitors are invited to attend the church of their choice.

12 to 1 P. M.—Lunch Hour.

1 to 2 P. M.—Sacred Concert by the National Guard Band of Enid.

2 P. M.—Dedication Program:

Invocation—Rev. John A. Callan, Department Chaplain.

Song—"Star-Spangled Banner."

Introduction of E. W. Marland and W. H. McFadden, donors of the first two billets of the American Legion Home School.

Presentation of deed to American Legion Home School site and billets by Mr. Marland to Frank P. Douglass, Department Commander.

Acceptance of deed by Commander Frank P. Douglass for the American Legion.

Address by Mrs. W. R. Marlin, of Pawnee, president of the Women's Auxiliary of the American Legion, Department of Oklahoma.

Address by Lieutenant Governor W. J. Holloway.

Benediction, Rev. Harry Lee Virden, chaplain of Nile Huff Post of the American Legion, Ponca City.

"America"—Enid National Guard Band.

3:30 P. M.—Polo Game, Ponca City Reds vs. Ponca City Blues, Lake Park Field, across the road west of the Marland Estate.

* *

(The Marland Estate will be open to visitors throughout the day with members of the All-Indian National Guard Company, of the Chilocco Indian School, acting as guides.

Back Page

The

AMERICAN LEGION HOME SCHOOL

PONCA CITY, OKLAHOMA

DEDICATION AND FORMAL OPENING

———

Sunday, June 17, 1928

———

E. W. MARLAND
Chairman Dedication Committee

Front Page

PROGRAM DEDICATION AND FORMAL OPENING OF
THE AMERICAN LEGION HOME SCHOOL

E. W. MARLAND   W. H. McFADDEN

TRUE benefactors of the American Legion are E. W. Marland and W. H. McFadden, whose generosity makes possible the opening of the first units of the American Legion Home School, for dependent children of Oklahoma boys who were killed or disabled during the World war.

Mr. Marland, who was chairman of the American Legion Endowment Fund campaign of June, 1925, has been the outstanding worker toward establishment of the Home School. After directing the successful campaign, he contributed the 120-acre site for the school, and then donated the cost of the first billet. He has also furnished both billets.

Mr. McFadden, who has for many years been active in child welfare work, contributed the cost of the second billet. He also established Camp McFadden, for Ponca City Campfire Girls, and it is there that girls in the Home School will spend a two-week vacation this summer.

The Marland and McFadden billets each represent an investment of more than $40,000.

UNSELFISH CO-OPERATION MARKS WORK FOR OPENING HOME SCHOOL

* *

THE Marland billet, the first unit of the American Legion Home School to be completed, is pictured at the bottom of this page. Although there is a slight difference in the exterior design of the Marland and McFadden billets, the interiors are the same, and each provides the utmost in efficiency and comfort. Both buildings are of Spanish design, stucco and tile, and of fireproof construction.

Each of the billets will provide a cheerful, comfortable home for 20 children. Already these 40 children are installed in the two billets, knowing greater happiness than they have probably ever experienced in the past.

But these 40 children are only a small per cent of those eligible to enter the Home School. The recent survey shows that there are more than 500 dependent children of Oklahoma ex-service men in destitute circumstances. Those already enrolled

PROGRAM DEDICATION AND FORMAL OPENING OF
THE AMERICAN LEGION HOME SCHOOL

were selected on the basis of the most urgent need, but many others are in dire circumstances.

Plans anticipate caring for every needy child of every ex-service man in Oklahoma. It is a gigantic program, and every citizen of Oklahoma—and surely every member of the American Legion—should have an active part in that program.

MRS. I. M. RITTENHOUSE

Characteristic of the spirit that marked American activity in the World war, unselfish co-operation has been extended in the work necessary to opening these first two units of the Home School.

Outstanding work has been done by Mrs. I. M. Rittenhouse, sister of Mr. Marland, and Miss R. M. Jolly, who will be director in charge of the institution. They accomplished much during the needy children survey in giving the American Legion a real picture of the organization's duty—and the duty of every citizen of Oklahoma—toward these unfortunates who are suffering because of war sacrifice.

Work of Jim Hatcher and Wesley I. Nunn, during the early days when the Home School was visioned, of Commander Frank P. Douglass and Adjutant Petit in handling the great mass of detail incidental to the actual opening of the Home School, of Tom Gammie, Howard Drake, A. W. Horton and A. L. Schall in completing the organization at Ponca City—all have contributed unstintingly to this great project. Dr. Frank McGregor served faithfully.

The Legion Auxiliary has again proved its worth to the Legion, its president, Mrs. W. R. Marlin and her entire organization having worked untiringly.

There are others who contributed much, but these can be numbered only by the measure of co-operation sought by the American Legion, for every one drafted did more than his share.

The American Legion is grateful—and we know these 40 children, our wards, are grateful, too.

MISS R. M. JOLLY

MISS RUTH DEWBERRY

MRS. PEARL MARKS

MRS. JESSIE HOBBS

HERE are the four women who will mother the 40 children of the American Legion Home School. Miss Jolly is a graduate of Orange Memorial Hospital and was a nurse overseas during the World war. Miss Dewberry, who is a graduate of Barnard College, and had postgraduate work at Oxford University, will be in charge of kindergarten work. Mrs. Marks will be assistant in the boys' dormitory, while Mrs. Hobbs will assist with the kindergarten work. All are experienced in child welfare work.

PROGRAM DEDICATION AND FORMAL OPENING OF
THE AMERICAN LEGION HOME SCHOOL

FOR THE CHILDREN OF TODAY— OLD SOLDIERS OF TOMORROW

* *

OKLAHOMA'S responsibility toward the children of ex-service men—men who were killed or disabled during the World war—is one that demands immediate attention. Several hundred ragged and undernourished youngsters have the right to a better chance, the chance to become healthy, happy, intelligent citizens.

But the vision that is coupled with the establishment of the American Legion Home School has looked beyond the immediate need. Within a few years the children of fathers who have paid the sacrifice in the World war will have grown to manhood and womanhood, capable of self-support.

Then there will be the old soldiers of the World war, just as now there are the aged veterans of the Civil war, thousands of them without means of livelihood, except through public charity. Although Oklahoma was a barren wilderness during the Civil war, today there are more than 2,000 Oklahoma veterans of that war in old soldiers' homes. When it is considered that Oklahoma had more than 90,000 men in the World war, the need for old soldiers' homes, 30 or 40 years hence, can be readily rdalized.

WORK toward establishing the Home School has just been started. The first two billets are merely a stepping stone toward the great unfinished task—that of bringing relief to every deserving child. But they will demonstrate the workability of the Home School plan, providing an argument upon which the American Legion may "sell" the finished project.

The architect's drawing across the bottom of these pages shows the Home School as it will appear when completed. At least seven beautiful buildings are planned, including an administration and recreation building, dining hall, school building, auditorium and dormitories.

When it is considered that nearly $150,000 has already been invested in the Home School, through the generosity of Mr. Marland and Mr. McFadden, it is readily seen that the sum of about $80,000 now in the coffers of the American Legion is no more than the proverbial "drop in the bucket."

If the American Legion Home School is to be a success—and it will be a success—every citizen of Oklahoma must be made to recognize his responsibility toward the Oklahoma boys who sacrificed all during the World war, and toward the children of those Oklahoma boys who now suffer because of that noble sacrifice.

The American Legion must bring home the need for this worthy institution to every citizen of Oklahoma.

(The Marland Billet is on the extreme left and the McFadden Billet the third from the right)

Page 6   *Page 7*

PROGRAM DEDICATION AND FORMAL OPENING OF THE AMERICAN LEGION HOME SCHOOL

WESLEY I. NUNN

JIM HATCHER

FRANK P. DOUGLASS

TED PETIT

OUTSTANDING among members of the American Legion who have contributed to the establishment of the American Legion Home School are these four. Mr. Nunn was Mr. Marland's personal representative in the Endowment Fund campaign. Hatcher worked hand-in-hand with Nunn. Commander Douglass took up the work where Hatcher left off. Ted Petit has handled the mass of detail accompanying plans for the opening.

FIGURES AND FACTS THE LEGION MUST FACE

* *

WILL the American Legion Home School fulfill its real purpose? Members of the American Legion in Oklahoma hold the answer to this all-important question. If every member of every post of the Legion will work to meet the quota in the Campaign from June 25 to June 30 there is no doubt about the successful future of the Home School.

The 40 children now being cared for are but a small beginning of a great work. Unless the Campaign is successful 500 other children will be deprived of the happy home provided for these 40. We must make good!

In 1925, the national American Legion organization inaugurated a Child Welfare Fund drive, and asked Oklahoma to raise $75,000 toward the national endowment fund. The Oklahoma American Legion drafted E. W. Marland as chairman. He not only was a large contributor, but gave a month of his valuable time. He also conceived the idea of raising a Child Welfare fund for Oklahoma, to which he also contributed in a big way. Some $80,000 was raised and the Oklahoma Child Welfare Endowment corporation was established at that time.

This Endowment Fund corporation has not had practical operation, in that the rules governing the investment schedule of the fund are of necessity too strict to provide any real interest earning. The fund has been in existence for two and a half years and the interest earnings have amounted to only about $2,600 which is, in itself, not an amount large enough to be of practical use.

It is the purpose of the Oklahoma Child Welfare Endowment corporation that a movement be presented to the State Legion convention at Shawnee during the month of August, to set aside this endowment fund and permit the principal to be used in connection with the Home School at Ponca City, and for other general Child Welfare work.

The American Legion Home School now includes only two billets, but Mr. Marland has pledged himself to gain support of

PROGRAM DEDICATION AND FORMAL OPENING OF THE AMERICAN LEGION HOME SCHOOL

enough other wealthy citizens of Oklahoma to erect several other billets as the need demands.

The job before the American Legion today is just this: An administration building must be constructed as soon as possible. This building will house the employes of the school and contain class rooms for the younger children, office equipment and library. It will also house the central kitchen and cooking unit and dining room for the School. At present cooking arrangements are being worked out in the separate billets, but this will not be a practical operation as the School increases in size.

Numberless prominent citizens throughout the state have been interviewed regarding the American Legion Home School and it is the general opinion of these men that the State of Oklahoma should pay the operating expenses of this Home in some manner. They are all agreed in saying that it is a responsibility that rests with all the people of Oklahoma to take care of these children of men who are, either physically unable to support their children or have given their lives for their country. It is, therefore, the plan of the Legion to raise enough funds throughout the state to practically complete the Home and maintain it until such a time as proper legislation can be enacted and an appropriation made by the State of Oklahoma for its maintenance. The Legion realizes that it will be impossible for the state to operate the Home School as a State Institution and is willing to accept full responsibility for the entire operation of this Home, provided the State appropriates the funds necessary for its operation.

The Legion is planning a drive to raise $180,000.00, which is based on $10 per member for the membership of the state, between June 25 and June 30. It is not our idea, however, to go to the general public for funds in this drive. After very careful consideration on the part of the men in charge of this movement, it has been decided that there are enough men of means in the towns where the various Legion posts are located so that the post's quota for this drive should be raised from among their ranks. There are, over the state, a goodly number of Legion members who are financially able to and who will give generously to this cause. It is unfortunate, however, that we do not have enough men among our ranks who are financially able to contribute this full amount. For this reason, we must of necessity approach the business men of the different communities in an attempt to gain their support and a cash contribution.

EACH POST'S SHARE

**

Campaign June 25-30

**

Name of Post	Quota	Name of Post	Quota	Name of Post	Quota
*Tulsa, No. 1...	$15,000	Rush Spgs., No. 80.	330	Granite, No. 177...	440
Collinsville, No. 2..	420	Eufaula, No. 82...	310	Grove, No. 178...	160
Cleveland, No. 3..	390	Wynona, No. 83..	350	Hartshorne, No. 180	940
Enid, No. 4...	5,180	Talihina, No. 86...	430	Elk City, No. 181...	1,110
Kingfisher, No. 5...	700	Pauls Valley, No. 87	890	Ryan, No. 183...	120
Thomas, No. 6....	130	Norman, No. 88...	1,900	Watts, No. 184...	160
Blackwell, No. 7...	2,080	Kingston, No. 89..	60	Heavener, No. 188..	180
Idabel, No. 8...	180	Weatherford, No. 91	1,130	Hanna, No. 189...	120
Marlow, No. 9......	830	Alva, No. 92...	1,120	Gotebo, No. 190...	150
Okmulgee, No. 10..	3,470	Mulhall, No. 93...	150	Pond Creek, No. 199	120
Ponca City, No. 14..	3,210	Ringling, No. 96...	270	Crescent, No. 200..	200
Muskogee, No. 15..	3,930	Pawnuska, No. 97..	2,910	Binger, No. 201...	150
Shawnee, No. 16...	2,990	Oilton, No. 98...	710	Healdton, No. 203...	800
Sand Spgs, No. 17..	480	Wagoner, No. 99...	160	Seminole, No. 204...	380
Muskogee, 19 (Col.)	440	Hitchcock, No. 100..	140	Okarche, No. 206...	330
Woodward, No. 19..	630	Nowata, No. 101...	1,000	Lamont, No. 209...	250
Ft. Gibson, No. 20..	150	Stilwell, No. 102 ...	200	Perkins, No. 211...	340
Stigler, No. 22....	830	Okmulgee 103 (Col.)	310	McLoud, No. 212...	900
Lindsay, No. 23...	470	Bartlesville, No. 105	3,770	Keifer, No. 213....	400
Anadarko, No. 24...	1,370	Waynoka, No. 106..	160	Minco, No. 215...	240
Pawnee, No. 26...	770	Waurika, No. 107..	180	Wanette, No. 217...	210
Sallisaw, No. 27...	490	Cushing, No. 108...	1,720	Caddo, No. 218...	170
Helena, No. 28....	210	Edmond, No. 111....	500	Muskogee, No. 219..	3,240
Lawton, No. 29...	3,690	Erick, No. 113...	310	Kaw City, No. 220...	540
Guymon, No. 31...	830	Hennessey, No. 114..	450	Boise City, No. 221.	190
Holdenville, No. 32..	1,020	Drumright, No. 116..	1,540	Spiro, No. 222......	240
Cherokee, No. 33...	190	Hobart, No. 117...	1,540	Gage, No. 223......	160
El Reno, No. 34....	2,240	Mangum, No. 121...	1,590	Wetumka, No. 224..	820
*Oklahoma City....	15,000	Wewoka, No. 122...	690	Apache, No. 225....	590
Sapulpa, No. 36....	3,270	Okemah, No. 123...	2,920	Barnsdall, No. 227..	400
Medford, No. 37...	160	Afton, No. 124...	220	Wilson, No. 231...	1,250
White Eagle, No. 38		Watonga, No. 125...	400	Fairfax, No. 232...	560
Durant, No. 39.....	580	Bristow, No. 126...	2,221	Boley, No. 234 (Col.)	400
Vinita, No. 40...	1,050	Burbank, No. 127...	240	Morris, No. 236....	440
Clinton, No. 41...	1,570	Avant, No. 128...	210	Allen, No. 238...	170
Purcell. No. 42....	850	Stillwater. No. 129..	2,660	Custer City, No. 239.	110
Altus, No. 44....	1,580	Mountain View, 130	200	Selman, No. 246....	250
Burlington, No. 45..	200	Skiatook, No. 131..	450	Canton, No. 247...	430
Antlers, No 46....	800	Poteau, No. 132...	810	Enid, No. 253 (Col.)	20
Carmen, No. 47....	310	Cordell, No. 134...	310	Stroud, No. 257....	960
Atoka, No. 48....	810	Marietta, No. 136...	430	Comanche, No. 258	170
Frederick, No 49...	1,220	Hooker, No. 137...	420	Braman, No. 259....	340
Tahlequah, No. 50..	630	Fairland, No. 139...	450	Tecumseh, No. 260..	430
Fairview, No. 51...	810	Claremore, No. 141..	1,530	Blanchard, No. 261..	410
Perry, No. 53.....	1,040	Hominy, No. 142...	740	Shamrock, No. 268..	510
Chickasha, No. 54...	2,610	Sayre, No. 146....	570	Eldorado, No. 270..	360
Duncan, No 55....	1,770	Miami, No. 147...	2,140	Hastings, No. 272...	400
Haskell, No. 56...	190	Sulphur, No. 148...	810	Mounds, No. 273...	310
Lone Wolf, No. 57..	360	Beaver, No. 149...	180	Wister, No. 280...	70
Guthrie, No. 58....	1,820	Picher, No. 150...	1,020	Port, No. 281.....	120
Hugo, No. 59......	670	Walters, No. 155...	410	Clear Lake, No. 284..	130
Chelsea, No. 60....	850	Carnegie, No. 156..	560	Capron, No. 287...	530
Freedom, No. 63...	270	Okla City 157 (Col.)	260	Jefferson, No. 289..	140
Chandler, No. 64...	1,010	Hollis, No. 159...	570	Sopher, No. 291...	240
Ardmore, No. 65...	2,400	Yale, No. 161....	1,210	Broken Bow, No.297	210
Webb City, No. 67..	940	Temple, No. 162...	330	P'huska, 298 (Col.)	280
Nash, No. 68...	190	Tishmingo, No. 164	500	Olustee, No. 299...	200
Konawa, No. 70...	1,050	Newkirk, No. 165..	550		
Tonkawa, No. 71...	1,050	Marshall, No. 167...	90	*Tulsa and Oklahoma City	
Ada, No. 72......	2,540	Okeene, No. 171...	160	quotas equalized at $15,000	
Quinton, No. 97...	240	Billings, No. 172...	460	each on basis of population.	
McAlester, No. 75...	2,390	Grandfield, No. 175	300		

"We Must Not Fail"

Five articles about the Administration Buildings

NEW SECTION WILL ENLARGE PRESENT HOME SCHOOL UNIT

~ Ponca City News ~

LIVING, DINING AND BEDROOM FACILITIES TO BE PROVIDED FOR MANY MORE CHILDREN; USE PRESENT HEATING PLANT

Contractors are busy over plans and specification for the addition to the American Legion Home School Administration Building. It is to be built so that the two will appear as a complete unit. Bid are to be opened at the office of Charles B. Duffy, head of the state welfare work for the Legion, at his office in the Community building the night of Thursday, July 9. The addition will represent an approximate cost of $16,500.

The plans, as drawn by G. J. Cannon, local architect, call for a building of two stories, without basement. It will join the present administration building so that the same heating plant may be used for both, and in order to work out other living room and dining room facilities. Accommodations are for 26 children to be housed here, with dining room facilities for 36. The first floor will have a large living room, dining room, and kitchen.

LEGION TO LET CONTRACT SOON
HOME SCHOOL BUILDING PLANS COMPLETE

The architect's plans for the new administration building at the American Legion home school are now in the hands of contractors. Bids will be received and the contracts let December 20 in the office of Charles B. Duffy at 7 o'clock.

The new administration building is to be midway between the two billets and of Spanish architecture. The general scheme will be similar to the two buildings already in use at the school.

The building will be of two stories and by having it, at least ten more children may be accommodated in the school.

R. G. Patton of Okmulgee, Department Commander of the American Legion, and Milton Phillips of Oklahoma City, Department Adjutant, will be here for the meeting at Duffy's office. J. Duncan Forsythe also will meet with the Legion committee members and the contractors.

HOME SCHOOL KIDS ENJOYING BUILDING
WATCH WITH INTEREST CONSTRUCTION OF NEW
ADMINISTRATION UNIT

Activities at the American Legion billets east of the city have taken on new zest since the new administration building was started. Work was begun by Dick Sherbon, contractor, the past week. Children in the home school were excited over "shooting the basement," many wanting to be on the scene of action. They were kept indoors, however, and watched the spectacular event from their windows.

Evenings at the home school are much more enjoyable since the new radios have arrived. The one in the boys' billet was presented by the eighth district of the American Legion and arrived Christmas day.

The following day another radio arrived. This was from Miss M. R. Jolly who is in West Orange; N. J. Miss Jolly is a former superintendent of the school. This radio has been put in the girls' billet.

Numerous pictures were taken of the children Christmas day with their Christmas trees and numerous gifts received from various American Legion Auxiliary units about the state. Many of the units have adopted a child each and have sent gifts accordingly.

Miss Dorothy Hillswick, new Superintendent at the school, has two new Matrons to assist her. Mrs. Inez Brown has arrived from Tulsa to take over the boys' billets. She formerly was with the children's hospital in Wichita. Miss Clara Salyers is the Matron of the girls' billet; she is a former school teacher from Tulsa.

Six more children are to enter school in the city the second semester, Miss Hillswick says.

James and Clifford Parks, two Home School children, are convalescing from tonsil operations.

DEDICATION OF THE ADMINISTRATION BUILDING. OKLAHOMA LEGIONNAIRES DEDICATE NEW HOME FOR CHILDREN

Ponca City ~ July 26 (Special)

Echoes of 1917 will resound here Sunday when a new building will be dedicated to dependent children of former service men. It will be the inaugural ceremony for the new administration building, third of a group being established here to care for dependent children. Milt D. Campbell of Cincinnati, National American Legion vice commander, will be the principal speaker. A statewide attendance is expected. The 65 children now in the billets will open the exercises. They will present an ensemble at 1:45 o'clock lasting 15 minutes. The entire program will not require an hour. Tom Gammie of this city, chairman of the state legion's child welfare committee, will preside. The invocation will be by Rev. J. M. Jones, of Yale, state chaplain, followed by a short welcome address by Miss Dorothy Hilseweick, superintendent of the school. B. G. Patton, state commander of the American Legion, will speak on the subject of "Oklahoma's Child Welfare Program."

Mrs. S. M. Singer Anadarko, state president of the American Legion Auxiliary, will appear for a brief address relative to the work of the auxiliary in connection with children of the school, and E. W. Marland, who donated the land and one of the billets, will give a short talk. The address by Vice Commander Campbell will close the event. The beauty and efficiency of the American Legion Home School, the Oklahoma legion's tribute to war dead and pledge to the living, has been further increased by the addition of its third building, the administration unit, for which the state legion appropriated $25,000. And annual state legislative appropriation maintains the institution. The new build was occupied recently, and with it in use the Legion was able to increase the number of children under its care.

Inside the two billets and the administration hall live 63 children, orphans or dependents of state legionnaires. The first two billets, named for their donors, E. W. Marland and W. H. McFadden, completed two years ago, house 24 boys and as many girls, and now the new combination administration building and billet makes a place for 14 children more. The complete, and dreamed-of, building will include, in time, at least seven buildings on the 120-acre site donated by E. W. Marland. Ages of the youngsters range from 3 years to 11. One is struck with the absence of that "institution look" found on the faces and depositions of Home children, and the fact that they are happy, contended, cheerful children, with more than the average allotment of intelligence, a noticeable lack of self-consciousness and a surprising store of courtesy toward their guests. They take much interest in their home, rising at 6:30 in the morning to make their beds, help in the kitchen and do the general house cleaning. Follows time during vacation months to read, garden, fish, and play or enjoy any kind of conceivable sport.

Their superintendent is Miss Dorothy Hilseweick, a former teacher in the Roosevelt school of Ponca City, who has made an unusual success through her work with and her understanding of children. She has been associated with the Home School for a year. Mrs. Jessie Hobbs, the assistant, had done teaching in the junior high school at Catoosa, before her coming here two years ago, at the opening of the school. Mrs. Anna K. Fain of Livingston, Texas, noteworthy for her work with delinquent boys, is the relief matron. Mrs. Maude Wallace is matron at the boys' billet. Herman Miller, bus driver and a familiar figure about the ground, is a World War veteran. The new administration building contains and excellent office for the affairs of the school. It is furnished with Walnut furnishings, an artistic vase of flowers, an unusual rug- the new building contains a number of beauty spots equal to those found in many private homes.

Children of the school enjoy a variety of activities - 12 girls attended the second summer camp season at Camp McFadden, and 10-year old Pauline Hill received the loving cup for the best girl camper. Girls have organized a literary society under the direction of Mrs. Hobbs and they present some surprisingly original programs. The boys garden, sweep and clean the walks, help with the landscaping, work in the kitchen, do the general housework for their billet and look after the younger boys of the school. Summertime means kindergarten twice the week for an hour, and a class in home economics instruction, personal hygiene, morals and manners, meets with Mrs. Hobbs on Wednesday. Miss Hilseweick, the superintendent, talks to the boys and girls on Thursday evening on character building, and on subjects of general interest to them. Friday means a free show anywhere downtown or swimming, also free at the municipal pool. Townspeople are kind to the children of Oklahoma Legionnaires. Two music teachers of the city give free instruction, 12 doctors and dentists serve freely for one month each in alphabetic rotation, and there are many others who give unselfishly. Saturday is shopping day, and Sunday the school bus takes the youngsters to the church of their choice for Sunday school.

The family tie is strong in members of the Home School. There are five families of four children, numerous threes, and a number of twos and only one child who has neither brother nor sister in the school. Fourteen children have recently arrived to take their places in the new building, among them 3 1/2 year-old twins, Marvin and Madeline Kinchen of Chandler. There are musicians in this crowd of Legionnaire children and a number of them have appeared in public recitals with Ponca City children. One 12 year-old boy, T. L. Rider, is a talented dancer.

ADMINISTRATION UNIT NOW UNDER CONSTRUCTION TO HARMONIZE WITH OTHER BUILDINGS

Workmen who are busy on the erection of the new American Legion Home School Administration Building, have an interested row of spectators, as shown in the accompanying photograph, most every day, for they are looking forward to the day of its completion.

All of the brick work has been done, and now workmen are ready to lath and plaster the inside walls. The outside remains to be stuccoed. It is hoped that the building will be completed in every detail in order that it can be dedicated on Memorial Day. These are tentative plans of the Committee in charge.

All of the children in the billets have been adopted by some American Legion Post, or Auxiliary Unit in the State, with the exception of two. 'Adoption' means the clothing of the particular child, and special attention.

Miss Dorothy Hillswick reports that the six new additions that came to the school about Christmas time have been adopted. A Legionnaire drove from Eric, on the Texas line, one day the past week and made a personal visit at the Home School. He arranged for the adoption of two. The Post at Vinita also will adopt two and the Hammond and Coweta units have arranged to adopt one each. There are two children who had been adopted by Auxiliary Posts during the past year, but the Posts are unable to care for them again, so Miss Hillswick says that these two are the only ones in the school who remain to be adopted.

All of the 48 children in the school are attending school, with the exception of a few of the youngest. Of the entire group ten are attending Hiss Helen Lucille Cooper's kindergarten class where she is giving them instruction free of charge.

LANDSCAPE AT LEGION SCHOOL ORNAMENTED BY FLOWER BEDS

THE ADMINISTRATION BUILDING AND ANNEX IN 1932

Roses, sweet-peas, flower beds and shrubs are to enhance the beauty of the grounds at the American Legion Home School as the result of efforts of H. L. Miller, ex-service man and driver of the bus that brings the children to and from school daily.

Miller has given a fairy touch to the landscaping already, as flowerbeds are underway, and trellises are being arranged for early sweet-peas. He puts in all of his spare moments gardening and landscaping on the grounds. As a gardener, Miller has had experience, for he was associated with Henry Hatashita, landscape gardener for the E. W. Marland estate, for the past two years.

Chapter Three

Thomas L. Rider

LT. COL. (RET.) T. L. RIDER RELATED HIS MEMORIES

"I came to the Home School with my three brothers, Roscoe, Leon, and Kirby. We were there in the spring of 1928, when the Home opened and was dedicated. That was quite a historical day and event, one of the most impressive things in my life. Mr. Marland, Mr. McFadden, American Legion and Auxiliary officials and hundreds of Oklahoma Legion members, including Herman J. Smith, were all present.

Most of the children in that first group, which wasn't too large, maybe thirty or so, were family groups with three to four children. Miss Rebecca Jollie was the First Superintendent, and her assistant was a lovely lady by the name of Miss Dewberry. Mrs. Lillian Hobbs and Mrs. Pearl Marks became the First Matrons. Each of them had four children with them. Mrs. Masters had four children, and stayed for a while as a relief housemother. We grew to love these supervisors but it took awhile, for it was a traumatic experience being separated from a mother or father in this strange environment.

Some of us older children helped plant the trees which now adorn the campus at the Home. The landscape architects were two Japanese gentlemen who were the official gardeners for the Marland estate and surely experts in their field. We knew them as Henry, the older one, and Matsumo. They were friendly and loved children.

Our first cook was "Thad." His last name may have been Stevens. Many people in Ponca City knew him. He was a wonderful black man with a great personality and cooking talent. He was there only long enough to get things organized and operating well, and then he left. He may have worked for Mr. Marland at the time, but later operated "Thad Bar-B-Q" on South Avenue.

It was several weeks before we acquired our first bus, a Chevrolet with a wooden body. Mr. Bird was the first driver. Until we got the bus, we were transported to Sunday school and Church, the movies, to the Bogan Swimming Pool, and to picnics by local families who owned automobiles. Most of them were affiliated with the American Legion, or were good church members. They were wonderful people. Among them was Mrs. O.V. Black, who had a baby daughter, named Polly. I remember thinking she was the most beautiful little girl I had ever seen.

By the time school started in September, we had our new bus with AMERICAN LEGION HOME SCHOOL painted on the sides along with a prominent American Legion emblem. That emblem became very important to me, and I think I adopted it as my own personal Coat of Arms. It is still very important to me, to all of us and the entire Nation. To us at Home it represented a new different life, with a great opportunity to go ahead and achieve something worthwhile if we would but expand effort, and make our ambitions known.

I was ten years old when I first arrived in Ponca City. My older brother was twelve, and the two younger brothers were eight and six. My older brother, Roscoe Jr., was the oldest of all the children in the Home at that time. Later, while attending high school, he went to the Oklahoma Military Academy at Claremore, where he finished the high school course, and possibly a year of college. We didn't see him after that for several years, except on rare occasions.

I became the oldest student at this point, and as such I assumed the responsibilities as the older brother. The little children accepted this and looked to the older ones for comfort and protection, and were generally easy to control, and were obedient. The task of looking after so many little ones was too great for the Housemothers, so they relied on the older students for this help. As a result, we naturally grew up as a fairly close family.

At first we had two buildings, the Marland Building for the boys and the McFadden Building for the girls. There were about twenty-five children in each building. Each had a nursery which accommodated six pre-schoolers. In fact, some of them were just beyond the diaper stage. I was in charge of the little boys. One of them is now a Doctor in Oklahoma City.

When I got to high school, I was finally allowed to go out for sports. Previously this was not allowed because of transportation problems. Miss Sexton was then our superintendent, and was sports minded along with her other keen attributes. She permitted me to stay after school and participate in team sports. This was the beginning of a phase of extra-curricular activities which allowed many of the Legion boys to compete in Junior and Senior High School sports where they were outstanding, even to the point of becoming State Champions. I think that our well balanced diet, regular hours and physical activities at the Home School contributed to this performance. It was always a good feeling to see a group of Home School students at a sports event rooting for one or several of our boys.

I graduated in the spring of 1936, at a time I shall never forget. It was a sort of sad time for me. I had no family there. But most of all, I was going to leave my home and my younger brothers. I was worried about what would become of them. I knew I was going to college, but I would have to do it on my own, for there were no scholarships established in those days for a Home School graduate. I had saved some money – enough for a couple of years, so I went to Tonkawa to Junior College, and then to Colorado State A&M College.

After finishing college in 1941, I worked for the Continental Oil Co. at Nocona, Texas that summer. That fall, on November 1st, I entered the Aviation Cadet program where I chose Celestial Navigation, and eventually graduated as a Celestial Navigator at the University of Miami, in Coral Gables, Florida. At this time I was commissioned a Second Lieutenant in the U.S. Army Air Corps. I was assigned to the Ferrying Division of the Air Transport Command and delivered combat planes to all parts of the world where our forces were fighting. Two years later, I was selected to go to pilot training. I went through that as a First Lieutenant. I graduated August 16, 1944 at Pecos, Texas. I chose B-17 Bombers and with more training I was assigned a crew and a four engine B-17 Bomber which I flew missions over Germany.

When the war ended in Europe we flew back to the States, I took a thirty day leave; and on July 4, 1945, I went to Ponca City to visit Mom and Pop Smith (Smitty).

After a couple of interim assignments and more schooling, I was selected to go to Tokyo as a pilot-navigator on General MacArthur's flight crew. I was stationed in Tokyo about two years, during the Occupation and then transferred to Hickam Filed new Honolulu to become Aide de Camp to Major General Bob Nowland who commanded the Pacific Division of the Military Air Transport Command. My duty also included that of a pilot-navigator. We flew throughout the Pacific.

Several months later we moved to San Antonio, Texas where General Nowland became Commander of Continental Division MATS. His responsibility covered both North and South America, and we covered it. He retired in 1950, and I was sent to Washington, D.C.'s Special Air Force Missions Group, where I was stationed for seven years. We flew special missions all over the world. In 1957, I was transferred to St. John's, Newfoundland to fly the Commanding General and Staff of the 64th Air Division, Air Defense Command. This was interesting in that it included arctic flying near the Pole and elsewhere.

After a two year tour there I returned to the States and was assigned to Dover Air Force Base, Delaware. I flew C433 propjets hauling heavy cargo to Europe and other places. I retired from the Air Force on November 1, 1963. I had completed twenty-two years in the Service.

THE RIDER BOYS: ROSCOE RIDER, JR. ~ CAPTAIN T. L. RIDER ~ LEON (JIGGY) RIDER ~ AND KIRBY RIDER

Once again, I didn't know where I was going. I had no home. Back in 1942, I had married the former Colleen Wallace of Ponca City, but one year later, she died. But, I decided to return to Ponca City for a visit. I traveled across the country on a long, un-thrilling vacation. I finally stopped in Fort Collins to visit friends at the University where I had gone to school. I was offered a job on the non-teaching staff in the Alumni Association as Assistant Secretary and Editor of the Alumni magazine. I took the job and two years later I bought an eighty-acre ranch, got married and started raising Arabian horses. The chores became so heavy that I resigned from teaching a few years ago, and we devote full time to the ranch.

Both of my younger brothers, Kirby and Leon (Jiggy), are dead. My older brother, Roscoe, lives in Dallas. I deeply grateful for all the opportunities afforded me at the Home School and especially the help from the Legionnaires and Auxiliary Units of Oklahoma."

HOME SCHOOL HAS FIRST H. S. SENIOR GRADUATE WITH 1936 CLASS

Ponca City News ~ Wednesday ~ May 20, 1936

CROW COUNTY AMERICAN LEGION COMMANDER IN CONJUNCTION WITH THE EIGHTH GRADE COMMENCEMENT EXERCISES IN THE HIGH SCHOOL AUDITORIUM HERE

The American Legion Home School is to have its first senior high school graduate in the history of the institution when T. L. Rider gets his diploma Thursday evening, among the 1936 graduates of the Ponca City High School.

Rider has made his home at the school since it was opened. Throughout his school career he has been prominent in activities and has ranked high scholastically.

The school's football and baseball teams and wrestling squads have had Rider as a member during his student days. In February his fellow students elected him as Best Citizen for the month. Last week he played the role of "Tommy" in the senior play by that name directed by Woodson Tyree.

In addition to school affairs Rider has been actively engaged in rank of Gold Palm Eagle Scout. In DeMolay work he was awarded the blue honor key for outstanding work in the local chapter and now is district junior councilor and a past master councilor. He was awarded a life certificate in Botts Business College to be used at any time.

Rider plans to attend the University of Oklahoma or Oklahoma A. and M. College this fall where he will take preparatory work for entrance examination for the United States Naval Academy at Annapolis, MD, the following year.

CAPT. THOMAS L. RIDER
ONE OF THREE SURVIVORS IN PLANE CRASH

August 22 ~ The Nocona News ~ Nocona, Texas

Capt. Thomas L. Rider, husband of the late Colleen Wallace Rider, daughter of Mr. and Mrs. Claude Wallace was one of three survivors in a plane crash in the Pacific Ocean August 17th.

Capt. Rider is one of General Douglass McArthur's staff stationed in Tokyo. Apparently 10 to 13 men aboard perished when the converted bomber ran out of gasoline enroot from Tokyo only a few minutes flying time from Hawaii. Three survivors were taken to Pearl Harbor by naval rescuers.

The group was flying to Washington from McArthur's headquarters to discuss plans for a Japanese Peace Treaty. Search units were ordered to watch for highly confidential documents that they were carrying.

Five shrouded bodies were brought ashore from the destroyer; the sixth body sank as coast guardsman aboard tried to recover it.

Capt. Thomas L. Rider, one of the survivors, said he was sitting beside George C. Atcheson Jr., General Douglass McArthur's political advisor and allied council chairman, as the helpless plane slid down toward the water. All aboard had been warned that the plane must be ditched.

Cap. Rider suffered a broken arm. The plane ran out of gas shortly before midnight Hawaiian time Saturday in the final miles of a flight from Kwajalein against headwinds.

Capt. K. R. Stills, at the controls, was talking calmly by radio with Lt. Charles Martin, a Hawaiian sea frontier officer ashore when the B17 hit the water. The plane's radio went out abruptly at 11:46 p.m.

Another survivor Mr. Huglin, a resident of Fairfield, Iowa, told what happened in the passenger quarters of the plane during the final minutes. He said the passengers were given 30 minutes warning that they might crash. They still took every possible precaution for a safe landing he said. Huglin said he believed the impact and high waves broke the plane in half where he was sitting. He could not remember how he escaped from the wreckage. Destroyers crisscrossed the crash area throughout the night, searching for the missing men or their bodies.

Capt. Rider entered the service in 1941. He was in the bombing of Berlin during the last war, and was in the service when the war ended. He has been in General Douglass McArthur's staff for two years.

Mr. and Mrs. Claude Wallace
sent the following telegram to Capt. T. L. Rider:

Keep your chip up "Chief," we are betting on you. Everyone is anxious to hear from you. Come home for a visit soon. Best wishes Claude and Mrs. Wallace.

Ponca City News ~ May 23, 1962

Maj. T. L. Rider, first high school graduate from the American Legion Home School, will receive the Legion of Honor of DeMolay Saturday at Guthrie.

The presentation will be made at 7 p.m. Saturday in the Masonic Temple. The ceremony will be open to the public.

Now serving with the U.S. Air Force at Dover, Del., Major Rider was an athlete and football star at Ponca City High School and entered the American Legion Home School with his three brothers shortly after it opened in 1928.

He has sponsored several scholarships in previous years for boys at the American Legion Home School.

**FIRST ROW: LINDA (STEWART) DUNDEE ~ MS. SUMMERS
BARBRA (MAHORNEY) ALUSI ~ T. L. RIDER
BACK ROW: TOM RATLIFF ~ BRUCE WYATT**

**TOM RATLIFF, BARBRA MAHORNEY ALUSI,
HOLDING KIRBY RIDER'S PURPLE HEART
PRESENTED TO POST 14 BY T. L. RIDER.**

A GENEROUS BEQUEST FROM T. L. RIDER

T.L. RIDER WITH HIS BROTHER, KIRBY RIDER'S PURPLE HEART

The American Legion Children's Home recently received an exceedingly generous gift of over $100,000.00 from the estate of Thomas L. and Betty J. Rider. T. L. was one of the first children to live in the Home School in 1928, and was our very first graduate. He went on to become a decorated war hero and left the military as a highly decorated Lieutenant Colonel. Before he passed away, he made his wishes known to his wife Betty that he wanted the Children's Home remembered in his estate. When Mrs. Rider passed away in 2009, we were remembered in her will in honor of her late husband. What a wonderful legacy to leave behind!

Chapter Four

Christmas Memories

BARBRA'S MEMORIES:

BILL BAILEY (61) AS SANTA CLAUS AND HIS MRS. CLAUS PAULA. HE IS SANTA ONLY FOR KIDS AT HOMELESS SHELTERS AND LOCAL SCHOOLS, AND HE DOES THIS FREE (HIS WAY OF PAYING BACK ALL THE HELP THE ALHS GAVE HIM AS A YOUNG KID).

Every year, way before the Christmas season began, I would try to dodge Mrs. Summers if I would see her first. I always owed her "my Christmas letter." It was a letter I was supposed to write to my sponsors every year telling them what I'd like for Christmas. I was supposed to have it written and on Mrs. Summer's desk the first of December so she could proof read it and put it in the mail. We were supposed to write about how we were doing in school and make a list of the things that we wanted for that Christmas. To me, writing that letter was very difficult because I didn't like to write letters. The good thing that came from the letter was I always ended up getting the things I asked for, which was nice. The only way I would manage to write the letter when I was in grade school was under the threat of not being able to go to the show on Saturday and I hated missing that. I usually ended up copying a sample letter from Mrs. Mayhue.

I remember how all of us girls in our dorm (the senior girls building) would gather together to decorate the tree. Mr. Summers would always bring the tree to our building. I never knew where he got the tree, but all the big boys would be with him to help unload it from his truck.

Then there were the long hours we girls spent cracking and shelling pecans for Mrs. Mayhue. Evidently there were pecan trees somewhere on the property, because she'd bring in huge sacks of them. We weren't able to quit until every last pecan was shelled. A group of us girls would sit on the bottom of the stairs, right outside of her bedroom door. Of course we were blocking anyone who wanted to go up and down the stairs. But this was a sure way of getting new workers; anyone who wanted to pass was made to shell pecans first. By the time we were finished, we would have eaten most of the pecans, although some did end up in the bowl.

We needed decorations so we'd pop a large pan of popcorn and string it on thread to put on the tree. I remember stringing cranberries as well. The younger girls always made new paper garlands at school so we'd add those to the tree. If we decided we needed more we'd get the little girls to cut more strips of paper and glue them together. By the time that they finished they all ended up with just about as much glue on themselves as they got on the paper.

When it snowed Mrs. Mayhue would always make snow ice cream for us. I would always volunteer to go out and get the snow, and for some reason it seemed like it usually snowed at night. I loved being out in the fresh snow. It was gorgeous and so quiet and peaceful. Mrs. Mayhue normally wouldn't let more than a couple of us go at a time. Besides enjoying the fun of being out in the snow, I wanted to make sure the snow that I was putting in my mouth was clean. I would take a big dishpan and we'd fill it up a couple of times. The recipe called for milk, sugar and raw eggs. To me the thought of eating raw eggs really bothered me. I guess the good taste of the final product blocked it out of my brain though.

Mrs. Mayhue would make huge amounts of candy for us. And making fudge was always a big problem for me. I never managed to let the stuff cool before I would try to taste it. I always would end up with a burnt tongue. I always liked how she told us to put a drop in a cold glass of water to see if it was done. Every year we made loads of candy and cookies.

Mrs. Mayhue would make new pajamas and robes for everyone in the building. I remember the year that she let me make the buttonholes for all the robes and tops. I thought I would never get finished. I did my best job, figuring that one of them would be mine. But she surprised me she made mine when I was at school. So we all got nice new pajamas and robes.

Butch Bryson would always come to our building when he was home from college. He would play the piano for hours and we would gather around him. We enjoyed each song that we would ask him to play for us. I always liked to play a joke on him when he would first come to the building to practice. Since the piano was at the bottom of the stairs. I would stand at the top of the stairs and say real loud. "Oh no, Butch is here and we have to listen to his horrible playing." He would respond in kind and it would be lots of laughs while he was there.

Christmas was the time of year that all of us kids went to the homes of our sponsors for the holidays. I remember my sponsors in Stillwater. Jerry Evans and I shared the same Sponsors but he only was invited to go there once when he was in high school.

I was only nine when I arrived at the Home on September 22, 1957 and one of the first things I learned was what a "Sponsor" was. One day after school Mrs. Mayhue called me into her room, when I entered I saw several large wardrobe boxes lying on her bed. She again told me all about these wonderful people called Sponsors and said that they had sent me these boxes. Opening the boxes I found a huge assortment of clothes. There were enough clothes in those boxes for all the girls in the building, but she told me they were all for me.

Mrs. Mayhue explained that one of the three coats in the box was for school, one for play and one to wear only to church. I had never seen so many beautiful dresses other than in a department store. She told me some of the dresses were just for school and some just for church, showing me the difference. She pointed out the clothes I was to wear just for play. There were lots of blouses and jeans enough so I would have many play clothes. There was underwear, socks, undershirts, and slips. Some were set aside especially to wear to church because we always saved our best to wear to church. I couldn't believe it when I caught sight of the red can-can slip to wear under my dresses; with layers of beautiful crinoline. It was the most beautiful petticoat I had ever seen and my favorite thing to wear.

Mrs. Mayhue told me to try on all the clothes to make sure that they all fit. She had a full-length mirror so I could see my reflection as I tried each new outfit on. I wore the can-can petticoat underneath each dress and I twirled and twirled around seeing the yards of red fabric as I twirled. I felt as though I was in heaven. She told me that my new Sponsors had sent all these beautiful clothes to me.

The traumatic experience of moving into the Home and finding my way emotionally was made easier by having these wonderful Sponsors. I met them face to face for the first time two months after I arrived at the Home. It was November and I was going to spend Thanksgiving with them. Mrs. Mayhue took me to downtown Ponca City to the bus station. On our way there she went over the things that she'd already told me, that these nice people had invited me into their homes in Stillwater for Thanksgiving. I had to remember to use all my good manners that she had been teaching me. I was to unfold my napkin and put it in my lap, keeping my hand over it. Use my fork to cut a small bite of food and put it into my mouth, chew with my mouth closed and not talk with food in my mouth. I was to keep all my clothes in order and place the dirty clothes in a bag she'd provided. Being a good houseguest was important to my being asked to go back to the Sponsor's houses. She told me repeatedly that good manners would serve me well throughout my life.

By the time she was finished going over all the rules and regulations it was time to get on the bus. I was to sit up front close to the driver if there was a seat available and I was not to get off until I was told it was Stillwater. She put me on a Greyhound bus for the 45-minute ride, which seemed much longer. I was excited, but mostly the excitement came from fear of the unknown. The bus arrived in the pretty town of Stillwater and a nice lady was there to meet me. She introduced herself as Mrs. Mary E. Smith saying she was the President of the women's Auxiliary. She seemed like a nice grandmotherly type lady with white hair. She carried my little suitcase and held my hand and we went to her car. I sat quietly and spoke only to answer her questions. The car stopped outside of a beautiful home. When we went inside she showed me to a bedroom that she said was to be mine. It was a large beautiful room with bright colorful flora window curtains. The bed was covered with a solid colored silk comforter that matched the curtains. I had never seen anything like it and it was so silky soft, I loved it. I arranged my tiny suitcase and kept it neat and tidy. If I touched something I would put it back exactly as I had found it. Mrs. Smith cooked me a lovely lunch and dinner asking me what I liked to eat. I was so young I had no idea what I liked or disliked. I would have to experience each food and just let her know. Of course, I was courteous when asked if I had liked the meal. I don't ever remember disliking anything that she fixed for me. She was an elegant lady and I really liked how she prepared such a beautiful table. I began to relax because it was just the two of us, and after dinner I sat quietly watching T.V. Settling into my new surroundings was easy and sleeping in the beautiful bed was wonderful, but still strange new surroundings all the same.

The next day when I awoke she fixed me breakfast and explained to me where I was going to go next. We got into the car and she drove me a short distance to a new house. I was going to have Thanksgiving with a different family. I was introduced to Mr. and Mrs. Colasco who had two older children, a boy and a girl. There was a lot of activity going on and I was kind of left to look around in the living room, which had a huge picture window that I could stand and watch all the people drive up to the house. I remember that it started snowing and I touched the window. All of a sudden, Mrs. Colasco appeared behind me telling never to touch the window again. Her scolding tone scared me and I felt embarrassed that I had done something wrong. Then she called the maid and had her clean the window where I had touched it.

One of the guests was Sharron who was five years older than me. She was a very kind smiling girl and I instantly liked her and she me. It turned out Mrs.

Colasco was her aunt. She said, "You don't like it here do you?" and I was afraid to tell her that I didn't, but she encouraged me to tell the truth. She said, "I live down the street. Come with me and I will take you to see my parents." We walked into her home and the atmosphere was so warm and inviting. She said, "Mother and daddy, look who I found. This is Barbra and she's going to stay with us." Sharron had been known to bring in stray dogs and I was just another stray that she made welcome. I felt an instant connection with this beautiful family. There names were Bryon and Aline Daniel, after many years I would refer to them to others as "mom and dad Daniel" to show that I had a family. The whole family, Sharron, Dana Kay and Gordie, all made me feel welcomed and every bit a part of their beautiful family. They could never, ever know just how I treasured being part of their family. The relationship that has lasted all my life. They valued me as a family member and I felt the love they gave me.

My first Christmas of 1957 when I was nine I was taken on a bus to Texas to stay with Mrs. Strom's son, a doctor. He was married, with a son and a mean, nasty daughter who was also nine. She made a point of telling me that Mrs. Strom was her grandmother and I wasn't welcome at her house. I felt sadder than I can ever remember feeling and I stayed in the room that I was sharing with the daughter girl. The doctor came up and asked me what was wrong and all I could tell him was my stomach hurt. It wasn't exactly a lie, but he gave me a shot and from then on I promised I would never tell a lie again. Thankfully, I never had to go there again.

I remember being at the Daniels' house when I was older and feeling a part of the family. Mr. Daniels was pointing to the packages under the tree that had my name on them. He asked me if I knew what was in them, I named off what was in each. He asked me how I knew what was in them. I told him what I had asked for and that I always got what I asked for. I think he would have loved to have taken everything back and exchanged them just to show me that I wouldn't always get what I had asked for. I liked him a lot and I had fun at their house. To me it wasn't about the presents it was the joy of feeling loved and wanted by them and being a part of their family.

Christmas time has always been my favorite time of the year, but as a grown up I have always felt a certain sadness, I don't really know why. I have a beautiful family of my own, making our own family traditions and I am most thankful for the love that we each share with each other. I think it may be a sadness that the past is gone.

Like Johnny I always remember all of you hoping and praying all of you the blessing of a beautiful Christmas...

Much Love Barb (1966)

JANICE (FRANKLIN) NEELY (1961)

Hi Barb... Yes, I remember the snow ice cream and the testing and of making candy...I also remember Christmas's at the Legion Hut that Bill mentioned which were exciting.

The girls my age all got a doll, it was great!!!! Hey, do you remember us getting on a bus in Ponca one Christmas going to Oklahoma City, Ok? That was one time that I went home instead of going to my auxiliary's. I must have been about 13 or 14 and really thought I was something else. Those were the days!!!!

It's funny what we forget, I don't remember the Christmas letter being hard for me, but I do remember that we would always send thank you letters after Christmas. I usually went to Pawhuska and the first Christmas I was there they had our picture taken with us looking at the tree (Glenda, John & I). It was my 10th birthday...wow!!! That's been a long time, some very good memories.

There were certainly a lot of us children, I remember Mrs. Mayhue's cooking in the summertime, and it was wonderful. Do you remember the time we went camping for a week at Mr. Summers' cabin on the creek, it was such fun and oh the wonderful food. We started a small fire because one of us hung a towel over a lamp. We made such good memories, we went swimming in our nothings and I wouldn't take everything off, just some of the girls were that daring. Anyway, that was so good to be with Mrs. Mayhue and having such fun. She was tops, the greatest mom that we could have ever had.

Have a wonderful Christ filled Christmas.
Love, Janice (Franklin) Neely 1961

BILL BAILEY (1961) WROTE:

I remember 100 screaming children at the Legion Hut, giving skinny Mike Sokol, wearing his ill-fitted Santa suit, fits about handing out presents. I remember always being awakened during the winter at 6 am and having someone yell, "Get out of bed!" Rushing to slop the hogs with ice on the ground. I remember breakfast when Dewey Snyder crammed a whole pancake in his mouth to show off to the other kids. And Mrs. Mayhue hollering at you and the littler girls to quit snickering at him and eat your breakfast. Butch Bryson playing Christmas songs in the cafeteria while we ate our supper.

And not knowing at that time, we were the luckiest kids in the world to have so many siblings and older folks who respected, and cared for, and loved all of us. Even though we've all gone in a thousand different directions, my life will always light up at Christmas time remembering those positive, pleasant, and powerful memories. Who among us would have ever thought while we were young and living at the Home, that those would be the times and memories that would be so precious to us now, all these many years later?

Bill Bailey

SUSAN (SUMMERS) MARKS (1965)

Like Barb, I find there is a certain sadness around the holidays too. When I was growing up, all of my family lived pretty geographically close, so it made it easier for us to be together during the holidays. We didn't do anything spectacular, but I remember being together with aunts, uncles, and cousins, just relaxing and visiting. We would set up a card table and work interlocking puzzles, play canasta, and drink Cokes. I remember the Cokes so well because mother never bought any Coke at the house. It was always milk, juice, or water, so having a Coke was a real treat for me. It was a time free of stress. My parents brought Mike and me up stressing that "family" was everything. I hold to that today, but now we are a much more mobile society and it makes it harder for us to get together. We have a daughter in Pennsylvania, a daughter in OKC that will have to work that day, and a son in the Dallas area, and none of them will get to come home this year. That saddens me, however, we have a daughter and son-in-law that will be in from Dallas for three days. I am trying to focus on the blessings we have in our lives, not the negatives, and that helps. On Christmas Eve, my ex-mother-in-law and her daughter will be coming to our house for lots of good snacks and conversation. We are all still very close, and I am thankful for that.

I think part of the sadness is that things are different than when I grew up. As a child I didn't have adult stresses to deal with. Now I have the responsibilities that go along with being an adult, and I think that takes a toll. As a kid, you don't have many worries, because the adults in your life have the burden of being responsible.

Christmas is supposed to be a time when we come together for sharing and celebration. I am going to focus not on who is not here, but on those that were able to make it. I am going to enjoy good food and conversation and the love I feel for those around me (whether near or far). I am also going to be thankful for food on the table, clothes on my back, and a roof over my head. All too often I take these things for granted and these are basics in everyday living. Once again, I wish all of you a happy holiday season.

Love, Susan (Summers) Marks (1965)

SANDY (BRISSEL) JACKSON (1967)

Hey there girl! Merry Christmas to you and all of our extended family!!!!!! Hope you have a great one. I will share the most precious memory of Christmas I had at the Home. Some of us kid's including Johnny and I were taken by bus to Bartlesville, OK. There were some families there that would take us kids in for the holidays, if you had nowhere to go. My mom was in Norman at that time, and my dad was at McAlester State Prison. The people who took me in were so wonderful. They asked me what I would like for Christmas, and I told them that I would like to see my dad. They called and talked to the warden at McAlester, and got me and Johnny (who was staying with a different family) passes in to see our dad. The father of the family I was staying with took us there on Christmas day to see our dad. What an exceptional family they were. I am sorry that I do not remember their names at all. (Old age gets you every time! HA) Anyway, that was the best Christmas I can remember. Everyone, have a very Merry Christmas, and a great New Year!!!

Linda Stewart Dundee had the record player that Susan Summers used to play her West Side album on. Linda says that to this day she has a fond memory of the West Side story. Since they played the record over and over she knew the words.

Ok, I know when I talked to Linda she says like me Christmas is her favorite time of the year. But there is also sadness about it as well. Do any of the rest of you find the holidays sad? Please let me know, as I would like to know if it's just Linda and I or are some of the rest of you affected?

Love ya! Sandy (Brissel) Jackson 1967

JOHNNY BRISSEL (1965)

As once more the bell tolls for Christmas, it always affects me in many and varied ways. I'm so thankful for the family I became close to in the Home School, and what a character building event it became for us all. I know without a doubt that it was the most profound event in my life that helped make me who I am today. Each and every one of you played a tremendous role in my life. I'm forever grateful for Mr. and Mrs. Summers, as many of you feel I'm sure that they became our surrogate parents who taught us values and discipline in our lives. I have endured many ups and downs in my life, but the Home School will be in my heart till I die, I don't think I would have had it any other way than growing up the way I did. I love each and every one of you and thank you again for all the memories. I have two wonderful sisters, Sherry and Sandy, and a brother, who have been there for me and I'll cherish the relationship with them forever, as I do for all my extended family from the Home.

We sometimes do not appreciate things in our life, and it only becomes apparent when you lose them. Even though we don't see each other often, you're always in my thoughts and prayers. Thanks to each and every one of you. May God shine down on you and yours, and may this next year be the most kind and rewarding to you all.

Love Johnny Brissel (1965)

DONNA (WILLEFORD) HAFFNER (1967)

Hi Everyone, I hope you and yours have a very Merry Christmas. I too have fond memories of the days at the Children's Home. As a matter of fact, those days were the best. My only regret is I didn't realize it then and make the best of it. I still get a lonesome feeling when I think about those days. I sure wish I could go back and redo. I don't have any complaints about today, just wishes of yesterday. Talk to all of you later.

Love, Donna (Willeford) Haffner (1967)

RITA (CHILDERS) HARTZOG (1967)

Hello to All… It's been a very long time since I have talked to anyone except Barb. Hearing all of your fond memories of Christmas Past makes me miss each and every one of you. I may not be in touch but my thoughts are always with you all. I do wish all of you a very Merry Christmas and a Blessed New Year. I will spend Christmas Eve with my children and grandbabies, and Christmas will be with friends.

My Christmases at the American Legion Home were always great, but also nerve wracking, I never knew where I would be going for Christmas and being kind of shy I was mostly scared to death. Wow!!!!! Time does have a way of changing all that. Tee-Hee..

I love living on the water in Florida, especially with most of my family here. My brother Bill is living in Texas but we are always in touch.

I lost both my oldest and youngest brothers, Larry and Danny Childers and we miss them terribly. My older sister Mary Childers (Bolding) is fine and of course Bill and I are great.

I would love to see you all and will share the information I receive from you with the rest of my family. Bill and I do the computer thing but Mary does not have the interest. I will try to get some pictures to share with you all, that is when I get one that makes me look great, so it might take awhile. Tee-Hee

Merry Christmas!!!
We Love you All, Rita (Childers) Hertzog (1967)

MICHAEL RUTH (MCADAMS) JONES (1963)

Oh yes how I remember Christmas at the home. Unlike Barb, I can't really remember doing anything to celebrate Christmas at the Home. Mrs. Mayhue used to pick me up on the day that school was dismissed and putting me on a bus to somewhere. She would always say, "These people have asked for a child like you and you will have a good time. Don't worry." I made a lot of friends and had a great time and boy did I get lots of presents but I always told them that I had to be back at the home a day before everyone else. That always caused a commotion among the help at the home. I loved it. I spent a couple of Christmases visiting with Mrs. Mayhue. Mostly we just drove anywhere she or I wanted to go to visit whomever. One year she and I picked up Linda Evans in a small town outside of Tulsa, that's when I met Linda's mother and her younger siblings. Mrs. Evans was a very hard working mother, it seemed she tried very hard to provide for her children.

The last Christmas I remember that I spent at the home was when I had my four children; we were all at Mr. and Mrs. Summers' house. I was going through a divorce at the time. Susan and her little girl Dama were there we all had lots of fun. The children of the Home were all gone to visit their sponsors, but Ale Joe the owl was there and entertained my four very young children. I can remember Mr. Summers becoming so angry with my two sons because they had let owl Joe into the gym. He was ready to kill them. I'm sure we all remember his temper. But we remember his love too. ----O.K. enough of my remembering, everyone, have a Merry Christmas.----

Love, Michael Ruth (McAdams) Jones (1963)

LINDA LU (STEWART) DUNDEE

Hi Barb... Your letter was really very sweet... I feel exactly the way you do only because of our past... I have so many memories of the Legion Home... most of them are funny as hell... They weren't at the time they were happening, but looking back on them they are now...

I miss Mrs. Mayhue to this day, what a grand women she was... and Mrs. Jackie Laird... she taught me how to tell time using the big clock in the dining hall... I remember one time you dumped out all my drawers because they were not neat and I had to fold and refold clothes until YOU agreed they looked neat enough, I hated you for that for a long time... I don't think you ever knew... I love you now... Gosh how we have grown all these years...

Back then we all had nothing but our Birthdays to call our own...Birthdays were our day no one could take away from us, right?

Christmas time was our time to get out of the home and go visit with real people, in real homes and be given all the attention we craved so all year long... It was truly the only time of the year I felt any kind of real love when I would visit with my sponsors James and Betty Sterling, and they spoiled me rotten. I love you Barbra. Barb, sweetheart, please take care and if you want to talk or cry, or laugh, call me, I am real good at all three... Bye doll.

Love to All, Linda Lu (Stewart) Dundee

BARBRA (MAHORNEY) ALUSI (1966)

I believe with all my heart that Mrs. Mayhue and Mr. and Mrs. Summers would have been proud of all of their great kids. Especially, how we all have stayed in touch as a family. I know that I am always saying it, but I'll say it again. I want you to know I am so proud to have all of you, and prouder still to have you as my family.

God bless all of you during this most beautiful time of year!
Love, Barbra (Mahorney) Alusi 1966

SANTA CLAUS PLANS 'BIG DOINGS' IN HONOR OF LEGION'S CHILDREN

The following story by Mary Bartram
Ponca City News ~ Wednesday ~ December 24, 1930

Santa Claus is a busy man, and Christmas is a busy season, but it's a safe bet that the jolly old patron is going to remember first of all in Ponca City the group of about 65 children at the American Legion Home School. In fact, it's a "sure thing," for Santa whispered to this reporter that while he will not have time to visit the school personally, he's going to have a whole battalion of helpers to do the job up right.

The Boys Club of the school, composed of the boys over nine years of age, has arranged a program to be presented in the living room of the girls' building. The girls have decorated a tree at one end of the room, and the program will be given around it. There will be Christmas carols, sung by a group of boys; and the children who are studying at the DeBrae Dancing School will give some dances. The kindergarten pupils are planning to represent Santa's Toys, each child portraying one toy in a characteristic poem, dance or song. One of the older girls is going to tell about the custom of celebrating Christmas. Some of the toys will be distributed after the program, each child receiving the same amount.

On Christmas morning, the children will find presents beneath the trees in the living room of the houses, as evidence of Santa's work.

There will be plenty of turkey for everybody Christmas noon, as Doctor McIlvane of Lone Wolf has sent his customary seven turkeys to the children, and the Frederick Post of the American Legion has sent some more. The tables will be decorated with miniature trees and Santa Clauses fully equipped with sleigh and reindeer.

Christmas day, also, the gift of the Norman Post of the American Legion will be set. This is a moving picture machine which was sent to all of the children. The pictures will consist of two nature pictures and a Felix comedy, and came from the Extension Division of the University of Oklahoma. Additional pictures will be secured as they are desired.

A few of the children are visiting the auxiliaries by whom they were adopted. They will spend the entire vacation, probably not returning until after the first of the year. There will be several visitors at the school on Christmas, including Department Commander and Mrs. Moody Nicholson, who have given a set of encyclopedias to the Home School.

Gifts have been sent in to the Home from various sources, in order that no child would be neglected. The members of the American Business Club drew names, and each member brought a present for a certain child. The local Chamber of Commerce sent individual boxes of candy to the children, and both the Tonkawa and Tulsa Posts of the Legion sent candy. The Brown-Dunkin department store of Tulsa sent a box of toys to be distributed.

The Auxiliaries which have adopted children at the Home have sent boxes to their children. The largest single gift is a sled; sent by the Perry Auxiliary to its children. Mr. and Mrs. Everett White of Okmulgee have subscribed to *Child Life* and the *American Boy* for the children.

This is the third Christmas to be celebrated at the American Legion Home School, which was dedicated during the summer of 1928. The site and one building were donated by E. W. Marland, and one building was given by W. H. McFadden. The Marland building houses 25 girls, the McFadden building houses 25 boys. A new unit, the Administration building, was dedicated last summer. It contains the office of the Superintendent, Miss Esther Sexton, and houses seven boys and eight girls. The school is maintained by State Appropriation, and the children are adopted by the American Legion Auxiliary Units, who clothe their wards.

AROUND THE CHRISTMAS TREE IN THE MARLAND BILLET IN 1929

FAR LEFT: SIDNEY MARKS ~ KIRBY RIDER (IN FRONT) ~ ERNEST MCADAMS

SEATED IN FRONT: SAMMY JACKSON ~ JOHNNY MARKS ~ UNIDENTIFIED ~ BILLY JAY SANDERS ~
ROBERT WILSON ~ VIRGIL PENROD

RIGHT BOTTOM ROW: LESTER GATTIS ~ UNIDENTIFIED ~ PAUL JACKSON ~ UNIDENTIFIED ~
T. L. RIDER ~ LEON "JIGGY" RIDER ~ CLIFFORD PENROD ~ UNIDENTIFIED

SECOND ROW STANDING: GENE RIGSBY ~ JUNIOR RIDER ~ JIMMY RIGSBY ~ UNIDENTIFIED ~
KENNETH GUNNING ~ JULIUS MARKS ~ LELAND HARDER
BACK ROW: MR. MILT PHILLIPS AND MRS. PHILLIPS (GUESTS) ~ UNIDENTIFIED ~
MISS DOROTHY HILSWICK, SUPERINTENDENT

Ponca City, Oklahoma ~ Monday ~ November 8, 1943

This is a letter I found amongst Mrs. Mayhue's scrapbooks.
Half of six lines are torn from the upper left hand corner of the letter.
It is the copy typed on brown paper.

Dear Santa,

If someone hadn't taken the pleasure to tell me that there wasn't any "Santa" which just about broke my heart until I found out it was really "Dearest Auxiliary" that had been so sweet to me and I'm truly glad because just think of all those lovely summer vacations that I would have missed if it had been Santa instead.

As I know no one better than I do you all, I feel very justified in saying that even if I wanted nothing this year, you all would take it upon yourselves to see that everything went just as it used to when you would receive the "chunky little letter" with a list of things in it that I would like to have and saw to it that I had a grand Christmas just as any little girl would have in her own home. I could go on to say that you all have been responsible (through all the years that I have spent at the Home here) for me to wake up early in the morning on Christmas day and enjoy opening all the lovely gifts that you had sent; but ah!, it would take more pages than I have and that is something which I shall never be able to thank you enough for. But in my own little way I do thank you for what I can! So keep this thought in mind that whatever you think of for me this Christmas I have the same thought in mind and anything would please me ~ clothes, toilet articles or eats would be just the things. So just do what you think best.

Well, for my grades now; (I just know you all have been sitting on the edges of your seats waiting to hear about them and us we have now approached the subject you may sit back and let your breath out with a big sigh), give a big smile and say "our prodigy has come through with flying banners except for one little hole in it". Of course it was an "effort put forth" but I think the teacher just got me mixed up with the blank face she saw sitting there answering 'here' to the name of 'Adams', but as it had no affects on my passing the subjects for the first nine weeks of this semester.

Chapter Five

More Billets and Improvements

When the first plans were made for the American Legion Home School, it was discovered that Oklahoma had over 500 children of World War veterans who were in need of help. The 40 children that chose to live at the Home in the spring of 1928 were just a small beginning.

Mr. Marland had pledged himself to gain support of enough other wealthy citizens of Oklahoma to erect several other billets as the need demanded.

The Legion pledged a drive to raise $180,000, which was based on $10 per member for the membership of the state. They did not plan to go to the general public for funds in that drive, but each Legion Post was to raise its quota from its ranks or, if necessary, from business men of the different communities. However, it became evident that if the Home School was to be a success, every citizen of Oklahoma must be made to recognize his responsibility toward the Oklahoma boys who sacrificed all during the World War, and toward the children of those Oklahoma boys who were suffering because of that sacrifice.

It was time for the American Legion to go on with their plans for at least seven buildings, including an administration building, dining hall, school building, auditorium, and dormitories. In September of 1928, the American Legion officials were ready to decide which building would be next. A conference made up of George Davis, Department Commander, Frank A. Douglass, past Department Commander and Ted Petit, Department Adjutant, along with local Ponca City Legion officers, members of the state executive board and E. W. Marland came to the conclusion that an administration building should be first. But they also agreed that the other billet for children must be added as soon as possible.

The cost of the administration building was set at about $100,000. It was to be the quarters for the Home School staff. The J. Duncan Forsythe Corporation began immediately to draw plans and work soon begun by Dick Sherbon, contractor.

The workmen had an interested row of spectators everyday that looked forward to the completion of the new building. They were the children in the Home, and they were really excited over "shooting the basement." Many wanted to be on the scene of action, but were kept indoors, however, and watched the spectacular event from their windows.

On July 26, 1930 the third building was completed and officially dedicated. Milt D. Campbell of Cincinnati, the National American Legion Vice Commander was the principal speaker. The 65 children living at the Home opened the program with a fifteen minute presentation. Tom Gammie of Ponca City and chairman of the state legion's child welfare committee presided. Short talks were made by Miss Dorothy Hilsweick, superintendent of the Home, B. G. Patton, state commander of the American Legion, Mrs. S. M. Singer, state president of the American Legion Auxiliary and E. W. Marland.

The new building, easily recognized by the bell tower, made it possible to bring 14 more children to the Home. They were among the group that performed for the dedication.

That summer was a busy time. It was the second camp season at Camp McFadden and 12 girls from the Home attended, with Pauline Hill receiving the loving cup for the best girl camper. Also, the girls organized a liter society under the direction of Mrs. Hobbs, Assistant Superintendent, and they presented many original programs.

The boys tended garden and helped Mr. H. L. Miller with the landscaping. The boys enjoyed working with Mr. Miller, who was also the driver of the bus that took the children to and from school. He was a former gardener associated with Henry Hatashita, a landscape gardener for E. W. Marland's estate. Mr. Miller and the boys gave a professional touch to the flower beds. They built a trellis for sweet peas and planted roses and shrubs.

Summertime also meant kindergarten twice a week for hour. A class in home economics instruction, personal hygiene, morals and manners taught Mrs. Hobbs on Wednesdays. Miss Hilswel the Superintendent, talked to the boys and girls or Thursday evenings about character building. Fridays meant a free show anywhere downtown, or they could go swimming free at the municipal pool Saturdays were for shopping, and on Sundays the school bus took the child to the church of their choice for Sunday School.

The family tie was strong in the members of the Home School. There were five families of four children, numerous threes, a number of twos and only one child with neither brother nor sister. Among the 14 that arrived during the summer of 1930 were three year-old twins, Marvin and Madeline Kinchen of Chandler. There were music clans two played in public recitals, and a twelve year-old boy, T. L. Rider, was talented dancer.

That fall, all the children attended thee Ponca City Public Schools except ten, who went to Miss Helen Cooper's kindergarten free of charge.

Also, that fall, plans were already in progress for a fourth building. I became known as the Annex. It was to join the administration building and would appear as one unit the same heating plant would be used for both buildings. G.J. Canon of Ponca City was the architect and the design matched the other buildings with stucco and roofs of tile. This addition made room for 26 children and dining facilities for 36.

Dedication was in November 1931, with the keynote speaker being Henry L. Stevens, Jr., National Commander of the American Legion.

The following year a garage building which also housed the laundry was finished.

A welcome addition to the Home School in the winter of 1937 was a new playground with tennis courts and equipment. Special ceremonies brought dignitaries of the American Legion for the dedication of the Fritz Blumenthal Playground. A bronze tablet with his name was placed in his memory. He had been a German citizen who later became naturalized and served in the American forces. In his will he stipulated that some of the funds from his war risk insurance should be used for a special project at the Home School. Joe Looney of Wewoka, Department Judge Advocate, gave the dedicatory address. The playground was accepted by S. Bee Crawford, chairman of the Home School Committee.

An announcement was made May 2, 1938, that a new building was to be constructed at the Horne. The American Legion Home School Building Corporation had met the Lay before in McAlester. Guy Conner of Ponca City chairman of the Home School Committee and I served as Secretary-Treasurer of the building corporation.

THE AMERICAN LEGION CHILDREN'S HOME, ABOUT 1935

He said the new building was to be a superintendent's billet, "The cost was estimated at $8,000, but an additional $2,000 would be needed for remodeling the Administration Building and furnishings for the cottage."

Joe G. Cannon was named architect, and O.W. Williams was low bidder when the contractors met with John Kennedy, of Pawhuska, a member of Soldiers Relief Committee. Williams' bid was $9,900, but the final cost was $8,560.00 The Conner Sheet Metal Works did the metal work, roofing and heating. Cooley Plumbing Company had contract on plumbing, and Clint Starr did the painting and decorating. Lumber and materials were furnished by the Baughman Lumber Company. The electrical work was done by A. O. Braker Company.

The five-roomed cottage was of modified Spanish architecture, light buff in color, to blend with the other buildings. It was located on the east side of the quadrangle on a spot that had been saved for that purpose. It was constructed of solid brick walls and covered with cement stucco. Inside, the house had oak floors throughout with the exception of the kitchen, which, was covered with linoleum, and the bathroom, which had a tile floor. A new type of plaster was used on the walls. It had insulating and acoustical plaster, a material that was supposed to pliable enough to withstand cracks. All the rooms were covered with wallpaper except the kitchen bathrooms which were painted. There was ample closet space in the bedrooms and a cedar closet in the hall. There was a part basement and a warm air circulating heating plant. It was designed so the refrigerated conditioning could be installed later.

The cottage was furnished and the selection of furniture and equipment was made by Mrs. John Kennedy Pawhuska.

J. H. Crosby, a superintendent, and his wife and daughter were the first to occupy the new home. They moved in Wednesday, November 16, 1938.

The Williams contract also called for remodeling of the second floor of the Administration Building, where the superintendent and his family had lived. This would make room for 12 more children. There were a total of 112 boys and girls at the Home when the work was completed.

Guy Conner, chairman of the American Legion Home School Committee, and Leonard Starke, a member of the committee, were in charge of the new building project.

When National Commander, Seaborn P. Collins of Las Cruces, New Mexico, came to give the address for the dedication of Memorial Hall, he said, "This building is proof that the people of Oklahoma are willing to take part in the American way of life."

Many Legion officials were present for the ceremony, but Clyde E. Muchmore, publisher of the *Ponca City News* and master of Ceremonies, gave a special praise to the Home School Committee, composed of Homer Tanner, chairman, M. L. (Dick) Atkinson and Professor A. D. Buck of Tonkawa. Mr. Muchmore said these three conceived the idea for the building and stayed with it until it was completed. Dick Atkinson had pleaded for the cause when he explained that the children had to use the dining rooms for study halls. Dishes, and everything had to be cleared away and the noise over before the children could settle down to study. Also in cold and inclement weather, they had no place play. The 96-by-60 foot building was to contain a gymnasium, library, study hall, office space and showers.

The building was estimated to be worth $75,000 to $80,000, but donations of labor and materials made up differences between $32,000 cash that was collected for Legion posts and individuals from all over the state. Organized labor, pledged by local craftsmen, had accounted for $16,000 of the estimated cost; while materials, equipment and. services donated by Ponca City building and related firms added $10,000 to the fund.

The fund had begun with a request of a contribution of 25 cents per member, but there were all sorts of activities organized to bring in much larger amounts. Some of the money was raised by posts and units having parties, dances, games or other fund raising methods. But many posts made direct contributions, and there were men like Senator Bola Kerr, past Department Commander, who gave, $7,500, and Dr. A. B. Rivers, a retired Okmulgee Dentist and past State Commander, who also gave $7,500. The businessmen of Ponca City gave $10,500 in cash, Tonkawa raised $4,800 and Enid gave $2,200.

Also, among the contributors was Major T. L. Rider, United States Air Force hero of World War II. When he learned about the proposed recreational building at the Home School he immediately sent a sizeable contribution. He had been a resident at the Home School from the time it opened until he was its first student to graduate from Ponca City High School eight years later.

When he sent his contribution, he wrote, "I have thought and dreamed of such a building for many years. I am glad to see it start. I want to be among the strongest advocated of the project."

T. J. LeFlore, J.R. Meek, Joe Miller and Robert Spray had been leaders in the all-out campaign, and along with the many contributors and workers who made it possible, could rightfully be proud when Memorial Hall was dedicated on December 18, 1954.

The gymnasium was dedicated to the memory of five men "who made the supreme sacrifice in giving their lives for freedom." They have all been residents of the Home School before they entered a branch of the service during World War II.

A marble plaque on the wall inside bears this inscription:

MEMORIAL HALL
Dedicated to the Memory of

Rubin Gooch	**Alvia Minor**
Porter Masters	**Carl Reynolds**

Elvis Reynolds
American Legion Home School Boys
Who Gave Their Lives in World War II
For God and Country

Mr. Muchmore told the story of a problem boy he had picked up in Oklahoma City and taken to the Home School. Upon arrival the boy was heard to say he wasn't going to stay at that "dump" very long.

"However, I accompanied him to the ball diamond, where promptly made a home run. From that time on Alvia Minor was a part of the School."

He became known as the ready helper of Miss Sexton, former superintendent. He went on to the University of Oklahoma, enlisted in the Navy during the war, and went down with a ship in the Pacific.

This school could be considered worthwhile for the saving of that boy Muchmore said.

Many people were praised that day, but no one was happier than the 100 Home School children. They at last had a place to do their homework and a place to play.

A photograph of a proposed dining hall was exhibited at the Department Convention in Oklahoma City in August of 1958. Earl Summers, the Home School Superintendent, and the Home School committee, headed by Joe Onstot and aided by Tom Willis of Ponca City and Ike Crawford of Enid were there to persuade members of tile posts and auxiliary units give financial backing to complete the building. Their argument was that the Home had a dining room and kitchen each of the dormitory units and the demand for more livingspace to house the increased number of children prompted the need for a centralized building. It would be built so as to utilize a garage which stood at the south edge of the School Circle. It would be constructed of concrete blocks brick veneer. The kitchen would have walk-in type refrigerator boxes and deep freeze units for preservation of food.

**THE AMERICAN LEGION CHILDREN'S HOME
IN SUMMER OF 1960**

After the completion of the central dining room, the other three would be converted into living quarters for the boys and girls.

Even though ground was broken in March of 1959, actual work could not begin because $66,000 was still needed to finance the project. But in October construction was approved, and the contract was given the Robertson Construction Company. There was still a shortage of $20,000. Among to plans to raise money was the selling of "bricks" at 50 cents each. More than 16,000 "bricks" were sold. Contributions by the Legion posts and auxiliary units and from individuals completed the fund. The donation of all his services by Ralph Burglund, architect, and the many discounts given by firms from which materials and equipment were purchased also played a big part in making the dining all a reality. When Rivers Memorial Hall was completed and the first banquet was held on the evening of April 23, 1960, the total cost of $72,000 had been paid.

Girls from the Home School served the meal which was given to honor Mrs. A. B. Buck, State American Legion Auxiliary President, and was hosted by her home unit, the Tonkawa Auxiliary. Mrs. Buck was praised for her loyalty to the Legion and Auxiliary child welfare program. Dinner music was presented by Norvel Bryson of the Home School.

The speaker was Major T. L. Rider who was introduced by Herman Smith, a former committee chairman of the Home. Smith said that Rider probably had done more to sell Home School than anyone else. Rider was the first Home School graduate, outstanding DeMolay, Eagle Scout, combat pilot and stationed with the Air force at Dover, Delaware. In his speech, Rider stated, "This home is no longer just a home but a shrine and let us perpetuate this shrine."

The next day was the 33rd Annual Home School Day, and more plans were made for extensive remodeling of the living quarters in the dormitories.

For the next five years there were continuous efforts to raise funds for the renovation of the four dormitories. The Home School Committee had estimated the costs for girls' dormitories at $65,000. But, eighteen months later when architect's plans and specifications were received from Ralph Burglund, and bids were presented, the lowest bid placed the cost $9,000. Funds for the original estimate had been set aside, but the committee was not prepared for the increased cost of labor and materials.

THE AMERICAN LEGION CHILDREN'S HOME ~ 1965

The Legion and Auxiliary members faced the challenge collecting the additional $30,000. The committee had faith that the goal would be reached so under the leadership of Ike Crawford of Enid, they proceeded by letting contracts in December, 1961, for the north wing of the girls' dormitory. Their plan was to get it finished and paid for and then schedule construction on the south wing.

This project proved to Oklahoma the real interest and care that Legionnaires and Auxiliary members have for their children.

The children and the Home School officials also cared. Along with Earl Summers, superintendent, the older boys saved over $1,000 in the contract price. They did a large portion of the demolition work. Temporary quarters for the girls were made in the recreational building. They seemed to think it was fun to "pioneer-it" for awhile. Everything had to be cleared out because the inside of the dormitory was completely changed, including doors, windows, plumbing and fixtures. More rooms were made with only two or three girls to a room instead of the open-type barracks for several girls to share.

In January of 1962, there were 23 girls in the north wing and 26 in the south wing. By March 1, the girls were able to move back to a modernized home and work was begun on the south wing. It was similar to the north wing, except it would cost more.

In March of 1964, it was three down and one to go, because the senior boys' dorm, Marland Hall, had been redone from top to bottom. Work men literally took the insides out of the building and started from scratch putting in new plumbing, heating and lighting. The high ceilings were lowered and three new rooms were made for the boys. Each room in the dorm accommodated four boys.

By April of 1965, the last of the four dormitories, McFadden Hall, had been refurnished. When the Legionnaires met for the dedication, they came within $2,000 of having enough to "burn the mortgage." Jack Newman of Ponca City was chairman the Home School committee. The other members

A BURNING OF THE MORTGAGE 1965

were Ike Crawford of Enid and Frank Throckmorton of Kingfisher. A $375,000 building improvement program had been concluded. The Home School had a capacity of 105 children.

In the fall of 1981, a priorities list was made of the largest capital improvements project ever planned for the Horne School. State Commander, Walter Rapp of Red Oak said buildings had gradually deteriorated and there would be a statewide drive to raise $300,000 for a renovation program to be completed in one year.

H. H. "Buddy" Champlin of Enid, president of Champlin Exploration was made state drive chairman, and Charles Casey, a Ponca City attorney, headed the drive in Kay County and the Ponca City are Carl H. Welch of Tulsa was chairman of the Home School committee, and Neal Winfield, Ponca City, and Elmore Meshew, Oklahoma City, were committee members. It would take many hours of donated time and effort by these men and many caring people from all over Oklahoma to carry out the plans.

The Huff-Minor Post 14 contributed $10,000 to start the campaign and Charles Casey's drive in Kay County was responsible for over one third of the project by donating more than $100,000.

Conoco, Inc. gave $10,000 toward the projected estimate of $40,000 needed for fire escapes. The fire marshal had said that fire escapes had to be installed in the four dorms in order to keep the required license for the Home. When Mertz, Inc. designed and installed doors on the second floor and the fire escapes for four buildings, Don and Forest Mertz presented no bill for the cost. This was all done in one month, so the Home could stay open. Thanks to the Mertz Brothers.

The Magbee Foundation of Tulsa contributed $60,000 for repair to the tile roofs which were 54 years old and leaking. The tiles had to be removed, and then put back over a cover of felt-like material that sealed the asphalt. The tile had been originally imported from Italy and broken pieces had to be replaced with tiles that would match as nearly as possible.

In April of 1982, when the Annual American Legion Children's Open House convened, it was announced that the campaign for $300,000 was short by only $35,000. By the end of July, the deficit was lowered to $14,000.

Besides the fire escapes and the tile roof repairs, several important improvements were made. Energy saving measures were installed to save on the cost of utility bills; such as insulation in the ceilings, new furniture, storm windows, lowering of some ceilings, circulating 52-inch fans, and conditioning.

Perhaps the most interesting improvement to the children was the built-in furniture in their bedrooms. A furniture wall was installed in each room, containing a chest of drawers, a wardrobe, a study desk, and a dresser with a mirror. Even the beds were built-in with storage space underneath. And everything on the priority list was ready before school started that fall.

The Legion and Auxiliary members had kept the faith.

CHILD WELFARE CONFERENCE AND HOME SCHOOL DAY NORTH WING IS COMPLETED; LESS THAN $12,000 NEEDED

April 1962 ~ The Oklahoma Legionnaire Newspaper

Legionnaires and Auxiliary members are invited to the annual Child Welfare Conference and Home School Day at Ponca City, scheduled for April 28-29, announced J. Earl Simpson, American Legion Home School Liaison Representative.

Everyone will have the opportunity of observing the remodeling project that has been completed on the north wing of the girls building. The furniture has been ordered and the high school girls will be living in the quarters on Home School Day.

Homer Tanner, Chairman of the Home School Committee, recently announced that approximately $12,000 is needed to assure the committee of sufficient funds to complete the south wing of the girls building.

Renovation of the south wing is expected to start on the south wing on May 1, 1962. Some four months will be required for the south wing to be completely remodeled.

The Home School Committee is anxious for all Legionnaires and Auxiliary members to see the north wing on Home School Day and during the Child Welfare Conference.

Simpson urges all Posts and Units to sponsor money-raising activities with the proceeds going to the Home School to raise the $12,000 needed by April 29. Checks are to be mailed to the Home School or turned in to the Home School by April 29 so the committee can start the south wing project.

Reports indicate that the new wing is something to behold as it is beautiful and modern in every respect and the project is one that all Legionnaires can be proud of in 1962. The cost of the completed project is $47,000 and the estimated cost of the south wing, yet to be renovated, is $45,000, with only $12,000 needed for the south wing project.

American Legion Posts and Units around the state are urged by Child Welfare Chairman Shag Allen, Vinita and J. Earl Simpson, Tulsa, to support the Home School by sending contributions on or prior to April 29, 1962.

The Home School project belongs to each Legionnaire and Auxiliary member in Oklahoma and the remodeling of the girls building will not be completed until the $12,000 is contributed to the Home School Committee. Now is the time to go to work and see that the funds are available on April 29. Your Post contribution will be of great value in the statewide project.

BEAUTIFICATION PROJECT CONTINUES AT HOME SCHOOL

Sunday ~ February 6, 1966 ~ Ponca City News

The year 1965 saw completion of the remodeling project at the American Legion Home School with the final $23,946 paid off in April according to the Home School Committee's annual report presented recently by Jack Newman, chairman.

Other work accomplished in 1965 includes a new roof on the laundry building and water proofing of the recreation building, a girls' dormitory, the superintendent's residence and the laundry building. The total of these contracts was $9,197, Newman said, and all had been paid or the funds were on hand to pay them at the close of business December 31, except for a balance of $1,856, still needed.

The chairman reported that some landscaping has been done as each of the remodeling projects was completed, with shrubs and flower beds set out and grass sodded around each.

He said the drive and the circle are still in need of beautification and there is need of curb and guttering on the drive to prevent erosion by rainwater. The committee would like to continue this project as its next step in progress at "the school." Newman added.

The report expressed appreciation to numerous people among them department officers and child welfare chairmen for both 1965 and 1966. Also named were Ralph Berglund, 1501 North Woodland and the Ponca City Medical Association, which has furnished doctors to see the Home School children, without cost, whenever they are needed.

Berglund, a Continental Oil Company engineer, has engineered and drawn plans for the complete remodeling project at the Home School.

Newman said the Home School has a capacity of 105.

MONEY GIFTS EXCEED $10,000 FOR LEGION HOME SCHOOL HERE

American Legion posts and auxiliaries in Oklahoma presented over $10,000 to American Legion Home School officials during the annual two-day child welfare program here Saturday and Sunday.

Funds contributed have liquidated the $10,000 bank note made to complete remodeling of the older boys' building on the Home School campus. Approximately $250 was collected in addition and will be used to start the fund for remodeling of McFadden Building, younger boys' dormitory.

Largest check for the American Legion School was for $1,700, given by the Enid organization. Tulsa and Bartlesville Posts and Auxiliaries gave checks for $1,000 each.

Remodeling of McFadden Building is the last planned improvement scheduled in the remodeling program begun three years ago. During this time, a new central dining room was built at a cost of $75,000 and three dormitories were remodeled and furnished at a cost of $55,000 each.

Over 600 persons attended the open house at the Home School Sunday afternoon.

Keynote speaker at the dinner meeting Saturday evening in the American Legion Hut was Dr. James L. Denis associate dean of medical affairs and professor of pediatrics at the University Of Arkansas School Of Medicine, Little Rock.

MR. SUMMERS ON THE LEFT

Lawrence Gregory, Bill Bailey, and Jess Wright are talking to each other about how it was to help in building the gym…..

LAWRENCE GREGORY

Seeing the pictures of the gym being built brings back lots of memories. As I view the pictures I can remember how we (the boys), has fun in spite of the heat and hard work. The skilled workers would call for more "mud." So, in a playful mood, we would mix more mortar and deliver "more mud" to the workers. I believe the boy standing by the cement mixer is Frank Wright. In the center of the picture, I am the third boy (L-R) wearing the white t-shirt. Those were the good old days….

Lawrence Gregory '56

BILL BAILEY

I remember the back foundation that we chipped through solid limestone bedrock to pour the foundation of that back wall for those cement blocks. We even helped the bricklayers pour the cement for that block wall. And I remember digging that awful sewer pipe trench between the north gym wall and the little boys' dorm down to the sewer manhole. It took two weeks, as I remember, with parts of the ditch being about ten feet deep. My blister memories still hurt today after fifty years. I remember the pipe troughs that Mr. Summers built to hold the banana oil to soak the oak 2 x 2 boards to lay out for the gym floor. Then we put the flooring in and were not able to walk on it for a week. The whole gym smelled like bananas for weeks. We also strung the wires to hold the fiber ceiling tiles. What a job that was! But it taught us how to work and take pride in creating something we treasured for years, 'our own gym.' I remember you and Babe saying, "Little boy get to work, it ain't going to get done by sitting there and looking at it." That phrase has always stuck with me even till today. The first thing is to get a job done and then sit back and look at it. These photos bring back great memories of a job well done.

Bill Bailey (61)

JESSE WRIGHT

Lawrence, these photos bring back a lot of old memories. Isn't that Benny sitting next to you and is that C.D. Pierce on the left? I didn't get to play in the gym but did bust a lot of rocks to make way for it.

Jesse Wright

LAWRENCE GREGORY

Hi Jesse, It's really good to hear from you. You have a good eye. Your comments have caused me to take a second look at this photo. I believe the boy on the left, looking straight ahead is C. D Pierce. I am not sure who the boy in the middle is. I, (Lawrence Gregory), am the one in the white T-shirt. Your brother Frank Wright is standing by the cement mixer. My brother Ben agrees with you regarding C.D., but not sure about the boy in the middle, maybe Bruce Wyatt.

Lawrence Gregory '56

Chapter Six

The American Legion Home School Committee

The Home School is under the direction of a three-man committee who selects the superintendent and staff. Each year the Department Commander of the American Legion appoints a Home School committeeman to serve a term of three years, and one man is retired. Thus, the Committee is composed of three Legionnaires at all times. These men give freely of their time and effort to provide children of deceased, disabled or destitute veterans the advantages of home, school and church.

This is the only home of this type anywhere in the world and is a work of which all Oklahoma Legionnaires and Auxiliary members have made possible through their gifts and time.

The men who served on the committee from the founding of the home in 1928 to the present day have each had difficult problems and emergencies to solve. They each deserve special recognition for their unselfish service. The following lists of names are men who served as chairman or members of the committee. Most of them served at least one term of three years, and some filled more than one term. Some have donated many hours of service after their term was over just because they were dedicated to helping boys and girls. They never stopped caring.

If any names are omitted from the following list of honor, it is because records were not available. These names have been found through researching into newspaper stories about the Home.

LEGIONNAIRES WHO HAVE SERVED ON THE HOME SCHOOL COMMITTEE:

~ W. I. Nunn ~ Herb L. Schall ~ Thomas G. Gammie ~ Charles B. Duffy ~

~ R. G. Ross ~ Clyde E. Muchmore ~ Charles Reed ~ J. Allan Brown ~

~ Joe Cannon ~ E. R. Turner ~ S. Bee Crawford ~ Perry Whiting ~

~ Guy L. Conner ~ Leonard B. Starke ~ M. E. Clawson ~ Herman J. Smith ~

~ D. Earl Jones ~ Charles Hull ~ R. O. Wilson ~ Harry McAnulty ~

~ Ralph Berglund ~ H. F. Rushing ~ Harold E. Wiley ~ Frank Ramsey ~

~ Coy Harris ~ Frank Carter ~ Homer Tanner ~ Lee Askey ~ M. L. Dick Atkinson ~

~ A. D. Buck ~ Joe D. Onstott ~ Thomas E. Willis ~ Ike Crawford ~

~ Jack Newman ~ Floyd Throckmorton ~ Leon Grace ~ Carl Welch ~

~ Neal Winfield ~ Elmore Meshew ~ Clyde Hickman ~ Maurice Hamilton ~

SUPERINTENDENTS

The Superintendent is hired by the Home School committee of the American Legion. He is to direct the activities and carry out the policies of the American Legion in the operation of the Home.

The superintendents have always lived at the Home. For ten years they lived in the dormitories and often were house parents, too. Between 1928 and 1936, six women served as superintendents and were called 'Directors.' There is limited information about them, except that they were highly qualified as child welfare workers and provided excellent training in personal hygiene, morals, social graces and the cultural arts. They were sincere in wanting to make good, productive citizens out of their charges.

In 1938, a separate billet was built for the superintendent and his family. At this time, the leadership of the Home became a husband and wife team, and the wife became an active member of the staff.

The following list is the names of women and men who served as Directors or Superintendents. There is limited information about some of them, but they must be mentioned because of their service to many boys and girls who lived at the Home. Some of the activities in which they participated are given in other parts of the book.

1928 ~ MISS R. M. JOLLIE

Miss Jollie was the first director of the Home and was there just enough to help with the initial organization. She had come to America after World War I from England, where she had been an army nurse. She was a graduate of Orange Memorial Hospital, and left the Home to return to West Orange, New Jersey. She did not forget the home or the girls in Marland Hall, because in 1930 she sent them a radio for Christmas.

Miss Ruth Dewberry was the assistant director, but was there for only a short time. The other helpers were Mrs. Lillian Hobbs and Mrs. Pearl Marks.

1929 ~ MRS. SUSIE DARLINGTON

Mrs. Darlington was an interim director following Miss Jollie. She was at the Home a very short time. She was an elderly lady, tall, stately and very kind toward the children. I described her as being much like a Victorian grandmother.

1930 ~ MISS DOROTHY HILSWICK

Miss Hilswick was a former teacher in the Roosevelt school in Ponca City, but had been associated with the Home School for a year before she became the Director. Mrs. Hobbs was her assistant, and she had taught in the Junior High School at Catoosa before she went to the Home School. Mrs. Anna K. Fain of Livingston, Texas was relief matron. Mrs. Maud Wallace was matron of the boys' billet, and Miss Clara Salyers was matron for the girls, Miss Salyers was a former teacher from Tulsa. Mrs. Inez Brown was another helper and was a former nurse from Wichita, Kansas.

1931 ~ MISS ESTHER SEXTON

Miss Sexton was born in Oklahoma, and graduated from Northeastern State University at Tahlequah. She taught school several years before going to the Legion Home. She was superintendent for three years. The older students were just beginning to enter high school, and Miss Sexton dealt with the problem of expanding the activities at the Home to include sports, drama, clubs, and social events.

Miss Sexton resigned in May of 1934. She soon was married to Owen Moss, an Oklahoma City attorney. They later moved to Lucedale, Mississippi

1934 ~ MISS VETA PORTER

Miss Porter was director of the Home for 15 months. She announced her resignation on September 9, 1935. She was to be married to Myron Oates, head athletic coach at Okemah.

Miss Porter was a former student at Edmond and Ada teachers colleges. She had taught at Paden for three years. There were 103 children at the home at that time. The buildings had undergone painting projects with the boys at the Home School doing the work. The gardens were enlarged and the playgrounds improved.

MISS VETA PORTER QUITS HOME SCHOOL SUPERINTENDENT SOON WILL WED; SUCCESSOR NOT YET SELECTED

Miss Veta Porter, superintendent at the American Legion home school the past 18 months, has announced her resignation in a letter to members of the American Legion home school committee. She expects to leave Ponca City in two weeks.

Miss Porter is giving up the work as director of the institution here as she is to be married to Myron Oates, head athletic coach at Okemah, September 28. The marriage will take place at Paden, home of Miss Porter's parents, at the First Methodist church.

Appointment of a new superintendent will fall to the home school committee including G. J. Cannon and Bee Crawford.

Miss Porter, former student at the teachers college at Edmond and Aida, came to this city after having been on the faculty of the Paden schools for three years. She succeeded Miss Esther Sexton who took a position at the statehouse in Oklahoma City.

During the superintendent's 15 months here the school entertained a number of distinguished guests including Frank Beigrano, national commander of the Legion. Governor E. W. Marland on a number of occasions, the president of the southern division of the Auxiliary, Mrs. Tom Gammie who is a candidate for the national president, the state commander. Cecil Harberson of Bartlesville, as well as many auxiliary and post delegates from points over the state. There have been numerous affairs for the school's staff doctors and dentists, dinners for honor students in the school.

The school's list of children has grown to include 103. During Miss Porter's 15 months as director, the projects with the boys at the school doing the work, the gardens were enlarged and playgrounds improved.

CROSBY APPOINTED HOME SCHOOL HEAD

The Ponca City News ~ Tuesday ~ November 19, 1935

WIFE TO ACT AS ASSISTANT, AND TO ASSUME DUTIES EARLY IN JANUARY

Mr. and Mrs. J. H. Crosby will be the new superintendent and assistant, respectively, of the American Legion Home School. They are to take over their duties officially January 20th following the present semester of school. Crosby is with the senior high school faculty as an instructor in English.

The selection of the Crosby's as directors of the school answers the committee's long-felt need for a man and a woman on the official staff. The committee in charge of the school includes Joe Cannon, chairman, and Bee Crawford, on the Home School committee. Notice of their selection has been sent the department headquarters of the American legion at Oklahoma City.

Mr. and Mrs. Crosby and small daughter are to move to the school immediately where they will familiarize themselves with the operation of the institution before taking over in January. Miss Ina Hedrick, who has been serving as superintendent since the resignation of Miss Veta Porter this summer; will remain in this capacity until the 20th of January, she plans to leave the school then. Mrs. Crosby will be her assistant.

MANY APPLICATIONS RECEIVED

Numerous applications from throughout the state had been received for the superintendent's job. The home school committee was assisted by Perry Whiting and Mrs. Leah Barrett in making the selection for the school.

J. H. Crosby is a veteran of the World war and a charter member of the Weatherford post of the American Legion. He has been teaching school the past 13 1/2 years and has his A. B. degree from Southwestern State Teachers College and his Master from the University of Oklahoma. In addition he has two summers' work towards his Ph. D. For two years Crosby was principal of schools at Lyman and Webb City. He spent a year on the faculty of Southwestern State Teachers college and for the past nine years has been on the senior high faculty in Ponca City.

MRS. CROSBY ALSO TEACHER

Mrs. Crosby has taught for nine years. She was in the Enid junior high school for five years and on the Ponca City junior high faculty for four years. She is a graduate of Phillips University at Enid, took her A. B. degree in 1927. In addition she spent a year in resident work at Sullins College, Bristol, Va., and did a summer of graduate work at the University of Oklahoma and a summer of graduate study, at the Colorado Teachers College in Greeley, Colo.

A statement from the committee says: "It is the opinion of the committee that this couple will conscientiously perform their duties, cooperate with the committee, and be very loyal to the Legion and the home school."

Previous superintendents of the school since its founding in 1927 were: Miss R. M. Jollie, Mrs. Susie Darlington, Miss Dorothy Hillswick, and Miss Ester Sexton Miss Veta Porter.

1935 ~ MISS INA HEDRICK

Miss Hedrick served as director until January, 1936. She filled a vacancy left by Miss Porter, and helped Mr. and Mrs. Crosby become oriented to the Home School.

1936 ~ J. H. CROSBY

Mr. and Mrs. Crosby took over the duties of superintendent January 20, 1936 following the first semester. They answered the long felt need for man and a woman team on the official staff. Mr. Crosby had been on the teaching staff at Ponca City Senior High. School for nine years and had taught English. He was a World War veteran and a charter member of the American Legion at Weatherford. He had and A.B. degree from Southwestern State Teacher's College, and a master's degree from the University of Oklahoma. He had worked two summers on a doctorate's degree. He had been a principal at Lyman and Webb City, and taught one year on the faculty of Southeastern State Teacher's College.

Mrs. Crosby had taught five years in Enid Junior High School, and four years in Ponca City. She graduated from Phillips University at Enid with an A.B. degree in 1927. She spent a year at Sullins College, and did graduate work at the University of Oklahoma and at Colorado Teacher's College in Greeley, Colorado.

Mrs. Crosby became an assistant to Miss Hedrick at the Home in order to become acquainted with the children and the work before Miss Hedrick left. The Crosby's were the first to live in the superintendent's billet.

1941 ~ GEORGE C. ABBOTT

GEORGE CHARLES ABBOTT AND HIS WIFE MARY ELLEN 1955

Abbott became superintendent of the Home School in September of 1941. He was graduated from university of Oklahoma in Norman, his native city. He was coach at the Norman High School and then went to Ponca City as coach and physical education instructor in 1923. He left coaching to take charge of the junior police patrol at the Ponca City police department in 1930, retaining that position until he became superintendent at the Home. Abbott had served more than a year at World War I. He spent time in France fighting in the battles of Muse/Atognne and St. Mihiel, and served in Germany with the army of occupation. After the war, he received the Distinguished Service Cross and the Croix r Guerre.

A total of 117 children were at the Home and by June, 1942, there were graduates of the American Legion Home School who were serving in the United States Military Services.

1948 ~ H. CLYDE POWELL

Powell was appointed superintendent and assigned his duties on February 19, 1948, succeeding George C. Abbott. For several years, Powell had been an elementary principal, and then for seven years he was a village consolidated school superintendent. He had a B.S. in Ed. degree from Central State College in Edmond, and a master's degree from the University of Oklahoma.

During World War II, Powell spent 30 months in the Army Air Corps. He was qualified by Oklahoma merit examiner as a test technician and as social welfare worker. He also had a civil service rating as a training officer and as a vocational advisor.

Powell was married and had two children. He was a member of the Methodist Church, Masonic lodge, Kappa Delta Pi, Phi Delta Kappa and the Red Red Rose. There were 115 children at the Home School.

1949 ~ LEROY BAKER

Baker came to the Home from Ardmore. He served as superintendent for two years, and then resigned to retire to Ardmore.

1951 ~ C. F. MCCAULEY

McCauley, a native of Abilene, Texas, came to the Home as superintendent in October of 1951. He was married to the former Leona McClaskey of Ponca City, and they had two children. McCauley was a veteran of World War II, having served over three years with the Second Marine Division, First Amphibious Corps. He saw duty in the South Pacific.

He had been employed as a district manager for Firestone, and previously was in the brokerage business for War Assets Administration. He worked as a district manager for Bardahl Oil Company at Corpus Christi, Texas.

McCauley served as superintendent at the Home School only until January of 1952.

Roy Pickens, State Child Welfare Officer or the American Legion in Oklahoma City, became acting superintendent until the Home School Committee employed a new one.

JANUARY 23, 1952 HOME SCHOOL HEAD WILL BE REPLACED

Fred Tillman of Pawhuska, chairman of the American Legion Home School Committee, said Wednesday that "C. F. McCauley has been relieved of his duties as superintendent of the home school located here."

Roy Pickens, state child welfare officer for the American Legion, Oklahoma City, is serving as acting superintendent until the committee can employ a new one, Tillman stated.

Members of the Legion Home School Committee are Frank Carter and Homer Tanner, both of Ponca City.

McCauley came here from Houston, Texas last fall to become Superintendent.

1952 ~ EARL N. SUMMERS

Commonly known as "Bucky," Earl Summers Tonkawa was selected as superintendent of the Home, and took over his duties on February 1, 1952. For several years, Earl Summers had been Superintendent of campus maintenance at Northern Oklahoma Junior College at, Tonkawa, from which he resigned to accept the position at the Legion Home. He was a veteran of World War II, having spent three years in the Air Force to hold the rank of sergeant. He was a graduate of college at Tonkawa. He married Lolabelle Summers on February 7, 1937, and had one daughter, Susan, and a son, Mike.

As superintendent, his objectives would be do everything possible to bring about a home atmosphere for the children in the Legion Home, and to keep in close touch with the teachers and administrators of the Ponca City schools. There were 117 children at the Home, and all of them attended the Ponca City schools.

Summers worked hard to carry out his goals, and served the Home School for 24 years. During that time there were many changes. The gymnasium and Central Dining Hall were constructed and all of the dormitories were renovated. There were also changes in the trends in education that required reorganization in order to meet new standards.

Frank Carter, chairman of the Home School Committee, said in his report of 1954, "The members of the committee are unanimous in the opinion that the moral, physical, and spiritual standing at the Home has reached its highest level, Superintendent Summers and his staff has made this possible." This progress continued throughout his administration.

Earl N. Summers died in May, 1976.

1976 ~ MRS. LOLABELLE SUMMERS

Mrs. Summers started her career as an assistant to her husband, Earl Summers, who became superintendent in 1952. After his death, she became acting superintendent, and served in that capacity until Charles F. Danley arrived to head the Home. She remained as assistant and worked in the office until she retired with 32 years' service on December 31, 1983. As part of her duties, Mrs. Summers spent considerable time visiting and speaking across the State on behalf of the Children's Home.

MR. & MRS. SUMMERS ~ WRITTEN BY THEIR DAUGHTER SUSAN SUMMERS MARKS

Dad:
Born: Earl N Summers, June 1, 1912, Arkansas City, Kansas
Died: May 14, 1976, Ponca City, Oklahoma
Enlisted in the Army Air Corps in 1943 (age of 31)
and was honorably discharged in 1946.

Attended and graduated from Northern Oklahoma Junior College. He worked to put himself through school as he was one of five children and his parents did not have the money to send him. He played "fullback" on the college football team and was nicknamed "Bucky." Very few people knew him by his real name. Everyone just called him Bucky. He also wrote the sports section of the school newspaper.

He married Lolabelle Holmes on February 7, 1937. He was an active member of the American Legion post in Tonkawa and served a term as Commander.

Mom:
Born: Lolabelle Holmes, October 16, 1916, in Hilldale, Oklahoma
Died: February 5, 1996, Ponca City, Oklahoma
Grew up in the town of Bliss, Oklahoma, now known as Marland, Oklahoma.

Attended Oklahoma State University for one semester, then, due to finances, transferred to Northern Oklahoma Junior College in Tonkawa. She took a job cooking, cleaning and ironing, for a family in Tonkawa. She made $4.50 a week plus room and board. She sang in an a-capella choir while in college and took voice lessons from Lena Sizelove. She also, from a very young age, wrote poetry. Her poetry was published in the Marland and Tonkawa newspapers. I have read two poems that she wrote when she was 12 and they sounded more like the work you would see from a college graduate. She very much liked the works of Alfred Lloyd Tennyson and I have her book of poetry by him.

She met "Bucky" Summers there and they were married on February 7, 1937.

Dad worked at the local lumber yard, then went to work for the college as the head of their maintenance department. During WWII, dad was stationed in California. He came down with meningitis and was very seriously ill. When he recovered, he was stationed in Tonopah, Nevada. Mom took the bus to Nevada to be with him. Mom worked at the base dry cleaners. Mom was the best country cook. Dad used to say that the guys on the base would beg him to take them home with him so they could eat mom's cooking, especially her gravy.

After WWII, mom and dad came back to Tonkawa, where they were dorm parents at the college. They also gave dad back his old job in the maintenance crew.

I was born on July 1, 1947. Mom and dad adopted me when I was one year old. They named me Susan Terrell Summers (the Terrell was my father's grandmother's maiden name) and they took me everywhere with them. They loved to square dance and play cards at friends' houses. They just loaded me in the car with my blanket and pillow and off we'd go. If I got tired I would just lie down and go to sleep.

In February 1952, we came to the American Legion Home School, as it was called then. I was four. What a change. I loved it. So many people around. Before I was old enough to go to school, I used to wait for the school buses to return each morning. Then I would hop on the bus and look for lunches (in the brown paper sacks) that were left (you could count on at least one each day). It was always a bologna sandwich with mustard and an apple or orange.

I was six when mom and dad asked me how I would like to have a little brother. I said yes!!!!! We went to Oklahoma City one day. We pulled up in front of this big white two-story house. Mom and dad made me wait in the car. It wasn't long until they came out to the car carrying a little boy. He was 10 months old and had blonde spiky hair. All the way home they asked me what I would like to name him. I don't remember any of the names I chose, but they clearly did not like my choices. Before we got home he was named Michael Earl Summers. He was born on September 16, 1953. The Earl was my father's first name. The minute we got home it was dinner time. We always ate in the Senior girls building. We walked in with Mike and the girls just went nuts over him.

Our parents raised us with good strong values: honesty, integrity, kindness toward others, a good strong work ethic and a strong love for God and Country, how to have a firm handshake and flag etiquette regarding the American Flag. I bet most people don't know that there are four verses to our National Anthem. I knew that and could sing all four verses before I was four years old.

Mike and I knew we were loved and wanted every day of our lives with them. To this day, we know just how lucky we were, and from our conversations together, not a day goes by that we don't think about them.

All the values they instilled in Mike and me, they tried to impart to each child at the Children's Home. They truly cared about each child. Their goal was not only to give food, shelter, clothing, and an education, but to teach those values that help you make your way in the world as a respected individual.

My dad was not an "I'll pat your back if you'll pat mine" kind of guy. The greatest thing he taught me was "to do it because it is the right thing to do, not because you expect some reward in return." This is basically how my mom and dad lived their whole lives, and I know we were all the better for it because we got to be a part of that.

- Susan Summers Marks

Chapter Seven

How It Was In the Beginning

MADELAINE KINCHEN MOSES REMEMBERS

MARVIN AND MADELAINE KINCHEN

My twin brother, Marvin and I were three years old when we first arrived at the Home School in 1929.

My first recollection has to do with sleeping in a crib in the downstairs dormitory of the Marland Building. I remember waking up in the night with the light shining dimly on the knobs of the dresser drawers. They looked like eyes – and I was afraid to go to the bathroom.

When the Annex was built next to the Administration Building, I lived there in the "nursery" with Ruth Lee Adams, Dorothy Reynolds, Erma Ruth Shannon and later Phyllis Mitchell. Bertha Justice, one of the older girls, slept there and took care of us.

We attended the Kindergarten in the Administration Building, in the room that later became the library. Mrs. Hobbs and Mrs. Sexton were the directors then, and taught the Kindergarten classes. In movies that were taken at that time, it shows that we had wash pans in the classroom to wash our hands and faces. I was even washing my eyes.

When we were very young, we gave lots of "productions," and invited people from town for the presentations. When we were in Kindergarten we did 'Tom Thumb's wedding'. Marvin and I were "married"; Ruth Lee Adams, Blossom Hobbs, Dorothy Reynolds, and Erma Ruth Shannon were dressed as the bridesmaids.

The Christmas that I was eight years old, we gave a production about Santa's toys coming to life. I was a big "French Doll," and was dressed in a blue acrobatic costume with a crepe paper skirt and bonnet. Someone took me out of a box, turned a key on my back, and I sang a song and did an acrobatic dance. Another group dressed like candy canes. Iris Marks was made up to be a "Negro Doll."

We also gave productions every summer at the carnival at Pond Creek. One summer, Iris Marks, Emma Faye Conrad and Dorothy Hobbs dressed in "Orange Blossom" costumes and did a neat tap dance. The "Real Hillbilly Band" was quite a hit. Clifford "Red" Bingham and his brother, Jessie, played guitars, J.R. tabor played a jug, and some other boys played a jew's-harp and washboard. Marvin and I had our own act. We sang "It's the Animal in Me," then he untied my crepe paper skirt, and I did an acrobatic dance.

THE FOURTH OF JULY PICNIC ~ BEHIND THE MCFADDEN BILLET IN THE 1930'S

The Fourth of July was always a lot of fun. We were given a lot of firecrackers - and we made them last all day. We went swimming at Wentz Pool, and then we had a picnic. Sometimes the picnic was below the hill by the McFadden Building. There were long tables with potato salad, baked beans, and lots of food.

Christmas was the best time. The evening before Christmas we decorated a big live tree in the living room with strings of popcorn, cranberries, silver icicles and colored lights. As presents arrived in the mail, they were locked up in a closet until Christmas Eve. On Christmas morning there was a clown with a pig and a dog that came to entertain us, and then Santa Claus handed out the presents.

One of the fun things we did was the making of fudge or popcorn in the evenings. We would pass it around to everyone. We kept the popcorn hot on the steam radiators.

In the summer we played games after supper - New York and Boston and Red Rover. One of our favorite activities was skating on the sidewalks. The girls went to Camp McFadden for weeks.

There was a "health kick" going around when we were young and the girls had to take sun baths out behind the dormitory on mattresses (which smelled terrible from sweat). Equally unpleasant was the fact that we were dressed only in our underwear. Even though we were very young, we were extremely embarrassed, because the boys had to walk by us on their way to the garden.

We had no air-conditioning, so we sometimes slept outside when it was hot – or on the floor by our beds.

After we were older, we had a drum and bugle corps with Alice McCoy as our Drum Major. We marched a lot of parades, and performed on the stage.

BACK ROW: MADELAINE KINCHEN ~ MARY PETERSON ~ RUBY ADAIR SEATED: ETHEL GREENWOOD ~ VIRGINIA WESTMORELAND ~ WILLA DEAN CAVENDAR

In 1939, we had a sextet composed of Ruby Adair, Willa Dean Cavnar, Ethel Greenwood, Virginia Westmoreland, Mary Peterson and myself. Mrs. J. Frank Ramsey was our director. She and her husband were both very active in the American Legion and the Auxiliary.

Another nice thing the Legionnaires and Auxiliary members did for the children at the Home, was to invite us to their homes for dinner, invited to the home of Clyde Muchmore. Mr. Muchmore was the owner and Editor of *The Ponca City News* at that time. He was a friendly gentleman; and his wife was a quiet gracious lady. Mr. Muchmore discovered that I had never had a chocolate malt, so on our "after dinner drive around town" he bought me a chocolate malt, and insisted that I drink it all. They were people of real quality. I'd like to thank them for sharing their home with my brother and me.

The people who probably had the strongest impact on my life were Mrs. Caldwell and Mrs. Hancock. Mrs. Edith Caldwell was the Matron for the big girls. She was a registered nurse, and certainly taught us cleanliness. We scrubbed the tile in the bathrooms on our hands and knees. She took care of our health needs. She gave us hot lemonade when we were in parades in the cold, damp weather. She was strict, but very fair. When we were spanked, we deserved it, and we never got away with anything. But we all loved her. Her influence as nurse must have been great because five girls in my group became registered nurses. They are: Jessie Masters, Marie Tabor, Juanita Baker, Ruth Lee Adams, and me.

Mrs. Florence "Mummy" Hancock was the most understanding person I knew when I was a teenager. She came to the Home when I was fifteen years old. I spent many hours in her room talking to her about how I felt and about life. I often wonder how I would have turned out without those long talks with "Mummy." She had lived in Edmond before she came to the Home in 1942. The American Legion had placed girls in her home previous to their coming to the Home School.

I am glad I grew up in the Home. I never wanted to be adopted. I have a store of good memories of the children and the Matrons. I feel lucky to have the kind of "bringing up" the Home School gave me.

- Madelaine Kinchen Moses

ALL HOME SCHOOL CHILDREN ENROLLED IN PONCA SCHOOLS

Ponca City News ~ 1935

For the first time in the history of the American Legion home school all of the children crowded into buses, Monday morning heading for city school to enroll as students. The children include seventy-three in the grades, all going to the Roosevelt School; twenty-four went to junior high school and six in the senior high. The children are brought to town and taken home again in the evenings by means of the home school bus.

THIS PHOTO HAS BEEN SPLIT SO THE FACES ARE RECOGNIZABLE. LEFT SIDE
THE HOME SCHOOL CHILDREN IN FRONT OF THE ADMINISTRATION BUILDING IN 1930

THIS PHOTO HAS BEEN SPLIT SO THE FACES ARE RECOGNIZABLE. RIGHT SIDE
THE HOME SCHOOL CHILDREN IN FRONT OF THE ADMINISTRATION BUILDING IN 1930

THIS PHOTO WAS SPLIT IN HALF SO THE FACES CAN BE RECOGNIZED. (LEFT SIDE) SEE PAGE 95 FOR LISTING.

THIS PHOTO WAS SPLIT IN HALF SO THE FACES CAN BE RECOGNIZED. (RIGHT SIDE) SEE PAGE 95 FOR LISTING.

STARTING FROM THE BACK LEFT

BUFORD JUSTICE ~ CHARLES RAYE HILL ~ KENNETH CUNNING ~ JESSIE BINGHAM ~ WENDELL MCCOY ~ WARREN MCCOY ~ PORTER MASTERS ~KIRBY RIDER ~ CLIFFORD PENROD ~ CARL REYNOLDS ~ JULIUS MARKS ~ DUANE MOORE ~ J R TABOR ~ GORDON CAVNER ~ SIDNEY MARKS ~ JACK DOVER ~ BOB WILSON ~ RAYMOND COLLINS ~ JIMMIE HAMESON ~ARLISS REYNOLDS ~ DELBERT ADAIR ~ BILL GREENWOOD ~ ALVIA MINOR ~ EARL HOOKER ~ LOYD HILL ~ ELMEER DUNLAP ~ JOHNNY MARKS ~ ELVIS REYNOLDS ~ PAUL MASTERS ~ CLIFFORD BINGHAM ~ STANLY CAVNAR ~ L. B. CONRAD ~ JUNIOR CHASTAIN ~ GENE CGASTAON ~ GENE AUGUSTINE ~ MARVIN KINTCHEN ~ WALTER MCCOY ~ THEO JAMESON ~ DORIS ADAIR ~ GENEVA PARKS ~ FAYE CONRAD ~ MARIE BRADSHAW ~ MAXINE BEATTLE ~ IRIS MARKS ~ LOUISE TABOR ~ JEAN SCOTT ~ ETHEL GREENWOOD ~ CHRISTINE PENROD ~ MRS. CROSBY ~ MR. CROSBY ~ MARION COLLINS ~ ELOISE OWENS ~ MIRTLE TAYLOR ~ BERTHA JUSTICE ~ LIELA DUNLAP ~ JESSIE MASTERS ~ ROSALIE CHASTAIN ~ JUANITA WESTMORELAND ~ BEULAH GUNLING~ MAE WILSON ~ PAULINE HILL ~ WAYNE HUMPHERIES ~ BILLY JAMESON ~ MAE OWENS ~ RUBY ADAIR ~ YVAUGHN VAN LOON ~ JUNE ARIGO ~ JANE TINER ~ MADELINE KINCHEN ~ JEFFIE WESTMORELAND ~RHEE PETERSON ~ BETTY TINER ~ LOUISE TINER ~ MACIE TABOR ~ MARY PETERSON ~ RUTH LEE ADAMS ~ PHYLLIS MITCHELL ~ DOROTHY WARREN ~ WILLODEAN CAVNAR ~ DOROTHY REYNOLDS ~ VIRGINIA WESTMORELAND ~ ALICE MCCOY ~ SULA KATE HOOKER ~ JEWEL MASTERS ~ JACK TABOR ~ ORVAL PENROD ~ VIRGIL PENROD ~ BERL GUSTIN ~ SUNNY MITCHEN ~ HOWARD TITUS

THIS PHOTO WAS SPLIT IN HALF SO THE FACES CAN BE RECOGNIZED. (LEFT SIDE) SEE PAGE 98 FOR LISTING.

THIS PHOTO WAS SPLIT IN HALF SO THE FACES CAN BE RECOGNIZED. (RIGHT SIDE) SEE PAGE 98 FOR LISTING.

CHILDREN OF THE AMERICAN LEGION HOME SCHOOL OF OKLAHOMA ~ APRIL 19, 1965

BACK ROW (LEFT TO RIGHT) DONNA COWLING ~ BARBRA MAHORNEY ~ JOHN GENTRY ~ DOUGLAS LECLIR ~ FRANK SMITH ~ SAMUEL COWLING ~ BRUCE LONG ~ EDWARD MCEWIN ~ EDWARD TURNER ~ JERRY EVENS ~ JAMES HAMILTON ~ DAVID SHEFF ~ JOHN WALTON ~ JOHN BRISSEL ~ SAMUEL SCHARNHORSST ~ GARY WAGNER ~ RICHARD SCHARNHORST ~ PASKELL LECLAIR

ROW 2 THOMAS MINER ~ ROBERT CASTLEBERRY ~ VAUGH LANTER ~STEVE REYNOLDS ~ WILLIIAM CARTER ~ JACK WALTON ~ BECKY LONG ~ GRACE WILSON ~ YVONNE LANTER ~ SHEILA SHELTON ~ RITH HAMILTON ~ DIANNA CASS ~ DONNA WILLEFORD ~ RITA CHILDERS ~ LAVONNE LANTER ~ DIANE COWLING ~ NANCY CURNETTE ~ SANDRA BRISSEL

ROW 3: LINDA TURNER ~ JEAN SLATER ~ GLORIA STEWART ~ LINDA COBURN ~ LINDA ROWE ~ PAMELA SHELTON ~ DENISE SHELTON ~ DARLENE WILSON ~ MARIE NICHOLS ~ CHARLENE WILSOON ~ WANDA HARJO ~ CAROLE STEWART ~ SUE CASTLEBERRY ~ JUDY WIDENER ~ BARBARA COX ~ JEFF ROWE ~ FRANK CHILDERS ~ RICHARD LEE ~ DAVID EVANS

ROW 4: ALLEN JOHNSON ~ ALAN RAY WHITE ~ CLARENCE THURSTON ~ JERRY FITZSIMMONS ~ NORMAN NEEDHAM ~ ROBERT WHITE ~ MICHAEL HENEHA ~ BILLY ROBINSON ~ DANNY CHILDERS ~ JIMMY STEWART ~ ROGER WALTON ~ DONALD WAGNER ~ BENNY HOWELL ~ GEORGE SIDES ~ GEORGE WALTON ~ KAY CHAMPLAIN ~ HELEN COBURN ~ MARY COBURN ~ LINDA STEWART

ROW 5: GEARY ROBINSON ~ LAMONOT LONG ~ GUY WALTOON ~ GEORGE PRIMEAUX ~ MARK STEWART ~ FRANK HARJO ~ JAMES WILLEFORD ~ STEVE ALLEN ~ VICKIE ROWE ~ CHRISTINE COX ~ LOIS ROWE ~ JOYCE ROWE ~ WANDA MURPHY ~ KATHLENE JOHNSOON ~ RONNIE HENEHA

ROW 6: ALAN WALTON ~ DANNY WHITE ~ LARRY ROBINSON ~ BRENDA ROWE ~ SUSAN PRIMEAUX ~ JEANNIE HARJO ~ DARLENE WALTON ~ SANDRA COBURN ~ EMMA MURPHY ~ GLENDA WARREN ~ TONY WHITE ~ DOUGLAS WAGNER ~ ENOS PRIMEAUX

Chapter Eight

House Parents

Perhaps the 'house parents' are the most essential staff members of The American Legion Home School. They work directly with the children. They are involved with them on a minute-by-minute basis. Their day starts around 5:00 a.m. and usually ends around 10:00 or 11:00 p.m. The 'house parents' live in the dormitories and accompany the children on all outings in the community and outside the community.

In 1982, Governor George Nigh made a proclamation declaring that a week should be set aside to honor all 'house parents' in Oklahoma. He said they would be honored for their dedication and patience in working with the most valuable part of our society, our youth.

That week was observed at the Legion Home in a special way, and Superintendent Charles Danley said, "The 'house parents' are truly the backbone at the American Legion Children's Home."

It is impossible to list the names of all the matrons or 'house parents' who have devoted their time, a great deal of hard work, and many times their lives to the children at the Legion Home. Their purpose has always been to provide love, care and discipline like that of a real parent.

The following story is about my housemother. I want to make it a tribute to all 'house parents' who loved and cared for someone else's children.

MRS. GENEVA MAYHUE ~ MY HOUSEMOTHER

From age nine through eighteen, my housemother was Mrs. Geneva Mayhue. Very little is known about her except that she was a mixture of the strongest and the softest. She knew just when to use the hand that was needed. She helped in the running of the entire American Legion Children's Home, but her life was dedicated to the girls assigned to her care. She tried to help them learn everything that they would need to know in order to face the outside world. She was a Christian and tried to live the way she thought God wanted. She was a faithful member of the First Baptist Church in Ponca City.

Sometimes we thought she carried the Church to the Home with her too much. We thought her talks were too long and complained that preaching on Sunday at Church was enough. But with all of the attempts to ignore her sermons, a great deal of her teachings sunk in. I remember many things that have helped me through the years.

She taught us to have self respect and to respect others. She told us, "You're as good as the very best, but no better." She also said, "Give the world your best and the best will come back to you." And we learned, "The world does not owe you a living."

We were blessed by having her as a 'Mother' who cared enough to want us to learn these important rules for our lives. Slowly she tested us and gave us chances to be trusted. If we passed the tests, she treated us with great respect. I was thrilled when I had passed her tests. I knew this meant love, attention and extra privileges which I was eager to get and she was eager to give. She also helped us with little things that were important to our young lives.

When I was ten years old I was a 4-H Club member. My sewing project was a handkerchief and a head scarf. It had to be hand-stitched; I thought my work did not look so good. Mrs. Mayhue told me she would wash and iron them for me. No one can ever convince me that the scarf and handkerchief were the same ones when she returned them to me. I won a blue ribbon on both of them. Every year Mrs. Mayhue washed and ironed my project, and every year I won a blue ribbon. She had the magic touch.

MICHAEL RUTH & MRS. MAYHUE

To be sick and in her care was the greatest privilege. I know many girls pretended to be sick sometimes just to get that extra attention from Mrs. Mayhue. The patient would be tucked into her big bed, and Mrs. Mayhue would make a special tray and carry it from the cafeteria with such love that everything tasted delicious. Every afternoon she had cookies made and waiting for us after school.

Her days were full and usually started at 5:00 a.m. She would begin by washing for about twenty girls and hanging the clothes outside on the clothesline. I remember one morning when I got up and looked out the window; I saw her standing ankle deep in the snow hanging out the wash. I went to help and in a short time I began to feel frozen and wondered how she could work so hard and what kept her going.

She sewed and made new clothes, mended the old ones and found time to make curtains and bedspreads for each room. One Christmas, her gift to each girl was a handmade robe and pajamas. I helped her by making the button holes (hundreds of button holes). But my reward was that she made my gift special and different from the rest, so I would have a surprise.

When I got older I helped with the younger girls. One time I had a little girl to care for and decided to cut her hair. I thought Mrs. Mayhue would have had a heart attack when she saw what I had done, but I was given the honor of cutting all the girls' hair for the whole summer. I didn't know if it was a reward or a punishment, but my real payment came when I was treated with the privilege of going to the beauty shop.

I knew I had earned her trust and respect when I was given the responsibility of babysitting on Wednesday and Sunday evenings while Mrs. Mayhue went to church. She received great joy from going to church and made a big deal of showing her appreciation to me. She made me feel proud that I was finally able to do something for her.

I shall never forget the day she called us all to a meeting. She asked us to look around the room and see who was sitting beside us. She asked us to try to understand that in five, ten or fifteen years that some of us would be taken by death. Then she told us that she had Leukemia and the doctors gave her less than a year to live. She explained that when God felt that her work on earth was finished that he would take her to Heaven.

MRS. MAYHUE AND HER 1957 CHEVY

Because of her inner strength and faith in God, she lived longer than the doctors had predicted. But the end did come in February of 1966.

During those difficult days of waiting, all the girls showed super devotion to her. I learned that the other girls had been getting the same special love that I had been getting. I can remember sitting with Sandy, Nancy, Grace and Donna at the top of the stairs listening to see if Mrs. Mayhue might need us in the night.

When she had to go to the hospital for periods of time to get blood transfusions, she asked Mr. Summers to not have a replacement for her but to "Let Barbara take care of the girls. She knows how I do things." This was the biggest test she ever asked of me. I had to make her proud!

Mrs. Mayhue didn't earn great fame or fortune while on earth, but the difference she made in the lives of the girls she helped should have earned her a golden cross that she must be wearing today. She gave her whole life to us – a life filled with love that will be with me forever. No statue was ever built for her. I found no record of her ever being at the Home except for two tiny snapshots. But I know she was there. To me, she was the American Legion Home! And all the girls she took by the hand, tucked into bed and kissed "good night" will say she was our 'Mother.'

Chapter Nine

Sponsors

Each of the students at the Home School is supported by an American Legion Post or Auxiliary Unit. The sponsoring posts or units, in addition to providing clothing, also furnish a sum of money for weekly allowances for the children – ranging from 25 cents to $1.50 per week, depending on the age of the child. They also provide Christmas and birthday gifts. Some of the sponsors take their "adopted" children to the homes of members for vacation during the summer months, and some children visit during the Christmas holidays.

My sponsors were the ladies of the Stillwater Auxiliary Unit #129. They picked me from some pictures of girls who needed a sponsor. I thought I had become the luckiest girl at the Home.

They always sent more clothes and spent more money than was required or expected. Anytime I needed anything, they sent it. I was invited into their homes for every holiday. During the first two years, I went visiting from house-to-house but they decided that was too difficult for me, so they let me stay at one place.

One Christmas, I was visiting in the home of Mr. and Mrs. Colasacco and I met their niece, Sharon. We became good friends immediately. She took me to meet her parents, Bryon and Aliene Daniel. From that time, I was invited to their home for every vacation, and I was treated like a member of the family. They also had another daughter, Dana Kay, and a son, Gordie. Their home was the warmest, happiest home I had ever known.

I loved helping Aliene with the housework and watching her cook—she was a good cook. She always made me feel special, even though she already had two daughters.

Bryon taught me how to make pizza, and how to change oil in a car. He took me to the Legion baseball games. He was my "Father" figure, and we had many father-daughter conversations, which I needed.

My Stillwater sponsors became my family. The year that I went to 'Boys and Girls State' a dinner was given when we returned. Each of us was introduced and our parents were asked to stand. I didn't expect anyone to stand for me, but when I was introduced, the Stillwater Auxiliary ladies all stood up. That was a very exciting and emotional experience.

**ETNA HALL
CHILD WELFARE
PROGRAM**

I can't remember all of their names, but I will never forget these: Alta Dotter, Mrs. E. R. Lancaster, Marynell Weilmuenster Lane, Mr. and Mrs. Coe, Myrtle Hope, Bernice Weeks, Irma Thomas, Etna Hall, Minnie Strong, and Mary E. Smith.

Mary E. Smith was a dear, special person to me. She had a clothing store, and she allowed me to do what most girls love to do - try on all the beautiful dresses, formal gowns, and furs. Also, when I visited in her home, she let me play "dress-up" with her jewelry and furs. She gave me a room all by myself, and the bed had a beautiful silk comforter. I felt like a princess. She fixed fancy breakfasts and super lunches and dinners. I thought she was an angel and I had gone to heaven.

The ladies of the Stillwater Auxiliary Unit #129 were the best parents a girl could have. I loved them all, and I still do. We keep in touch.

BARBRA MAHORNEY WITH HER ADOPTIVE PARENTS 1984

AUXILIARY DAY MRS. MARY E. SMITH

Chapter Ten

Biographies

THE LAWRENCE GREGORY STORY

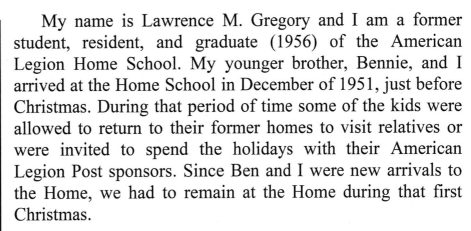

My name is Lawrence M. Gregory and I am a former student, resident, and graduate (1956) of the American Legion Home School. My younger brother, Bennie, and I arrived at the Home School in December of 1951, just before Christmas. During that period of time some of the kids were allowed to return to their former homes to visit relatives or were invited to spend the holidays with their American Legion Post sponsors. Since Ben and I were new arrivals to the Home, we had to remain at the Home during that first Christmas.

Let me regress a little with some background information, only because it might help explain the real reason and goals of the Home School. Ben and I were from Hartshorne, a very small town in Southeastern Oklahoma. Our ailing Mother was working day and night, taking in washing & ironing while trying to raise four boys without the support of our father, who was a World War I veteran, and an alcoholic and did nothing other than cause us grief. Mom had to finally kick him out of the house for he was such a poor influence on us boys. Although he lived in the immediate area, he did nothing to help us. My Mother died suddenly of a heart attack and we were left with only our elderly Grandmother to care for us. My loving mother knew her days here on this earth were short so she initiated our acceptance to the American Legion Home School. She talked to us about this and it was decided that although our Grandmother was more than willing to keep us, it would just be too much for her. So, when my mother passed away, my older brother Amon went into the Navy, Ben and I went into the Home, and my baby brother, John Paul, stayed with my Grandmother. John Paul was only two years old at that time. So you can see, almost overnight, our family was scattered like pieces of broken glass. That's not to say we didn't keep in touch for we were always a close-knit family. Thank God there was an American Legion Home School for children like us. Kids through no fault of their own were left with no home and no support system. At that time, situations like ours was the express purpose for the American Legion Home School to exist.

Now back to life as I knew it at the American Legion Home School in the 'Fifties.' The administration and some of the personnel at the Home were fired for various reasons, shortly after Ben and I arrived in 1951.

Mr. Earl (Bucky) N. Summers was then hired as the new Superintendent. As I reflect back on those wonderful years, I can now see how education, work ethics, vocational skills, self-esteem, family values, home ownership & security seemed to be some of the major goals and objectives for the kids.

All of us were involved in the everyday activities at the Home. Each of us was assigned weekly chores that ranged from washing dishes to cleaning the bathrooms. In addition to this, everyone was expected to make his/her own bed each morning and keep their room nice and neat at all times. The older boys were involved in all kinds of construction, maintenance and farming projects, whereas the older girls were responsible for most of the laundry chores such as ironing everyone's clothes.

As kids go, we worked very hard. We were never abused or overworked, but we learned how to work together as a team and we soon learned what it felt like to successfully complete a worthy project. We built everything from barns to barbed-wire fences. One of our major projects was the construction of our office/gymnasium building as we were the helpers for the local journeymen from Ponca City who volunteered their time on this construction project.

Doing such things as hauling hay, trimming trees, cutting the grass, caring for the animals, painting dorm rooms, laying tile, driving the tractor, and a thousand other things, helped each of us kids learn how to take responsibility for our "home" thus allowing each of us to claim ownership of the place that we called HOME. That's why I can say with pride... "This is my Home."

During my years at the Home, we had our own school buses and went to the regular public schools in Ponca City. We were encouraged to do well academically and to participate in the various school activities. At that period of time, there were a number of us boys from the American Legion Home School that were very good athletes (football, wrestling, etc.) and many awards and honors were achieved by our group. Many of us went on to earn college degrees in fields such as Law, Medicine, Education and various other professions. Since I am much older now at 70 plus years, I have come to realize that we were truly blessed and that we actually lived the "Golden Years" of the Home School.

I could relate many wonderful stories of my time at the Home School but the most important thing to remember is, with about One Hundred Twenty kids and a dozen employees, ~ "WE WERE ONE BIG FAMILY." We learned how to live together in peace and harmony. I learned to love and respect all my "brothers and sisters" at the Home and I will cherish those friendships forever.

Thanks for listening,
Lawrence M. Gregory (1956)

ALICE GRISSO COFFMAN ~ CLASS OF 1958

November 1, 1949 was the day that I arrived at the home with my siblings, Glenda age 8 and my younger brother Alfred (Al) age 6 and in the first grade.

We came from a rural Seminole farm where we had been living for about 5 months with our grandparents and attended Bowlegs Elementary School.

The school year had barely begun and it was far closer to cut across fields and wade creeks and walk through the woods than to walk to the school bus stop. We were beginning to get behind in our school work because we could not walk to school when it rained as the creeks were much too high.

One day we Grisso kids were called to the office one by one and met with two gentlemen who brought us a Picture post card of the home and let us know we would be leaving our grandparents and going to live in these big buildings in a place called Ponca City that we had never heard of. I remember wondering if they had a school cafeteria like the ones in my third grade geography book, all the while fighting back tears and trying not to show how frightened I was. When I returned to my fourth grade classroom my Teacher asked me if she could see my post card and announced to my class that I was going to be leaving and moving to this beautiful home in the picture. This took place on a Friday around the end of October and after school on the walk home, we discovered that we had all been to the office and talked to these men. I knew that my Daddy would never let this happen and I was telling him as soon as he came home which he did every weekend as he was a truck driver. We barely reached our yard and my dad drove up carrying a bag of apples and let us know he had arranged for us to go to live at the American Legion Home in Ponca City so that we could go to school and his elderly parents would not have so many (5) little kids to take care of.

The following Monday must have been the last day of October and the end of the 9 weeks we went back to school. My 4th grade teacher asked me to stay in at recess. I hadn't a clue what was going on and wondering if I had gotten in trouble on my last day at Bowlegs School.

She had made arrangements for a surprise going away party with all the other girls who showered me with new socks, underwear and a head scarf or 2 along with some other things.

On the morning of November 1st my dad arrived to take Glenda, Al and I to Seminole where we met with someone who drove us to the Capitol building in Oklahoma where we were shown around the building and met with Mr. Leroy Pickens who took us to Ponca City. We arrived just in time for lunch. This was the week or month the staff was eating in the Big Boys building. We later referred to the buildings as Senior and Junior buildings but at that time the buildings were Big and Little Boys and Big and Little Girls and we also called the house parents, Matrons, I don't recall that at the time there were any couples or men over any of the kids. Mr. Baker was the superintendent and Mr. Grizzel and his wife were billeted in the Big Boys as he was in charge as assistant Superintendent.

We were shown the restrooms so we could wash up for lunch and after lunch we stayed and played at the Big Boys building. After school was out one of the little girls was sent to take us to our dorm in the Little Girls building. The house mother was Mrs. Eads and they sent Al on to the Little Boys where his housemother was Mrs. Allgood.

I loved this place where I had so many of my own age, to do things with and a ride to school on a nice school bus that came right to the door.

I lived at the home for the next 8 years. During that time the boys built the gym and we met a lot of people and went a lot of wonderful places. We worked but I don't recall it being very difficult work but had to make our beds and take care of our personal things and as we got older we were required to iron twice a week and do kitchen chores.

I was fortunate to be sponsored by the Ponca City American Legion Auxiliary who sent me to Campfire Camp every summer and elected to sponsor me and Patsy Shaffner to Girls State, one of the most memorable weeks of my life.

After graduating in 1958, I attended Central State College at Edmond until I met and married my first husband James Baldwin in 1962. We moved to Norman, Ok, and I went to work at Zales and dropped out of college while putting hubby through. We had one daughter, Jamie Michele, who was born in October of 1967. We divorced in 1976 and I then met and married Douglas Coffman. Doug and I have 2 daughters, Deon Loelle and Darci Lynelle, and I have 4 grandsons and 3 granddaughters.

Douglas passed away on August 29, 2007 and I retired August 29, 2008 when my company closed their call center and we were given the option of becoming home agents. Due to some unusual circumstances I opted to take my retirement

I do some painting and handcrafts and read, but my favorite past time is emailing and chatting with my friends on the computer.

Alice Grisso Coffman ~ Class of 1958

SANDY BRISSEL ~ CLASS OF 1967

First memory is getting to Ponca. Sherry and I traveled by train. When we got to Ponca, there was no one there to pick us up. Sherry being of sound mind and body went straight for a pay phone to look up the number to the home. Me, I started bawling! I was in the only in the 4th grade, she was in the 7th. While Sherry frantically tried to get someone on the phone, I dried my tears and started looking for ways to get into trouble. Looking around, I spotted a police car. I went running over to them and started talking a mile a minute. They loaded us in the patrol car, and off we went to the station. I told them, well; we got picked up for not being picked up!!!! Go figure! I need to backtrack a moment, and tell you that I had such a love and admiration for John Wayne at this time. I felt that he was our hero, knight in shining armor, savior. I just knew that at any given time, he would show up and save my family from all of the "bad people" and bad things that had happened to us prior to going to the home.

That said I was not prepared to meet him in person, only in a smaller stature. When Mr. Summers came to liberate us from the Ponca Police, I took one look at him and said, "I think I will call you JW." He said okay, but why? I said you look just like John Wayne, only smaller. Mr. Summers then became my hero, my dad, and my knight in shining armor. We understood each other from the moment we met. On report card day, we stood in one long line, all waiting to go in and see Mr. Summers. I don't know what everyone else was thinking, but they always managed to scoot me to the front of the line. Always saying, you go first, Sandy, you will get him in a good mood. (What were they thinking?!) I flunked P.E., for refusing to suit up. (I also flunked home economics.) What a crazy bunch of kids! Funny thing is, I always left his office with a smile on my face, and he always had a chuckle for me. He was an amazing man. I was nothing but trouble.

Mrs. Mayhue, our housemother, was another wonderful person. I know she could have killed me sometimes, but she always had faith that something good would come of me. I got where I could write just like her, and forged her name and notes many a time. Once, Barb and I went to Anthony's loaded with a "note" that was supposed to have been written by Mrs. Mayhue, saying I could buy some clothing and charge it. I did. Sometimes I would get so mad at her, I would put sand and dirt in her snuff can. We baked a birthday cake for her made with ex-lax which was strong laxative in the amount we put in. I did this with the help of Barb and Nancy.

Sandy (Brissel) Jackson ~ 1958-1967 ~ Garland, TX

WILLIAM HENRY "BILL" BAILEY ~ 1952-1961

I was born April 11, 1943 in Enid, Garfield County, Oklahoma to John Elwood and Laura Kathryn (Lowe) Bailey. My Father in the United States Army was from Monmouth County, New Jersey. He met my mother who was a Lieutenant in the Army Nurses Corps at Ft. Sill, Oklahoma. Brother Donald Eugene was born in Enid on January 24, 1945. My parents were divorced in 1946 and Mother returned to Enid while Father moved back to Highland, New Jersey. Mother went back to nursing at the General Hospital (now Baptist) in Enid and worked there until 1969 when she retired. Because she worked shift work, Don and I were left with family and baby sitters many day and nights. As we grew older, many times we played for hours without parental supervision. We were enrolled in Adams Elementary School and I completed the first three grades. In the summer of 1952, our Uncles and Aunts in Enid realized that Mother was not supervising us closely and we were getting into mischief, so a decision was made to find a place for us to live.

My brother and I were brought before a County Judge in Enid, Oklahoma and given a choice to go to Stringtown Reform School in El Reno or someplace called the American Legion Home in Ponca City, Oklahoma. Unknown to me, Uncle Henry Lowe, supervisor of Peerless Ice Cream in Enid, went to his friend Clothing Store owner Ike Crawford, a Legionnaire, and they made arrangements for us to live at the American Legion Home. On August 29, 1952, my Aunt Margaret Weaver drove Mother, Don and I to the home in Ponca. There we met this rough looking man by the name of Earl Summers who was the Superintendent of this Legion Home.

Don was placed in the Little Boys Dorm and I in the Big Boys Dorm with a house parent named George Watson, who I believe was a minister, who shortly thereafter was replaced by house parents Kenneth and Jeanette (Stephens) Porter. I was a small kid of 60 pounds at nine years of age and surrounded by the big guys who were very intimidating.

Barney and David (K.D.) Calvert, Frank "Babe" Wright and his brother Jesse, Raymond "Peewee" Elliot, Neal Trostle, Freddie Reynolds, Lawrence Gregory, Sherman Harris and others who today I consider as big brothers; and, Keith Mason, Clifford Overturff, Jim Wheeler from Enid, and Lee Osterhaut who were my age. For the first three months I was miserable and it was hard to go to sleep at night in a room filled with other kids; and, to eat in the dining room downstairs with 30 plus boys. Maggie Pugh was our cook and we had lots of good food that I had never eaten before. Pancakes were served on Saturday breakfast, corn bread and beans for lunch, and always hamburgers for supper. Every Sunday after service at the First Baptist Church a special noon meal was served on pressed red and white-checkered tablecloths.

Shortly thereafter, I learned about the word "work." They took me to the alfalfa field below the pig and cattle pens to haul hay. I refused to pick up the hay until, I believe Jesse Wright said, "If you don't work, they don't feed you here." So two scrawny kids, Jim Wheeler and I earned our keep that summer picking up and hauling hay. This hard work gave me my first sense of pride and accomplishment.

My sponsor was the Bethany-Warr Acres Legion Post in Bethany, Oklahoma that provided us with clothes and spending money and would let us visit during the summers. Ida Bianchi, from that Auxiliary was very kind to both Don and I.

I attended Garfield, Lincoln, East Junior High, and High School in Ponca City, earned the rank of Eagle Scout with the help of Scoutmaster Lee Askey and went to Philmont Scout Ranch in 1959 with the Dodd twins and others. I was selected to attend Boys State in the summer of 1960 and at high school was selected for Student Council, Senior Rotarian, and Ponca High School Citizen of the Year in 1961. I spent three years wrestling under Coach Grady Penninger and Ponca and our team won three straight state championships. I earned above average grades. On graduation in June 1961, I knew that the American Legion Home had taken a young rebellious boy and after 9 years turned him into a productive citizen through hard work, constant encouragement and with the help of many caring adults.

Wanda Faye Streeter of Ranch Drive and I met, courted and were married in June 1962 in Enid. Our first son Christopher Everett Bailey was born in Ponca City, Oklahoma in 1963 while I was going to junior college in Tonkawa. During my last two years in college I attended OSU in Stillwater and in the evenings worked as the home's laundry man. In summer I took the kids swimming at Wentz Pool and spent a week with the boys at the Will Rogers Scout Camp near Cleveland, Oklahoma.

I received my A.S. degree from Tonkawa, Oklahoma Jr. College and my B.A. and M.S. degrees from Oklahoma State University in Stillwater in 1965 and 1968. We moved to Tampa, Florida in 1968 after accepting a position to teach high school biology and coach the wrestling team at Chamberlain High School, Tampa in Hillsborough County, Florida during 1968-1969 to undefeated city-countywide championship. Our second son Allen Carroll Bailey was born at Tampa General Hospital. Wanda and I were divorced in 1969. I later moved back to Ponca City, Oklahoma in October 1969 and took a job with the city as the head chemist at the city sewage treatment plant under City Manager Clarence Fulkerson.

My second wife Paula McComb Simpson from Boise, Idaho and I met in Ponca City while she was working at Conoco Oil Company and we married in April 1971 and honeymooned in New Orleans. We moved to Corpus Christi in fall of 1971 and I accepted a Fisheries Research position with the Texas Parks and Wildlife Inland Fisheries Division in San Antonio in March 1972. I stayed with the TPWD fisheries in San Antonio, Kerrville, and Port Arkansas, Texas until July 1977. My last supervisory project involved spawning saltwater estuarine red drum, flounder, and spotted sea trout in lab tanks, hatching their eggs, and stocking these fingerings in Texas power plant freshwater cooling lakes to control rough fish populations. This was the first aquaculture project of its kind in United States to that date; and, received worldwide recognition from fishery professionals in other countries after publishing a scientific paper describing our successes.

After leaving the TPWD, I attended Corpus Christi State College and entered the M.S. degree program in Computer Science. This special training let me accept a programmer/analyst job in San Antonio at United States Automobile Agency (USAA) Insurance Company and stayed there 1982-84. We moved to Antioch, California in fall, 1984. I was employed one year by the Stauffer Chemical Company and then moved to Citibank New York in Walnut Creek and on Sansome Street in San Francisco from 1985 to April 1999 when I retired. My last project was to draft the national requirements for the Citibank check debit-credit card that is now used around the world. Paula and I retired in San Antonio 2002, with our two daughters and three grandchildren. Our oldest son Chris lives in Oklahoma City while the youngest son Allen lives in Broken Arrow, Oklahoma with three other grandchildren.

And there isn't a day that goes by that I don't thank the Summers, Porters, Mrs. Mayhue, the Fowlers and the American Legion for giving me hope, determination and confidence to succeed. And a day doesn't go by that I fail to remember all of my 100 plus American Legion home brothers and sisters. Oh, the stories that can be told about those nine years at my Home.

William Henry "Bill" Bailey ~ 1952-1961

DONALD EUGENE BAILEY ~ 1952-1962

I was born on January 24, 1945 in Enid, Garfield County, Oklahoma to John Elwood and Laura Kathryn (Lowe) Bailey. My father was from Monmouth County, New Jersey and met my mother a Lieutenant in the Army Nurses Corps at Ft. Sill, Oklahoma. Brother Bill Bailey was born earlier in Enid on April 11, 1943. Our parents were divorced in 1946 and Mother returned to Enid while Father moved back to Highland, New Jersey. Mother went back to nursing at the General Hospital (now Baptist) in Enid and worked there until 1969 when she retired. Because she worked shift work, Bill and I were left with family and baby sitters many day and nights. As young boys we played for hours without parental supervision. We were enrolled in Adams Elementary School and I completed the first grade under the watchful of eye of Principal Esther Hinshaw. In the summer of 1952, our Uncles and Aunts in Enid realized that Mother was not supervising us closely, so a decision was made to find a place for us to live.

My brother and I were brought before a County Judge in Enid, Oklahoma and given a choice to go to Stringtown Reform School in El Reno or someplace called the American Legion Home in Ponca City, Oklahoma. Unknown to me, Uncle Henry Lowe, supervisor of Peerless Ice Cream in Enid, went to his friend Clothing Store owner Ike Crawford, a Legionnaire, and they made arrangements for us to live at the American Legion Home. So on August 29, 1952, my Aunt Margaret Weaver drove Mother, Bill and I to the home in Ponca. There we met this rough looking man by the name of Earl Summers who was the Superintendent of this Legion Home.

At 7 years of age, I was placed in the Little Boys Dorm and Billy in the Big Boys Dorm. In this Little Boys dormitory were twins Bill and Bobby Dodd, Benny Gregory, Calvin Reynolds, John Machon, Bobby Appleman, Johnny and Dewey Snider, Billy Lee Osterhaut and a lot of other children. Our Dorm had many house parents during the years but it was a nice place to live and make life-long friends. We missed our mother but she came to visit about twice a year. I acquired many new skills including farm work and taking care of animals.

I attended Garfield, East Junior High, and High School in Ponca City, earned the Life Scout rank under the tutelage of Scoutmaster Lee Askey and went to Philmont Scout Ranch in 1962 with Bobby Appleman, Jerry Evans and John Mahorney. I was elected to the City Council in Brundage Hall at Boys State in the summer of 1962. In high school, I participated in the Glee Club and was a member of the track and football teams.

My sponsor was the Bethany-Warr Acres Legion Post in Bethany, Oklahoma that provided us with clothes and spending money and let us visit during the summers. Ida Bianchi, from that Auxiliary was very kind to both Bill and I.

After high school, I spent some time with Mother in Enid and then I moved to Corpus Christi, Texas in 1963 where my Aunt Margaret Weaver had moved from Enid. I met and married first wife Judy Barbara Harpnel in January 1965 and daughter Monica Lyn Bailey was born in December 1965 in this city. We divorced in 1967 in Nueces County, Texas and Judy moved to the Bay area of California.

In February 2, 1968, I enlisted in the U.S. Army and after Basic Training was assigned to Kessler AFB in Mississippi for Air Traffic Control School for 13 weeks, 20 weeks in 1969 at Ft. Walters for basic helicopter trainings and 16 weeks at Hunter Stewart AFB near Savannah, Georgia for Advanced Huey Helicopter School. The Army shipped me to the Vietnam War Theater in WOC Co. D. Third U.S. Army where I served for two tours until 1971. I flew many combat and rescue missions from various helicopter bases. At Fire Base Eagle I was over sprayed with Agent Orange and that would later cause me severe medical problems. The Army promoted me to Warrant Officer and I was awarded two bronze service stars, a Republic of Vietnam Campaign, and Army Commendation Medal. On August 19, 1971, I was honorably discharged from the Army and returned to Corpus Christi, Texas.

By 1972, I had moved to Houston, Texas and two years later in 1973 was the manager of a large Carpet World Store. There I met Velma Jack Holmes from Beaumont and we were married in May 1973 in Harris County. In May 1976 our son Dameon Gene Bailey was born. Velma and I were divorced in August 1977 and then I returned to Corpus Christi, Texas. She later married a Rogers and moved to the Tulsa area with my son Dameon.

In 1981 I returned to Corpus Christi and found work as an Army helicopter repair mechanic at the Corpus Christi Naval Air Station in the Aradmac Helicopter Repair Unit and spent the next 15 years at this job working on army hueys that had been sent for repair and reconditioning. On June 15, 1990, Corey Snelson from Potowattomie County, Oklahoma and I were married in Corpus Christi, Texas. However our marriage was short lived and we divorced in 1996. The Aradmac

Officials in October 1996 gave me a medical retirement due to a neurological disorder compounded by the over spray in Vietnam and the effects of volatile hydrocarbon cleaning liquids used in the Aradmac repair shop.

I spent about a year in Antioch, California with my brother Bill and his wife Paula and then Phoenix, Arizona and Fort Worth, Texas. I now live in Galveston, Texas near the downtown area. My son Dameon Bailey-Rogers lives near Fayetteville, Arkansas while my daughter Monica Eckstrand lives in the San Francisco Bay area.

My 11 years at the American Legion Home helped me to understand that determination and hard work always gets a job done. I always wonder what became of my many home school friends.

Donald Eugene Bailey ~ 1952-1962

DONNA WILLEFORD HAFFNER

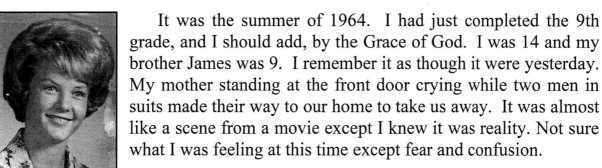

It was the summer of 1964. I had just completed the 9th grade, and I should add, by the Grace of God. I was 14 and my brother James was 9. I remember it as though it were yesterday. My mother standing at the front door crying while two men in suits made their way to our home to take us away. It was almost like a scene from a movie except I knew it was reality. Not sure what I was feeling at this time except fear and confusion.

It was a bright, sunny Tuesday morning and we rode with these strangers for what seemed like hours until we stopped at this large statue of a woman and little boy. I stood in awe of this large magnificent monument not knowing the name; history or meaning of what I was soon to learn was the "Pioneer Woman." The men had taken us to the museum, but, as luck would have it, they were closed on Tuesdays so we continued our journey to what was to become our new life, new way of living and new home.

Once we reached the American Legion Home School (ALHS), I was taken to one of the girls' buildings while James went to one of the boys' buildings.

While James house parents were Mr. and Mrs. Fowler, Ms. Mayhue greeted me. What beautiful, blessed people they all were with love and compassion for each of us. I think I knew then, we would be all right. Ms. Mayhue gave me a bible on my 15th birthday, which I still carry to this day. She had a great love for the Lord, which she shared with us over the years.

The first few months I thought I would die from loneliness, I would cry myself to sleep. I didn't think the hurt would ever stop, but after about three months, I could see better times ahead. It did help by keeping us busy with required chores. The boys would work in the yard, cafeteria, and the fields and the girls would do ironing (isn't this a lost art?) and cafeteria chores. And to our surprise! No one died.

Now comes the fun and memories. As for the memories....Wow! Where do I start? I remember days at school, Saturdays at the movies and Sundays at church. In the summertime we would go swimming, home visits with our families and also our sponsors and in the fall, we would go shopping for school clothes. I can still remember "visiting Sundays" that once a month when family came to see you, I can't remember one time my dear sweet Mother didn't come. My favorite time, though, would have be the Christmases at home with my Mother and family.

When April would roll around, we knew we had to prepare for "Auxiliary Sunday," the day set aside for all sponsors, veterans and VA Post to visit the home. This preparation required days of extreme cleaning and inspections by Mr. Summers (a Saint in his own right). And again to our surprise, we all survived.

I do recall one memory of a boy named Clarence. He resided at the PMA (Ponca Military Academy) and they were all forbidden. I slipped out one night to "baby sit" and would have gotten away with it, except for one person telling Mr. Summers. If my memory serves me correctly, that person was Barbra Mahorney. Still laugh about it to this day. Thanks Barb, you probably saved my life.

Of all the childhood memories I chose to cherish they are the ones of my stay at the home with Sandy, Johnny, Barbra and all the others, too many to name.

While too young to know at the time or to appreciate the opportunities granted me, I do know now these were the best times of my life and help mold me into the person I am today. I would like to say to all I met and loved from there "Thanks for the Memories." May God richly bless you all.

Donna Willeford Haffner ~ Ponca City, class of 1967

NANCY CURNUTTE BUTLER

My family consisted of my mom and dad, Pete, my 16-year-old brother, Ann, my older sister who was 15, and me, the youngest at 9-years-old. Ann and I had birthdays six days apart. She was born September 15, 1942 and I was born September 21, 1948. I was nine at the time that I arrived at the American Legion Home School. We were told that Pete was too old to go with us to the American Legion Home; instead he was taken to the Tulsa Boys Home.

My dad was stationed in Italy during WWII as a Gunnery Sergeant; he got shot twice and was honorably discharged. He came home and became a truck driver but drank a lot and had many flashbacks of the war.

The day we were sent to the foster home in Tulsa, daddy was drunk and having flashbacks. He started threatening to kill my mom while she was ironing. His threats escalated until he pulled me over close to him and put a pistol to my head. He kept saying that we were all a burden and he didn't need any of us. I was scared to death. The gun was still pushed against my head and I heard it "click." For some reason it didn't go off. Mom was terrified and rushed over and grabbed me and put me behind her and daddy passed out. Mom was scared and was crying. She took me to my little friend's house, telling me that she would have Ann come and get me. I was to stay with my friend until she came. She was going to leave a note for Pete telling him to stay at the house.

Mom went to the courthouse to tell them the situation at home and they wouldn't let her go back to the house, telling her that they would have the police waiting at the house for us kids when we got home. They did an emergency protective order for us three kids.

Ann and I arrived back home and the police arrived around 3:00 and they wouldn't allow us to go inside. The police had taken daddy into custody and he evidently had fought with them and they "billy-clubbed" him and took him to jail. Mom had a nervous breakdown and went into a hospital for mental health care for two years. Daddy was ordered to never have any contact with us kids again. I only saw him one time after that, I was 26 years old, married and living in Kansas when he came to see me.

We kids were taken to the Sand Springs foster home; a group home in Sand Springs, Oklahoma near Tulsa. We stayed there about six months until it was arranged for us to go live in the American Legion Home School in Ponca City,

Oklahoma. One day Ann and I were introduced to a nice man who had come to the group home. He told us we were going for a ride with him in his nice car and he'd feed us lunch. On the way he told us we were going to like where we were going 'cause it had lots of kids there.

On the day we arrived at the Legion Home it was rainy and dreary, much the same way that I felt. I had no idea where Ann and I were going but it seemed we were taking a long time to get wherever we were going.

When we first arrived at the Home we drove through the gates. There were kids running around outside. We were taken into a large building; the first people I saw were Barbra Mahorney, Avon Appleman, Donna Cowling, and Star Lowe. It was close to dinnertime and Barbra asked me if I wanted to play and showed me the room that I was going to be sharing with her and Avon. I was feeling very scared and sad and Barbra kept telling me that everything was going to be all right. Barbra took me to the top of the stairs and let me ring the bell to call everyone to dinner. In the dining room I couldn't eat or drink because I was so scared and upset in my new surroundings and I couldn't control my crying. The main thing I remember was how Barbra kept saying that everything was going be all right.

Mrs. Mayhue told us that I was going to be separated from Ann and that she would live in the big girls' building and I would stay in the little girls' building. I had never been separated from Ann in my life! Barbra took me to our room where there were bunk beds. I had brought all my belongings in a paper sack, which contained all my clothes. I didn't have much. I wore my only pair of shoes and I had no toys. Barbra took me to a closet that held all the supplies: towels, sheets, toothbrushes, and toothpaste -- it looked like a small store. She told me that the bottom bunk bed would be mine and she helped me make the bed. Barbra slept on the top bunk.

I remember crying and sneaking out of the room at night and going to the big girls' building so I could sleep with Ann. She shared the room with Janice Franklin, Mary Thurston, Roberta Battie, Judy Mingus, and Loretta Mann. For a long time, I had managed to sneak over there and had never gotten caught. One night when I got into the bed thinking it was Ann's bed, it turned out that they had changed the beds around that day and I got into Loretta's bed instead of Ann's. I scared her as much as she scared me, but she got really upset with me for being there. Ann calmed her down and said she'd take care of me.

I believe Ann had dated Billy since we first arrived at the Home. We were there for two years before he graduated from high school in 1959 and left the home and worked at the Safeway in town. They got married when she got pregnant at the age of 17 and had to leave the Home. The baby was born on September 14,

1961 in Tulsa. They moved in with Billy's mother. Ann got pregnant with her second child and on one visit to the doctor during that pregnancy it was discovered that she had toxemia. When she went to the hospital to deliver the baby she realized that the doctor had been drinking. She had a cesarean, but her baby girl was stillborn due to the affect of the toxemia. She had to go to Oklahoma City to be on kidney dialysis. Fortunately, my boyfriend, Jack, had a car and he drove me three times from Ponca City to Oklahoma City to visit with Ann.

Her condition worsened and she got congestive heart failure and kidney failure and pneumonia. My last trip to see her was one week before her death. Shortly before her death she told me that she was going to go home to heaven and she told me to finish school no matter what. She said she was going to be fine where she was going and that she would always be with me. She always called me a "spitfire."

She had lived thirty days after the baby was born; she died December 30, 1965 and was buried on January 1, 1966. Ann was always loving and caring to me and I always felt she was more of a mother to me than my own mother.

The summer after 8th grade Mr. and Mrs. Payett took me from the Home to California, planning on adopting me. The first thing they did was to change my name to Sabra Louise Payette. But when it came time to finalize the adoption papers my mother refused to sign. It didn't take me long to figure out all they wanted was for me to be their housekeeper and I hated it there. Mrs. Payett called Mr. Summers to tell him about mom not signing the papers and she let me talk to him. I told him that I hated it there and he told her to send me back to the American Legion Home. After spending a year in California, I flew into Tulsa and my aunt and uncle picked me up at the airport. I spent the night at their home and they drove me back to Ponca City.

By this time Mrs. Mayhue had moved to the big girls' dorm as the "dorm mother" and Barbra was now in that dorm, so we roomed together from then on. While in California I was so unhappy and had gained a lot of weight. Barbra noticed the clothes that I had brought with me and she told me that we needed to get me some new clothes and change my hair to a new up-to-date style. The next evening we were out riding horses and Avon fell off her horse and broke her arm.

I had fond memories of stealing juice and coffee from the cafeteria. Barbra would stand outside the bathroom door in the main cafeteria as guard to make sure Sandy Brissel and I wouldn't get caught drinking coffee in the bathroom.

After our building had been remodeled all the bedrooms had their own bathrooms. We used our bathroom to get together with girls from our dorm; like

Sandy Brissel, Donna Willeford, and Grace Wilson. Carol Stewart and Rita Childers would crawl across the roof from the other girl's building to join us. We would gather together in the bathroom to eat the stolen "merchandise" of all the ingredients to make a tuna fish sandwich and even had tomato juice. Barbra would sit in the sink because it was so cramped. I would smoke a cigarette, but had the window open to blow the smoke out of it and throw it out if we heard Mrs. Mayhue come up the stairs. When she did come up she'd say she smelled smoke and we'd deny that we were smoking. The other girls would hide in our closet and Barbra and I acted like we were brushing our teeth but Mrs. Mayhue would always ask me if I'd been smoking again. After she left five or six girls would come out of the closet. Before coming to our room Sandy and Donna would make up their beds with pillows to make it seem like they were in them and were asleep.

One day we were in the Gym and I was on the trampoline and I almost broke my neck, which took weeks of recovery. I was 10 when I noticed how hairy my legs were and decided to shave my legs for the first time. I was using a razor blade that had two sides and you inserted it into the shaver and screwed it down. I cut my leg so bad that I had to be carried to Mrs. Mayhue's car for her to drive me to the hospital for treatment.

I had problems with in-grown toenails and both my big toes stayed infected and hurting all the time. Mrs. Mayhue had taken me to the doctor to have them operated on. I could tell that he immediately liked me a lot. He did the surgery and put bandages on and gave me medicine to take for the pain. Mrs. Mayhue took me straight from there to school. While I was walking between classes Tank, a huge football player, stepped on my toes. He felt so sorry for me that he picked me up and carried me to the nurse's office and I had to be taken back to the hospital to have them re-stitched. I remember vividly being in a lot of pain but for some reason, Mrs. Mayhue wouldn't give me the pain relievers. The good thing that came from meeting the foot doctor was he asked me to choose a couple of my friends and he'd take us all with his family out on a boat to go skiing. I choose Barbra Mahorney and Sandy Brissel to go with me and we had a ball that day learning how to ski. The first Kentucky Fried Chicken had just opened up in Ponca City at that time and we were delighted to have chicken, cold slaw, potatoes and gravy and it was delicious.

Looking back on my time living in the Home the only good memories I have are of growing up with all the kids. I didn't have any other good memories and I hated old lady Dacus who had been my housemother when I was in grade school. She always told me, "You're so dumb, you won't amount to nothing but a slut and you better keep your pants on if you don't want to end up like your sister Ann." As a teenager "Old Lady Mayhue" always grounded me. She would always tell me that I would never amount to anything and I would turn out just like my sister. In high school, if I was one minute late coming back from a date, I wasn't allowed to go on another date again for a couple of weeks.

All in all, my nine years at the Home was a trying time for me, I had lost my one sister, whom I loved dearly. After Ann's death nothing ever seemed to be the same for me. I finished high school and even got some college credits. I was married for 34 years before my husband died; I have a daughter and two handsome grandsons. I work in the healthcare field and am good at my job. All in all, I am a happy person and love the connection with all my alumni sisters. I have been especially close to my longtime roommate Barbra Mahorney Alusi for these many years.

Nancy Curnutte Butler (1957-1966)

DIANN COWLING

Donna (10), Diann (9), and Sammy (8) Cowling came to the Home School on November 2, 1957, the same day our father was sent to prison in McAlester, Oklahoma. My mother, Alice, had died on December 20 the year before. We were made wards of the state and could come to the ALHS because our father was a WWII veteran. Even though it was a dreary, dark, and cold November day as we rode from Muskogee to Ponca City, we were assured that we would be together. We had visited at least 3 other orphanages in Oklahoma before Daddy's trial, but we did not like any of them because we would not be with Sammy. Over the next few years, we came to understand that Mr. Summers, Supt. of the Home School, was right -- we were together and the ALHS was really more of a home than an institution. We were safe, cared for, sent to local schools and churches, and developed good living habits by being given responsibilities and duties that were commensurate with our ages. Even though I can only speak for myself, over the next 9 years of my life I was encouraged to learn and excel in school and to care for and get along with the over 100 children who lived there. We were in a lot of ways a "Big Family."

Not only did I excel in school; I had many honors and awards for a Legion Kid. I was the first girl in my PoHi class in the National Honor Society and the first ALHS child to represent Oklahoma at Girls Nation after attending Girls State in 1965. I received two or three small college scholarships my senior year. I completed my B.A. degree at OSU in 3.5 years and was on the Dean's Honor Roll 6 of 7 semesters. I worked several jobs and paid my way through school since when I left the Home there was only $25.00 in my account. Unbeknownst to me, Mr. Summers had met a man at the American Legion convention in 1967 who sent me a small yearly check from the C. J. Wrightsman Fund, based in Ft Worth, Texas, during most of my college years. I remember finding him in 1970 when I moved to Texas and went by his office to thank him. He was very surprised and said that no one had ever done that before. It was during that brief visit that I found out it was Mr. Summers who had given him my information. In my mind, Mr. Summers and Valla Dacus, my housemother, were the two people who influenced me most while I lived there.

In addition, I was so fortunate to have a wonderful sponsor: Unit 40, Vinita Auxiliary and Post who just this year (2010) celebrated their 90th Birthday. Unlike Donna and Sammy who really did not know their sponsors well, I went to visit, wrote letters back and forth and always got to ride in the Will Rogers Rodeo Grand Entry every summer in Vinita. I got a cowboy outfit from the Buffalo Ranch in Afton every year and it was always fun to visit girls my age there and to spend most Thanksgivings and Christmases with the Cravens family. On my first visit to Vinita, I met Nadine (Cravens) Garber. She was President of the Auxiliary that year and in charge of visiting arrangements for Johnny Walton, the boy the Post sponsored, and me. Eventually, Johnny lived in Vinita and married a local girl. Unfortunately, he was killed in a car wreck sometime in the 1970s. Nadine's family more or less adopted me and even to this day, at 62.5 years old, I am still a member of her family and she is "Mom." So many times, I have wished that Donna and Sammy could have had those wonderful adults and role models in their lives who would love, encourage and support them as the Vinita ALA did for me. In July 2010, I visited with the new President of the ALA while I was visiting "Mom." There are still a few of the older members that remember me and one of the newer Past Presidents that remembers me coming to the Rodeo and she is just a few years younger than me. Since I graduated and left Ponca City, my life has been blessed and God, my Father, has been holding my hand. Moving to Austin in 1970, I accepted a Governor's Fellowship to get my M.A. in Public Administration at the University of Texas at Austin. During my public service career, I worked in the Governor's Office of Early Childhood Development for 9 years and have spent the last 28 years in commercial real estate specializing in selling and leasing office properties. As "Mom" has pointed out recently, I have been able to travel the world for business and pleasure, own real estate, and be a loyal Corvette driver for the last 35 years.

Whoa…that is enough about me; on to Donna and Sammy. Sadly, I won't have as much to tell about them. I lost Donna to cancer in June 1991 at the age of 44 and Sammy died of a seizure 9 months later. Although the 3 of us never talked a lot about living at the ALHS, I know they both felt safe and cared about by the staff and the other kids.

Donna, being the oldest, couldn't wait to grow up, get married, and have at least 6 children. She was a typical girl of the 60's. She went to college for a while and then met Larry Ellis and married in September 1965. Donna was very shy and a little overweight when she was younger. Boy, how that changed. She was good looking, a big flirt in high school, and had a lot of friends, male and female. She surprised all of us by entering the Ponca City Jr. Miss contest in 1964 and her talent was sewing. She made and modeled a dress, suit, and an evening dress. Sammy and I were so proud of her. She and Larry did have 4 daughters, 7 grandchildren, and 2 great grandchildren. They all still live in or near Ponca City. Although Larry remarried after Donna's passing, we all still get together and I enjoy visiting them on my limited trips to Ponca City. My fondest memories of my sister are: <u>One</u>, she sewed all the children's and Larry's clothes, including coats until finally going to work when all the girls had started to school. She was once a Deputy Sheriff and worked for many years at Conoco, Inc. <u>Two</u>, she would escape to Austin a few times over the years for a Sister vacation. She was always a fun person to be around.

Sammy, my precious little brother, who I not only feel like I raised and before his death served as his legal guardian, was a sweet and kind person. The only reason he never ran away (although announcing many times to the contrary) was he always wanted to be with his family, even though he only had Donna and me. He was very close to his housemothers, Mrs. Sanders and Mrs. Fowler, and was not a rough or mean boy. He liked gardening, cooking and doing chores or favors for the Mother figures in his life. I guess he never got over losing Mother just a few months after his 7th birthday. He was in the Boy Scouts and helped take care of the Indian Totem pole that stood by the gymnasium for years (may still be there). He graduated from high school in 1968 and by the Fall of that year was shipped to Vietnam as an Army PFC. As was the case with many veterans from that war, he came home a different person.

**DONNA, DIANN AND SAMMY
COWLING 1953**

Although he was proud to have served his country, the public did not treat him very honorably when he returned. That had a profoundly negative effect on his image of himself and his confidence. Over the next 15 years or more, he managed to hold down some jobs here and there and spent a lot of time in rehab. However, he never found himself or received the medical attention he so desperately needed. He was mugged in Tulsa at Christmas time in 1988. After several surgeries to remove blood clots on his brain, he eventually recovered but took a lot of medication and had seizures from time to time. He was granted a full disability by the Army in 1989 and moved to Ponca City in 1991 where he lived until his death in March 1992. He is buried next to our Mother in Porter, Oklahoma.

Footnote: In 1993, the State Capitol in Austin was expanded and remodeled. They sold sidewalk pavers to raise some of the funds for that work. I bought one and inscribed it with "Donna, Diann, and Sammy Cowling." Since they did not live to grow old with me, I have one place where our little family is still together. I miss both of them a lot but have fond memories of our years together at the Home School.

I want to thank Barbra Alusi for encouraging us to share our stories. This has been a small way to share the wonderful story of God's grace in my life. Jabez's Prayer is still working for me today. God continues to bless me, expand my territory, keep me from evil, harming no one; and all the while still holding my hand.

Diann Cowling

ALFRED GRISSO ('59)

Alfred Grisso went to the American Legion Home School in 1949 at the age of six years old and left in 1955. After running away from the home several times Mr. Pickens, the Child and Welfare Chairman, made arrangements for him to go live with his Dad in California. He says he never disliked the home, he just wanted his Dad and now realizes that he would have been better off if he had stayed at the Legion Home. He attended high school in Vallejo and was a member of the school swim team. Alfred went into the Navy at age seventeen and spent four years stationed in the Gulf of Tonkin, from 1959 through 1963. His 4 years of duty were at the beginning of the U.S. entry into the Vietnam War. Following his service, he returned to California and has lived there most of his life. He now owns three homes in California.

Alfred was a foreman for a shipping company in Oakland, California while he lived in San Leandro, California; after retiring he moved to Tracy, California for a few years and was a partner in a Thai restaurant in the Bay area. Just recently he has moved back to San Leandro so he can spend more time with his grandkids. He has three children: two sons and a daughter. He has two grandsons and two granddaughters. Alfred is single but has had a wonderful lady friend in his life for the last 30-plus years. They like to travel and spend time with their family.

Alfred Grisso ('59)

GLENDA GRISSO BARBER

I went to the American Legion Home School when I was eight years old in 1949 and remained there until I graduated from high school in 1959. After graduation I attended business school in Bartlesville, Oklahoma and worked for a CPA in Seminole for 3 years and also worked a year in Oklahoma City before I married. My husband and I have been married 47 years and we lived in Houston, California and Florida before returning to Tulsa, Oklahoma in December of 1979. We owned and operated nine convenience stores in the Tulsa area for several years called Barber's Superette. After the stores were sold we put in paint and body shop which we had for 14 years in Tulsa. We sold the shop and our home to retire in the country.

We now live in Bowlegs, Oklahoma (I was also born in Bowlegs in 1941) on 40 acres with a 7 acre pond we stocked with fish, which is a big change from living in the big cities for so many years. At first it was way too quiet for me but now I enjoy the quiet and we have all kinds of little critters running around in the yard -- oh some not so little too. If you are up bright and early you can see the deer drinking from the pond and a little baby squirrel sitting on my patio eating my dog's food. My little Chihuahua is my baby now, we call her P.J.

We have two children, a daughter, Kristy, who is married and lives in Sapulpa, Oklahoma with her husband, son and daughter. Our son, Travis, lives in Glenpool, Oklahoma with his wife and two daughters.

I keep busy with the grandkids' activities and sewing, and I like to crochet. My husband and I like to sightsee on our Goldwing motorcycle when the weather is nice. We plan on doing some traveling once my husband retires again. The closest I have gotten to that is my passport. Just can't seem to get him retired.

Glenda Grisso Barber

LUTHER K. GRISSO

Luther K. Grisso, known to his friends and family as L K, was born October 8, 1944 in the town of Seminole, Oklahoma. There were 6 of us Grisso kids and the oldest 4 lived at the American Legion Home. Luther attended Kindergarten through 12th grade and graduated from Ponca City Senior High. While there he made the rank of Eagle Scout and attended Boys State.

After graduation Luther joined the Air Force and was stationed in Japan and spent 4 years there. He spent his tour of duty during the Vietnam War as a cryptographer, which is the practice and study of hiding information; he would decode messages from the enemy. He was also trained as a computer operator by the Air Force and was alerted to Korea and Vietnam during the Vietnam War but never shipped from the base in Japan.

After being discharged Luther returned to Norman to attend Oklahoma University on the GI Bill. During the summer he spent time traveling around the country and even traveled south of the border into Mexico. While at O.U. he majored in English and History, and met and married his wife, Suzan Marie Hollowell. They have two daughters: Laura Marie, the oldest, and Rachel Ann. They are both graduates of O.U.

After Luther received his degree, he went to work for the state of Oklahoma in the Public Defender's Office as an investigator. He later retired to concentrate on his writing and art, but found himself back working for the State in the Child Support Division for the DHS, part time. During his spare time Luther still writes short stories and poetry and does sculpture. He is still working in clay and has yet to find anything that he feels is good enough to cast in bronze, which is his goal.

Written by Luther's Sister Alice Grisso Coffman

LINDA STUART DUNDEE

Being 9 years old when I first arrived at the American Legion Home School in August 1959, I remember as if it was yesterday; it was scary for sure, but then again I remember instantly having the feeling of security and that everything was going to be fine, if not better. I and my brothers, Jimmy and Mark and my sisters Carole and Gloria were living as wild children before arriving at the American Legion Home School. A year earlier our Mother Rose had passed away with Cancer at the age of 32, it was August of 1958, leaving us 5 babies behind. Our Father J.R. Stewart worked out of town, in Tulsa and he was away all week. He would hire ladies from the town of Stilwell to stay and keep us from killing ourselves or maybe each other, but I, being such a non-conformist, just ran them off. Oh goody! What fun. But this was the catalyst in having my Dad send us away, that and the heart trouble he suffered from.

My Father really did try and keep us children together with him but he just did not have the cards in his favor. He had fought in WWII as a Navy man, making his children eligible to be placed in the home. He brought us to Oklahoma in August 1958 (he was from Oklahoma). One day he sat all of us children down and explained to us we were going to take a long trip to a town called Ponca City. I don't know how my brothers and sisters felt but I wasn't going, no way. I was thinking, Wild Indians, wow!

The next day Daddy hauled us into his pick-up and took us to downtown Stilwell and sat us down on the courthouse steps. We were sitting outside of the courthouse when a big black fancy car drove up and two tall men stepped out. They spoke with my Father for a few minutes and then introduced themselves to the five of us and off we went, it was a long drive and we were tired when we arrived. The sun had just started to fade; there were lots of children riding around this large circle in horse drawn buggies. There was lots of laughter, smiles and they waved to the little people in the big black fancy car.

A new start to a new way of life meant going to church for the very first time, I couldn't remember ever going before. My housemother Mrs. Mayhue turned out to be a God-fearing, loving, sweet and kind-hearted woman. She expected wonderful things out of 'her girls'; although I lived for a time when I first arrived with Mrs. Dacus. I have no comment except to say, she was way beyond strict, and was hated by most of the girls. She did have a few favorites who seemed to like her too.

Other house parents who stand out in my memory were Mrs. Sanders, Mr. and Mrs. Fowler, they wanted us to grow up and be good Americans. We were taught to love God, our Country and our family. To be responsible and work hard and never give up no matter how hard things would get, things do change in time.

But I have saved my favorite for last; she was really SPECIAL TO ME, which was Mrs. Jackie Laird. She was our head cook and was always kind to all of us kids. How many little girls can say they were taught how to tell time from a real life trick rider from the world famous 101 Ranch Rodeo? She took me to visit the E.W. Marland Mansion in Ponca City before it was opened as a museum. The trip was made special as she told me so many stories about herself while cooking for Mr. E.W. Marland back in the 1930's... I am so blessed for having Jackie in my life when I was just this little pigtailed girl with wild blue eyes taking it all in with such excitement.

I recall watching from my window when I first arrived; as Mr. Fowler was taking away all my old rags that I called clothes, and my one pair of old shoes. The thing that I missed most that he was carrying away was my sweet stuffed Panda Bear that Santa had given me last Christmas, it had been the only present I received that year. It is the one thing that comforted me when I felt lonely.

I remember feeling that I was going to die from loneliness, missing my Daddy and not being able to see my little brothers because they had been placed in a different building, and having to eat all their meals there too; so I was just so lonely. I remember it was dark that first night when I was sitting eating dinner, I looked over to my right and I saw all these girls who were all different ages, sizes, and colors. I got the feeling I was not going to be lonely for long and sure enough, for the next 9 years I was surrounded with all the "sisters" one could ever wish for. Before long I realized I had about 30 new brothers, not counting my maternal brothers. At that time I realized that I was blessed and have been ever since.

I know in my heart I would not be the successful woman I am today, if not for the American Legion Home School. I was raised right, I had the best role models a little girl could have, and the best "family"... God Bless. I raised my son with love, but with the same strict principals that I was raised with.

God Bless All the American Legion Kids!

Chapter Eleven

Scholarship Fund

DONNA COWLING ~ BARBRA MAHORNEY ~
RICHARD & ROBERT HOYT

Two gifts of $500 each were designated as the foundation of a scholarship fund for boys and girls of the American Legion Home in August of 1956.

M. L. (Dick) Atkinson, who was heading the Home School Committee, announced that E. L. Gosslin and H. L. Apple of Oklahoma City had hoped the money could be used to begin an Educational Fund for the children of Legionnaires to help them start college training.

Atkinson explained, "Students leave the Home when they graduate from high school. Some are able to get assistance from a benefactor. Others are awarded athletic or scholastic scholarships, but the average graduate has to hope to secure summer employment and part- time positions in college to enable them to continue their education."

Atkinson later designed a plan that would help produce funds to enable those capable and willing to continue their education past high school. A small herd of Shetland ponies unlocked the door. The project began with the donation of a single gelding plus a saddle and bridle by Jack McClure and Don Stewart of Pawhuska, in 1957. Within the year, pony growers across the state had increased the herd to 12 with donated ponies. It was composed of 10 mares, one gelding and a stallion.

Each of the ponies was assigned to an individual boy or girl for care and management. The proceeds from the sale of colts were banked in the name of the individual in charge of the pony. Upon graduation from high school, the fund could be used to get a college education. If the youth did not use the opportunity, the money reverted to a scholarship assistance fund at the school.

JEAN WHITAKER ON A HOME
SCHOOL HORSE

The boys at the Home furnished almost all of the labor in providing a shelter for the expensive ponies rebuilding an old barn frame which was located on the school grounds. It was moved to a more favorable location, was covered with sheet aluminum and stalls were constructed.

The school furnished hay and other feed that could be raised on the grounds of the Legion Home, but the cost of other feed was deducted when the colts were sold.

By 1961, the Ponca City High School's "Citizen of the Year," Bill Bailey, had built up a scholarship fund of $2,000. The next year, he enrolled in Oklahoma State University at Stillwater.

At the dedication of Rivers Memorial Hall in 1960, T. L. Rider made another plea for help for boys and girls who graduate from the Home. Rider had been the first graduate from the Home in 1936, and knew how hard it was to be "out on your own" after graduation. He admonished that, "now the seed is sown, let us make the ground fertile, by continuing this program beyond graduation." He said, "We must not let these children fly in space without direction but as guided missiles."

He suggested that the Legion and Auxiliary members give graduates direct and personal encouragement and guidance through visits and establishing contacts on various campuses.

It was not until April, 1978, that the Home officially kicked off a drive to establish a scholarship fund for its youth.

This thought was conceived by two Oklahoma City men, who remembered how hard it was when they left the Home, and were faced with wanting an education despite a total lack of funds.

They were Frank R. Smith, who has a Master's degree in economics and works for the Oklahoma City Urban Renewal Authority, and Ken Coe, Oklahoma City attorney.

Smith was fortunate to have had someone in the community of Ponca City who gave him encouragement and support, even though it wasn't monetary. Coe joined the service as soon as he graduated and later used the GI Bill to attend college. Both men said they "hit the streets cold" and they wanted to make it a little easier for those following them.

When Smith heard about the death of Earl N. Summers, who had given over 24 years of his life to the Home, Smith decided that a scholarship fund should be

started as a memorial to "Bucky" Summers, who had done so much for the children. This would be a way to continue that help – by helping young people with their future. Smith called Coe, who agreed to set up the trust fund at the Security Bank and Trust Co. of Ponca City.

The Earl N. Summers Educational Trust Fund is now available, and loans can be granted from the fund, interest free, to students who graduate from high school while living at the Home.

A five-member committee was established, with the Home Committee chairman and the Home superintendent as permanent members. The funds are invested for the greatest return so that eventually the interest will be loaned and the funds become self-sustaining. Repayment of the loan is based on an honor system when the student is able.

Legionnaires, Auxiliary members and all who are interested may contribute to the fund so that boys and girls from the Home can seek vocational training, attend a trade school or get a college education.

BILL BAILEY WITH PONY

Chapter Twelve

Busy Days at the Home School

My day usually started at 6:00 a.m. If it was my turn to have "kitchen duty," I got out of bed and was dressed at 5:30 a.m.

I went to the cafeteria, set tables and served when everyone else arrived. After breakfast, I helped to clean off tables and sweep the floors. There were some kids who were the cooks' helper; we took turns washing dishes, a job that was hated by all.

Back in the dorm, there was more cleaning to do. Some chores were assigned on a month-by-month basis.

Then it was time to get dressed for school. The Legion Home had its own buses and bus drivers, and we boarded the buses at 7:45 to go to the Ponca City Public Schools.

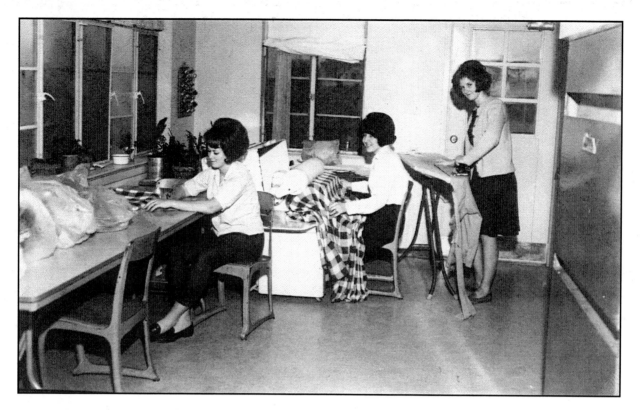

LAUNDRY ROOM 1965
~ NANCY CURNUTTE ~ BARBRA MAHORNEY ~ SANDY BRISSELL

The elementary kids carried sack lunches, which had been prepared by the older girls. Each sack contained two sandwiches, two cookies and a piece of fruit. The Home School had its own milk cooler at McKinley elementary school.

In spite of what we might have said at the time, most of us looked forward to going to school. We were able to participate in many of the school activities – sports, plays, music. Many of the Home School students excelled and received awards and scholarships.

At 4:00 p.m., the buses were at the school to take us back to our after-school chores. But, first, we changed clothes.

The older girls helped with the laundry. On Mondays and Wednesdays, I ironed shirts for the boys, and on Tuesdays and Thursdays I ironed my own clothes plus the clothes for one of the smaller girls.

The older boys took care of most of the farm chores – plowing, planting, and harvesting feed crops, caring for the cattle and hogs, keeping incinerators clean and hauling off trash. Some of the boys had "kitchen duty", and helped in the laundry. They did heavy linens in the laundry, but personal clothes were usually done in the dormitories. The smaller boys helped with the garden and yard work. We ate dinner at 6:00 p.m., and again the "kitchen duty" was rotated.

**IRONING IN THE LAUNDRY ROOM: WILMA
THURSTON ~ JANICE OVERTUF ~ UNKNOWN**

If good grades were maintained, there was no enforced study hall, but the Home School employed a Ponca City teacher to help the High School kids. My fourth grade gym teacher, Don Smith, has helped with the study hail for years. He also worked in the summer as recreational director.

There was a piano in each dormitory, and kids who wanted to take music lessons could practice each evening. Mrs. Ralph Burglund gave lessons free of charge.

There were also typewriters and sewing machines for kids to practice their skills. Study hall lasted from 7:00 to 9:00 p.m., and at 10:00 the lights went out.

Friday night was different, there was no study hall, and during football and basketball seasons, the older kids went to the games and usually to the dances afterward.

Saturday morning was extra-cleaning day, changing beds, scrubbing and washing floors. After lunch, we were off to the movies and down town shopping. Each child was allowed $150 a year for clothes. We could select our own clothes, but if we made an unwise choice, we were stuck with it. Saturday night was date night for those who were sixteen or older. We had to be in by 11:00 p.m., or at a reasonable time after the movies were over.

There was no sleeping late on Sunday morning, because we were up and off to church. We could choose the church we wished to attend. I went to the First Baptist Church. It was fun, because we had a chance to socialize with some of the friends we had made at school. I sang in the choir, went to all of the church dinners and attended Vacation Bible School in the summer. I was able to go on trips out-of-town with the church. I got to visit the Baptist Children's Home in Oklahoma City, and spent a week at Falls Creek Assembly Camp near Davis, Oklahoma.

We never felt isolated at the Home. We became a part of the community in Ponca City. We could do everything and more than most kids who lived in private homes with their families.

Each summer, we were entertained by the 101 Ranch Rodeo. We went to Tulsa to the Shrine Circus. The policemen of Ponca City treated us with fish fries and pizza parties. The firemen took us to Oklahoma City to the Zoo, and to Spring Lake Amusement Park for picnics. We also visited the Atkinson Pony Farm near Oklahoma City. We were always invited to the Kiwanis Pancake Suppers. We could go swimming twice a week at Wentz Pool. The Campfire Girls spent two weeks at Camp McFadden each summer, and the Boy Scouts went to Philmont Scout Ranch. We also could belong to 4-H Club and the FFA.

My days were very full, and I led an active life. We were taught to work but the work was well balanced with time to play and have fun. There were always plenty of activities to keep us busy and out of mischief.

In spite of all the activity, we were normal and broke rules from time to time. But, we all knew the punishment that went with each offense. We knew exactly how long we might be grounded. We seldom thought up anything new to do. Everything had been done or tried many times by the ones who were there before us. The discipline was firm, but was administered without partiality.

Like most kids we sometimes felt "put- upon," but we usually accepted the routine because it was expected of everyone.

I have learned, since leaving the Home, that I was very lucky to have had the care and opportunities that were made available at the Home School.

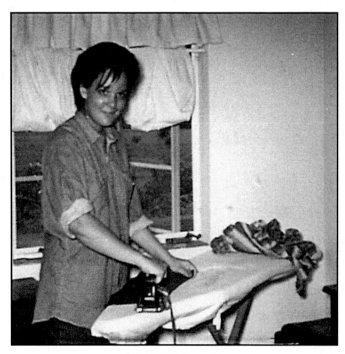

SUE CHAMPLAIN

Chapter Thirteen

Memories

DR. PAUL L. MASTERS RECALLS HIS YOUTH

"I came to the Home at the age of three, along with the first families, the Marks, the Riders and my family, the Masters. Mrs. Pearl Marks was the first Matron, and our mother, Edna Masters, was the first cook. She stayed only a few months until others were hired.

My memories of the home are most part happy ones. I was never mistreated – punished, but never mistreated. I was bullied once in awhile, but that tends to make one stronger in the long run – or at least wiser.

I am grateful to the Home School for many things. It was a place to grow up and receive a first-class education in the Ponca City School System. I think growing up in a semi-rural climate was a very healthy type of environment for all of us. I worked every summer on the surrounding farms, baling hay and on threshing crews. I also caddied at the Country Club.

Then, World War II sort of snatched us all up in those years between 1939 and 1945. I believe all of the boys around my age went into one branch of the service or another as they graduated and reached the magical age of eighteen.

The saddest memories I have of the Home are about those who aren't with us any more, especially those who were killed in World War II. I believe I knew, personally, each one very well. Avia Minor was older than me, but he was a nice young man. Rubin Gooch was my age, and a tougher boy never lived. Elvis Reynolds was a good looking athletic type. He played the lead in our Senior High School class play, it was about a young man going to the service, and he had to sing. This was the first time I ever heard him sing. Gene Gutin was killed in Hawaii during a leave. He was a fighter, and he won the "Golden Glove" fighting award for boxing in Oklahoma City about 1939 or 1940. I remember my last fight with Gene. I lost. We became very close friends after that. My big brother, Porter Masters, was more than that. He was my protector and my Father image, and was always – always telling me to study hard and get an education!!!! I will always treasure my memories of him! He was 1st Lieutenant in the Air Force, and was a pilot on a B17. He was killed while in training in 1944.

I used to regret not growing up in a regular type home, but as I grow older, I can see there were many pluses to the way we were raised and subsequently there are no real regrets.

My Auxiliary sponsor was the Tulsa Unit. They stayed with me throughout those lean years – many years ago. I am, and will remain, eternally grateful."

Dr. Paul L. Masters

WENDELL MCCOY REMEMBERS THE KIDS

"As I sit here writing this letter, I am thinking that many of the boys and girls are now grandmas and grandpas. But I remember the boys and their nicknames: Alvia Minor was "Major Hoople"; Charles Ray Hill was "Chicken" and his brother, Lloyd, was called "frog"; Robert Wilson was "Pete"; T.L. Rider was "Tick" and his brother Leon was "Jiggy"; Jesses James Bingham was "Ears" and his brother. Clifford was "Red"; Duane Moore was "Corky"; J.R. Tabor was called "Moe"; Julius Marks was "Hooch"; Buford Justice was "Donkey"; my brother, Warren, was "Itcho"; and I was called "Coon". I was greatly saddened when Arthur Warren informed of the passing of Julius Marks. He had been one of my best friends.

Those were great days and they will never be forgotten. We were the lucky ones in those days, because the depression and the "dust bowl" were hard on everyone. My thanks go to the American Legion and especially to the Forty and Eight Post at Fort Sill for the help they gave me – and Louise Tabor and her brother Jack.

I was never able to get rich, but whatever success I have had, I owe it to the time I spent at the Home School, which was eight years."

Wendell McCoy

MEMORIES FROM DOROTHY REYNOLDS HAMBY

"I came to the Legion Home in 1930 and left in 1940. My sponsor was the American Legion Post at Duncan. They were always doing nice things for me.

Besides the Christmas presents and clothes, they sent me a pretty Easter basket and something for my birthday. I certainly appreciate all they did for me. I probably would not be doing the things I am today if I had not had their support at the time in my life when I really needed someone.

I am especially thankful for all the wonderful people who took care of me when I was a little girl; Mrs. Edith Caldwell, my Matron; Mrs. Pearl Murray; Mr. George Fults. We couldn't have had any better. I loved them all, including the cooks and the other workers. That is the only home I ever knew, or can remember."

Dorothy Reynolds Hamby

NEITA D. STEELE ROGERS

Ponca City ~ class of 1942 ~ Written by her Son, Frank Rogers

My Mother, Neita D. Steele Rogers, was born on July 24th, 1923 and was raised in Waurika, Oklahoma. She moved to ALCH in about 1933, when her Dad, a WWI veteran, was unable to continue to support his family due to a terminal illness. She had three sisters and they were all adopted by families in the Waurika area. Making the trip alone to Ponca was especially difficult for her. She graduated with honors from Ponca High School in 1942 and was named to Oklahoma Girls State and was a member of the Ponca High School debate team that won the State Championship her senior year of high school.

She married Hobart Allen Rogers on February 28th 1942 and they enjoyed 40 years together in Ponca City before Neita passed away in 1983. She turned down a scholarship to Vassar College in New York to marry Hobart. She stayed on at the American Legion Children's Home after graduating from high school for a couple of years while Hobart was in the Navy during WWII. She drove a bus taking the Legion kids to and from school and helped with their laundry and schooling. Neita's children are Bart Rogers of Tulsa, Frank Rogers of Ponca City, and Randy Rogers of Islamorada Springs, Florida. She raised her three sons in the same way that she was raised at the American Legion Children's Home… in a very strict but very loving way with God always by their side. She taught them to appreciate all aspects of their lives and to be thankful for every single day that they were able to spend with their family members and friends.

With her family surrounding her in the hospital while she was dying of lung cancer, she once again offered a prayer of gratitude to her adult mentors at the ALCH for raising her like she was one of their own children. She was truly blessed to have been given the opportunity to live at the ALCH during her youth! She passed away on January 1, 1983.

Frank Rogers

FROM GENEVA C. RANTA WRITTEN AROUND 1990

I was so young when I first went to a home in Sulphur, Oklahoma, then to a home in Edmond, Oklahoma. So I don't remember my first impression of the Legion Home. I went to the Home because my mother died and my father was not able to take care of five (5) children properly.

The most important things I learned at the Home were: self discipline, to set goals for oneself, self-confidence and above all to be able to take care of myself when I became an adult. I do not feel that I missed out on anything in life by living in the Home. I feel that the Home was the best thing that ever happened to us. It gave us security, discipline and a means to get a good education and to make our life better in all aspects. The matrons became my surrogate mothers.

The fondest memories of "fun times" in the Home were going to the swimming at the city pool and at Wentz pool in the summer; playing outside in circle after meals with both boys and girls; having big 4th of July celebrations, taking sewing classes and dancing lessons in summers and having our own girls traveling softball team. Those are just a few - too numerous to mention all of them.

The special people were Mrs. Davies, Little Girls Matron - a very warm caring person- who made us all feel right at home when we arrived the first time. Mrs. Murray, Little Girls Upstairs Matron - also a very caring person and always had time for each one of us. Mr. and Mrs. Abbott- Superintendent and his wife really changed things at Home for the better when he came. I worked in the office for him and he always showed he cared for us all and only wanted the best for us. Really wanted us to set high goals for ourselves and be the best that we could be.

I never felt ashamed to be from the Home- we were called "Legion rats" etc. but that made us strive harder at school to be accepted. We were good athletes (both girls and boys) and participated on various school teams. We participated in clubs and became cheerleaders, queens and held school offices of the various school organizations. In my case –my P.E. teachers – Mrs. Kingdom- Jr. High and

High School and Mrs. Velma Mitchell were my second mothers and influenced me greatly. They were always there for me and they expected the best from me and I tried hard to live up to their expectations of me.

I feel good about myself today and I have never been afraid to tell people I grew up in the Home. I'm proud to tell them and discuss it. I know where my roots are and I have gone back many times. In fact when I was teaching in Tulsa-many years ago, I took our school's tumbling team over to perform for them. The kids had a ball doing it.

The Home today (the 1990's) is certainly not the Home, as I knew it. When we came, we stayed till we graduated from high school. We were then on our own and I still see some ex-Home kids I grew up with from time to time.

I shall always be grateful for what the Home gave to me. Without it – I would probably have been a country bumpkin.

I graduated from Central State University- thanks to the Home helping me get started. I married a well-educated man from Illinois. We have been married 33 years and have 2 lovely daughters who have graduated from Texas Tech University at Lubbock, Texas.

I hope I have instilled in them many of the things I learned at the home including trust, honesty, good morals, good work habits and above all, being a good useful citizen in one's community. Everyone must give back to their community- whether it is volunteer work or with their donations.

I have spent my entire adult life being around children - either teaching, working with girl sports teams and the last 7 years working at Westwood Junior High School being Secretary to 2 Assistant Principals.

I look at a lot of kids at school and wish they had had it as well as I did growing up. I feel blessed and proud to have had the privilege to live in the Home for eleven (11) years.

Geneva C. Ranta

LAWRENCE M. GREGORY ~ CLASS OF 1956

A very long time ago in a faraway place called Ponca City, Oklahoma, there was a very unique dwelling that housed about 120 kids (boys & girls), ranging from about six years old to about 18 years old. The unusual thing about this place was it represented a safe haven for kids that were in need of a home. As I remember, one of the requirements to be accepted at this home was predicated on the fact that at least one of your parents had to be a Veteran.

This place was almost magical for overnight you could wake up in the morning and all of a sudden you had about 120 brothers and sisters. WOW! Now, one could view this as a good thing or you could see it as less than the best situation. Some of the lucky kids that joined this family settled right in and made the best of the situation. Then there were always a few for various reasons had some difficulty accepting their new surroundings.

The place that I am referring to was called The American Legion Home School. It was one of a kind. I was sponsored by the American Legion of Oklahoma. I feel God had a hand in directing the men and women that initially made this Home a reality.

Now, just imagine how one might feel, as a child, if one day you are uprooted from everything and everybody that you have know all your life and suddenly placed in a totally new environment. We were not bad kids; we weren't troublemakers, but poor unfortunate kids simply in need of a good safe home. Well that is what happened to my brother and me. As I look back on those days I now realize that God knew what He was doing all along. He had provided a safe haven where kids like me could grow into young adults and be somewhat prepared for the tough old world we were about to face.

I believe God provided an avenue for each of us to join this growing family. I truly believe that being placed into this Home was one of the best things that could have ever happened to my brother and me.

From day one we learned to take responsibility for our own actions. Each of us at the Home was assigned duties that contributed to the welfare of all. We helped in the kitchen, moped floors, cleaned restrooms, etc. This was in addition to keeping our beds made and our room neat and tidy. The older boys also took care of the buildings, grounds, farm animals, and all other special building/construction projects.

During my years at the Home I was given the opportunity to experience first-hand what it feels like to put in a full days' work. We learned to farm, take care of animals, raise crops, do carpentry, painting, tile-work, bail and haul hay, etc. You name it and we probably did it. We developed work ethics that were second to none. This may sound like a slave labor farm but to tell the truth by doing these projects, we actually acquired a feeling of ownership of this Home ("We built it and it was our Home").

As you may know our Home was built just out of town on farm acreage. Therefore: We had to be bused into Ponca City to attend the regular public schools. At that time we owned our own buses and transportation was provided courtesy of the Home. We were encouraged not only to do well academically but we were also encouraged to take part in any and all extracurricular activities.

One can only imagine how kids and some people like to feel superior to others simply because of their social status within a certain community. I suppose this kind of feeling comes naturally as part of human nature. As a kid, I always referred to it as the "pecking order." Well, Ponca City was no exception. Many times kids from the Home were treated with less respect and dignity by their peers at school simply because the kids from the Home were considered less worthy and treated as the outsiders. Therefore some of the Home School kids were not included in certain social "cliques" within the school community. This negative attitude toward the Home School kids never did set well with me and I was determined to turn this situation around.

Some of us at the Home School knew we had to overcome this negative stigma and as a result we worked very hard to become the best at whatever we chose to do. During my tenure at the Home there were a good number of very talented and athletically inclined boys living at the Home. Through honesty and hard work these same individuals earned the respect of their pears at school and the community at large. As a result, some of us became student leaders and were elected to key positions within the school structure.

Many awards and honors were earned by this group of individuals during this period of time that I have chose to call "The Golden Years" at the Home School. No longer were we considered as the outsiders for we formed student friendships that still exist to this very day.

Personal character traits that were formed through honesty and hard work during those difficult teen years have proven to be the key to the success of these ambitious individuals. Each of these young men matured and took their place as productive citizens in today's society. As I recall, three of these boys became teachers/ coaches, one became a doctor, one an attorney, three were electricians, and several became businessmen and many of them served honorable in the various branches of our military services. I have no doubt that the self- discipline, hard work, and self-confidence instilled in each of us as young men at the Home School contributed to our success as adults. I personally thank God that there was an American Legion Home School available for me during my time of need.

Lawrence M. Gregory ~ Class of 1956

THE WRIGHT FAMILY

Wesley Frank, Jesse Lee and Marie Louise Wright arrived at the American Legion Home in Ponca City, Oklahoma in 1948. The three Wrights were the children of Jesse Jackson and Vergie Marie (Hobgood) Wright and all were born in Walters, Cotton County, Oklahoma. Frank, the elder brother, was born on March 13, 1937 and came to the Home at the age of 11. Babe, as the kids called him, graduated from Ponca City High School in l955 and served in the United States Air Force from 1956 until 1960. In 1961 he met Delores Peterson. On one of the early dates, he took her to his home which was the American Legion Home. In October of 1962, Frank and Delores were married in Oklahoma City, Oklahoma. A son Michael "Todd" Wright was born in 1967. Frank worked as a bakery route driver for 40 years and retired in 1999. He enjoyed golfing, fishing and traveling with Delores. Most of all he enjoyed his three grandchildren, Shelby 12, Taylor 9 and Hayden 5. Frank would tell everyone that he would not be the person that he became if it had not been for the Home. Frank passed away on May 30, 2010 at home in Midwest City, Oklahoma.

Jesse, the middle brother was born in 1940 and came to the Home at the age of 7 and left in l955. He served in the U. S. Navy from 1957-1961 and the U. S. Marines from 1961-1965. Jesse married Anneita Hall in 1962 in California and two children, David and Teresa were born to them in Riverside, California. Jesse worked for many years as Vice President and General Manager for a Heavy Equipment and Parts Firm and retired in 1999. Jesse now lives in Northern California in the town of Valley Springs and enjoys golf, fishing gardening, traveling and visiting with his daughter Teresa and three grandchildren ages 29, 23, and 22. Anneita passed away on February 5, 2010 and their son David passed away in 1980 at the age of 14.

Marie Louise was born on March 13, 1943 and came to the Home at the age of 5. Louise, as the kids called her, left the Home with her two siblings in 1955. Louise married Robert Reed, a police officer on February 6, 1966 in Enid,

Oklahoma. Louise was a beauty operator and housewife. Louise and Robert raised three children, Michelle, Eddy and Shanna Reed in Enid; and, have nine grandchildren. Louise passed away in Oklahoma City on October 13, 2005.

JIM WHEELER

April brings back all those wonderful memories that came with Auxiliary Day. There was much excitement of the day and anticipation of the visits with those people that gave of their time to be with us on this special day. All of us kids were dressed in our Sunday best and Mr. Summers seemed to be everywhere at once to make sure it came together right.

Special memories of my sis, Beverly and you singing in the gym come to mind. I remember thinking what a great voice Beverly had and "when did she learn how to sing?"

I was proud and a little surprised that my little sis was growing up so fast. I remember little about what you three had on except they were long dresses in pastel colors with high heels...you all looked so nice and if I remember correctly you sang "Tammy."

I don't remember when exactly the dinner bell rang but I do remember Mrs. Fowler seeming to ring it until she was pretty much sure we were all there for the meal and if we didn't show up she would send someone to look for us.

The cleaning before the big day remains a nightmare and I hate painting to this day, but it was all part of the big lesson of how working hard will help you make it through life. Mr. Summers was a genius at inspiring us to work hard, although we saw it a little differently at the time. He was a great man, being the Dad that I never knew and my only regret is that I did not spend more time with him.

Every April my thoughts return to all those many years ago, when we celebrated Auxiliary Day.

Jim Wheeler ~ class of 1961

RAISING HOGS

By Lawrence Gregory

This little story may sound unusual at first but I think it might give you an inside look at one aspect of our daily lives as teenagers. Neal (Mouse) Trostle and Frank (Babe) Wright were members of the FFA (Future Farmers of America) at Ponca City High School and one of their class projects was to take part in the yearly livestock show at the County Fair that was held each Spring.

One evening, Neal and Frank, my roommates, and I were sitting around discussing this issue. Although I was not a member of the FFA, I had many friends that were, so I asked if I could take part in this project. We all decided that the most logical animals to raise, in our situation, would be hogs. We went to Mr. Summers with this proposal and he gave us his approval. We also received a little pep talk and were reminded that we all had chores and duties at the home which took first priority. Then one weekend, Mr. Summers took all three of us out to a local hog farm where we were allowed to select the breed and piglet of our choice. We had to pay for these animals with money from our own bank account. This was also true of any and all expenses that involved raising them. In addition, we were required to keep records of all our expenses so we would know, at the end of the project, if we made a profit or took a loss.

Then the work began. We had hog pens to build and maintain and, of course, the daily feeding and watering of the animals. Each of us had our own hog pen and cared for our own animal. We were able to collect and use table scraps from the dining halls and also were given access to the corncrib, which held the corn we raised and harvested from our own fields. We had to shuck the corn with a hand crank and then added that corn to the hog feed we purchased from the feed store.

One cold morning, before we were to leave for school, we discovered that one of the home school pigs was missing. We notified the house parents of the situation and told them we were going out to search for the pig. We put on our winter coats and hats and headed back down the hill to start our search. This meant that we would have to miss school for our school bus was ready to leave. When we got down to the pigpens we noticed the missing pig was actually snuggled up under part of the wooden structure, safe and sound.

Now if you were a kid, what would you do? Since we had already missed the school bus, and knowing that it would be about a 10-mile walk to school, as the crow flies, we decided to take a day off, (something I had NEVER deliberately done before) and go "looking" for that illusive little pig. So, away we went, out across the fields, and made a day of it. We were a little cold and hungry when we got back home but we had a good day together, just enjoying nature. The "lost" pig was now back in its pen, so I guess you could say, "All's well that ends well."

Then, came the day to take the hogs to the livestock show. We had to care for our hogs and have them ready for the arena, show and sale. Since this was a two-day event, we were given permission to attend the fair. Most of the participants were allowed to bunk down in the hay or sleep on cots in one of the barn lofts. That too, was an interesting experience. When our numbers were called, we took our hogs into the arena for the showing and buyers in the stands would then bid on the hogs. I know that when I received the check for the sale of my hog, and balanced my account, I showed only a slight profit but the total experience was priceless.

Lawrence M. Gregory ~ Class of 1956

BILL BAILEY − (1952 - 1961)

My younger brother and I came to the home in October 1952. Mr. Earl (Bucky) Summers had just assumed the superintendent duties after leaving his plant managers position at NOJC in Tonkawa and was new to the job when we got there. I believe Legionnaire and NOJC Professor Dewey Buck probably recommended Bucky for the job. And sun-tanned, chain-smoker Roy Pickens from the Oklahoma Welfare Department was there every few weeks to counsel Bucky and to make the transition go smoothly. My experience with Roy is as follows below.

This was about the time that I ran away from the Home and hitchhiked back to Enid. My mother was aghast when I showed up in Enid and she called family friend and Legionnaire Ike Crawford of Enid to calm the waters with Bucky and get me back in the Home. Part of this negotiation had my mother paying so much a month for our upkeep to keep me there.

Pickens was there for a visit when they dropped me off back at the home. Well, Pickens got me in an office in one of the buildings closed the door and sat me down about 3 feet in front of him. He sat there for a few moments looking me over and not saying a word. Finally he lit a cigarette, inhaled deeply and blew the smoke into my face and he leaned over and looked me directly in the eyes. I said "Oh Damn" to myself as his stern look told me that this slender, grizzled old man had my future in his hands.

He firmly spoke for the next few moments, telling me that my family couldn't take care of me and my extended family didn't really want me around. After hearing that, I sat there with tears rolling down my face, coming to grips with the realization that there was no one that loved me left, except maybe my mother who now had no say in the matter. It was then the internal rage left at being cast out, and it was replaced by a big hole inside me. I felt betrayed, ashamed, alone and probably guilty that everything was my fault. He had scared the Hell out of me. I got quiet, as words just would not come to me.

He said the choice was mine, either stay here at the home, or go where the Enid Court judge wanted to put me in Reform school, at Stringtown, in El Reno. Pickens kept talking to me and I continued to say nothing. I just sat there sobbing, as any nine-year would do, struggling inside and not really hearing his words.

Finally he leaned back in his chair realizing how the little 9 year old in front of him probably felt inside. He then he got quiet, shifting in his chair probably looking for the right words to calm and assure me knowing he'd scared me to death. After a moment, he said that the ALHS, American Legion Home School was willing to take care of me, feed and clothe, even educate me and was willing to help me to grow up to be a good man. The choice was mine alone. We visited for a few more moments. He pushed his chair back; got up and looked back sternly from the door as he left and said something like "Are we alright now." I nodded my head yes, while wiping the tears from my dirty face.

It took a while to understand that it was my decision to take his advice. For weeks I cried myself to sleep, until one day the big kids around me became my family and big brothers. I realized that I finally belonged to someone and somewhere. My extended family was now strangers as my new family now provided my home.

To this day, if it weren't for Roy Pickens, I would have perhaps been a career criminal, wanderer around in this life, becoming a cynic with no chance at a family life. Instead tough constant love and a tough old man let me see the light. And it worked. However these memories still are fresh as the day they happened. This same story could be told with the hundreds of kids who came to the home and met men like Roy Pickens. My story turned out OK to this day. But those few moments of his time with a scrawny little boy can never be repaid.

Bill Bailey ~ 1952-1961

This is a letter written to me from Bill Bailey

Barbra...

We keep a group of chickens housed in the old Quonset hut below the old laundry and east of the pigpens. Everything was going good until a few of them got sick. In a short time over a hundred chickens came down with something akin to coccidiosis or Newcastle's, where they were walking drunk all over the hill below the big boys building. They would eventually fall over paralyzed and struggling with yellow-greenish stuff running out of both ends. And the smell was enough to "gag a maggot" as some of the kids later said. Years of raising chickens in this hut had built up the poop 2 inches thick on the file and it was solid as a rock. This unsightly, smelling, and disease-ridden mess probably harbored the germs that started this epidemic.

When Bucky realized that all these chickens were going to die, he ordered us to pick up the dead and dying birds and toss them in a big pile (I believe inside the old Quonset hut). We kids used pointed sticks to pick up the birds, as no one wanted to touch them. We then caught all the apparently healthy stragglers and killed them adding them to that same pile. We then poured gasoline on the inside of the hut and set that building on fire. Never forgot the smell of a bunch old dead chickens roasting in that fire. After a couple of hours all that was left was ashes and some melted metal parts.

When the new metal chicken house was built below the gym, lessons learned helped to treat their drinking water with antibiotics to keep the caged and bunched up birds healthy. Part of that prevention program to keep the leghorn egg layers healthy was the poop patrol, every other week someone had to scoop the poop into the old manure spreader and spread the poop on the alfalfa or wheat fields. It wasn't as bad in cool weather, but in summer the maggots and flies were abundant in the gooey mess. So getting the poop in this spreader was like scooping up water. If you drove the tractor pulling the spreader it was OK, but the kid that sat on the front of the manure spreader and had to hold the long metal lever to get the chain drive going to power the floor paddles, usually ended up covered with the slimy poop being thrown out of the spreader in all directions.

Bill Bailey 1952-1961

LEGIONNAIRE FLOYD THROCKMORTON

June 27, 1984 ~ List of Former Board Members

Fred Tillman ~ Tahlequah Oklahoma

Homer Tanner ~ Ponca City, Oklahoma

Leon Grace ~ Ponca City, Oklahoma

Ike Crawford ~ Enid, Oklahoma ~ served 26 years the longest term as a board member.

Jack Newman ~ Ponca City Oklahoma

Carl Welch ~ Tulsa, Oklahoma

Floyd Throckmorton ~ Kingfisher, Oklahoma ~ Served 18 years 2nd longest term as a board member.

No board member is compensated for services, not even any travel expenses. During my time 1957-1966 the home school ran full capacity at all times.

During that time income for expenses came from donations from various Posts from around over the state of Oklahoma, together with donations from the "blue cap" veterans of Oklahoma, and some from outside Oklahoma.

The Home owned approximately 240 acres of land, on which alfalfa was harvested and various feed for cattle, which the Home owned. Some few steers were butchered for use in the "galley" to feed the children. And all of the cattle were Angus, originally purchased and donated by various legionaries over the state. The cooks in the galley (kitchen) are professional and are carefully checked each month by the Oklahoma Health Department, which the Home always welcomed.

The children were taken to school each day in two school buses, and are taken to the church of their choice each Sunday. Occasionally we received a child who was not religiously inclined. In that case, since they are not required to go to church, their job on Sunday mornings was to peel potatoes. Shortly afterwards they asked to go to church on Sunday.

There was a Boy Scout troop, and our younger girls were members of Blue Birds, and worked their way to become a Camp Fire Girl. Transportation was furnished for all their group meetings.

During the summer months each child is assigned work to do by the respective housemothers and housefathers. Occasionally the older boys were allowed to do menial work outside the home, such as farm work for nearby ranchers and farmers. The money earned is deposited to their account, and portioned out, as their needs require.

Only on rare occasions did any children leave the grounds without permission. Right now I only recall one, junior in HS who got as far as Dallas and telephoned the superintendent to pick him up and bring him back. That boy completed his education and is now an assistant funeral director in Enid, married and has two children.

We operate strictly on a tight budget. I believe the annual budget during this time of 1984 amounts to something like $175,000 annually. This may seem quite a lot but we strive to give the kids the best, in order that they will make better citizens and future taxpayers.

One of our most ardent supporters of the Home is Mr. Jack Swank of Enid Oklahoma, who incidentally is the department Commander of the State of Oklahoma. He has never served on the Home's board, but has spent many years in raising funds for the Home.

As to medical services, one of the many doctors in Ponca City is assigned duty to the home on stand-by call. The medical association of Ponca City manages that particular section, and to the best of my knowledge, has never made a charge against the Home, except on one occasion surgery and hospitalization was necessary for an appendectomy.

Another faithful financial supporters is Mr. and Mrs. Chas Hassing of a town in Southeast Oklahoma (address unknown by me, and he is a banker).

An annual event which attracts hundreds of individuals is held on the first Sunday following Easter, and is referred to as Child Welfare Day, (our kids call it Auxiliary Day) at which time many notable veterans attend, meeting the children, and at the same time thousands of dollars in donations are turned in.

Modern laundry facilities are available to all children, with the girls doing the laundry for everyone, while the boys are in charge of policing the area. At all times the whole area is spotless. The flag is flown every day in the center of the compound and it is the obligation of two boys to raise the flag at 7:30 a.m. each day. It takes only a short time to learn the meaning of the flag and what it means.

Two exceptionally dedicated persons are Earl Summers and Lola-belle Summers. Mr. Summers was the superintendent for 24 years, who died of a coronary in 1977, while Mrs. Summers retired in 1982 after 29 years of dedicated service to the Home and the children. She would receive hundreds of Christmas cards each year, some even from foreign countries.

Our dining hall is one like a picture book, being clean and immaculate at all times. It was built in 1960's, and the money was raised by raffling off a new Buick Sedan, which raised the necessary funds $48,000 to build the dining hall.

The taxpayers of Oklahoma have never contributed to the home, except for a "per diem" for each child, but not near enough for the necessities of food, clothing, maintenance, insurance, etc.

I sincerely hope that I have been helpful in some small way. Kindest regards and best wishes.

Sincerely,
Floyd Throckmorton

LINDA ROWE STEPHENS

I remember the first year in the home me and 4 other girls decided to run away. I stole Diann Cowling's bra and put it on and stuffed it with toilet tissue so if we had to go to the bathroom we would have some with us. When I got finished stuffing it looked like I had some really big bosoms… LOL. I was only 11 years old and I was all toilet paper, if you know what I mean. But as it turned out we got caught at the bottom of the hill by Mr. Summers. He was in his El-Camino. Thank God I was fairly new so I didn't suffer the consequences. I only got one spanking from him all the time I was there and that was years later when he spanked me with the paddle for running away. He asked me why I did it and I told him I just wanted a vacation from the home, and he chuckled. I knew he liked me 'cause my best friend Gloria Stewart wasn't that lucky and it was my idea to run away again. I felt bad for Gloria.

Linda Rowe Stephens

ALICE GRISSO

PROM: ALICE GRISSO &
BEN GREGORY

You are a tough personality, a real survivor. Ever notice those who have had it the hardest, are the most compassionate and loving of individuals? A broken heart mends stronger than before, makes us tough and able to face whatever comes our way. Some things are more fearful when they have never happened. But once we face the fear and get through it we realize we can go on. And we realize that we are stronger for having had the experience; that is as long as we didn't let it beat us, making us better off for having had the experience. You are certainly one who has overcome great adversity. The idea of a sabre plant certainly applies to you -- a tenacious, thorny desert plant with a thick hide that conceals a sweet, softer interior, suggesting that even though they are rough on the outside, they are delicate and sensitive on the inside.

Love, Alice Grisso

LINDA STEWART DUNDEE

I have so many memories of Avon, she and I 'hung out' together. Avon was only 2 months older than me. She is the one that got me started "smoking" in the play house behind the building... she and I would sneak off down below the hill to the park to meet the PMA boys.

One evening Avon and I decided to try to run off after dark. It was late one night during the summer and it was damn hot, we couldn't have picked a hotter day to decide to run off. Anyway, I got out the window and met up with Avon and we ran to the edge of the hill and jumped, we were trying to keep Mr. Summers or Mr. Fowler from catching us. I was so scared I was shaking all over my body; my heart was in my mouth. Oh my God I was scared. Well anyway we got to the bottom of the hill and we were bleeding real badly. Our legs, hands and arms were cut up and we tore up our clothes on the sharp rocks, brush and tree trunks while trying to climb up and down the hill. We were only gone for about an hour and decided to return, we hurt so much.

I realized I was too much of a scared chicken and decided to go back up the hill to my building, go back through the same window that I came out of and act as nothing happened. I was trying to act like I hadn't tried to escape, except that I had all this blood dripping from my body... cuts everywhere. When I got back to my bathroom I cleaned up my muddy face and hands, feet and legs, God they hurt. I finally had to go see Mrs. Andrews (house Mother in 1964), and asked her for some band-aids. Well, she wanted to know what I needed band aides

AVON APPLEMAN

for, and why I needed so many. I told her that I had tried to shave my legs and cut them up to bits. She grounded me for a week or so, reminding me I was too young to shave my legs, only girls 16 and older could shave their legs. I still have the scars to prove it. The funny part -- I never got caught for attempting to run away but still managed to get grounded for something else, how fair is that? This is one of those funny stories that are true.

In 1966 I got this little bikini for the summer; really, it was just a stupid two-piece swim suit. God forbid Mrs. Mayhue would ever consent me wearing a bikini at age 14. Anyway I wore it one day, thinking I was the sexiest girl around the Wentz pool, I dove off the really high diving board and when I hit the water, yes, you guessed it, my strap broke, and off it went into the wild blue yonder. I was mortified for years when I would remember it, I'm still affected by that terrible experience, God help me. Oh, and by the way, a really good looking guy of about the age of 16 brought me the top after I came up from under the water (a girl can hold her breath just so long). I was going to deny that it was mine, but being "topless" made it was obvious that it was mine. I died again, as I pictured me going way up in the air and jumping, falling into the water without a top... I have to say the attention was all mine.

I could go on forever... she and I really thought we were "HOT." We did cheers out in the circle in the middle of the campus, hoping our tops would swing open and the boys would see our bras. Ha ... funny then... I could write a book.

Good afternoon sweet girl. Barb, what a wonderful writer you are. I started reading what you'd written and I just couldn't stop, I had to know the end of this tragic story. You and I have so much in common, your family story is so familiar to me. The lives of so many of "us" from the American Legion Home School were so similar to the one you wrote about. When I read your story I cried. I love you sis, and I am so sorry you had to go through what you did and Thank You God for Sallie, for your sake. I think this story is wonderful in the way you told it. We are supervisors, aren't we sis?

You are a good writer, and yet you're asking me to write down my stories, I am not a good writer. Are you sure you want me to write about my memories of living with my mom and dad and growing up in the Home? I do have some truly "funny" stories that will make you laugh your ass off. I will write them down, but just for you, because you have asked me too.

When I remember living and growing up in the Home you are one that stands out far more then some, Avon is another. Sandy Brissel and Susan Summers, Donna Willeford will, hell, a lot.

Barb, we are SPECIAL.... I HAVE ALWAYS KNOWN THAT AND HAVE NEVER FORGOTTEN, NEVER WILL.

One Saturday after being at the movies Avon and I decided to go to this big department store named Kress's, just across the street from the Ponca Theater. Avon was just 3 months older and she and I hung around together and had all kinds of "adventures" together. Some I will tell you about and some I won't. The one that I will tell is as follows.

So here we go... off to the Kress's Department Store, case in point, we had zero money to spend, or maybe 3 dollars between the both of us. Anyway we were going to do some shoplifting, stealing. Avon took a pair of real nylon hose in a package and I took a powder Compaq called "Angel Face" and I stuffed it down my purse. Avon hides hers in her blouse and off we went out the door. I don't know about Avon but I was shaking all over. As we walked out the door and thinking we were safe, laughing and smiling and making all kinds of noise that people make when they think they pulled off a good one. We heard this awful, awful low male voice behind us. "I need the two of you to come with me back into the store" (word for word, I never have forgotten). I really was scared now, and cool Avon, was not showing any signs of fear. She looked at me and then at the man in the suite and so calmly said, "Sure."

This man took the two of us to the back of the store and opened a door to an office. He suggested we have a seat and we did, I was just about to fall off of the chair I took right onto the floor, I was shaking and my palms were sweating, I had blurred vision to boot. I just wanted to disappear and take Avon with me. About 40 hours later, (ok, 5 minutes) this policeman walks into the room. Oh my God, I am dead!! And I am only 15 years old. He didn't say much but did instruct both Avon and myself to go with him and we did. He led us out into the alley, and there was the biggest, blackest, cold steel police car I ever did see. Avon was in the front and me in the back seat and off to the Police Department in the Civic Center right on Main street we went.

They found Avon's stash, the hose in the package but I denied everything, and as they emptied out my purse there was nothing there. Sooo. It was Mr. Fowler who came and took us back to the Home School and we were grounded for the next 500 years. But not until after we heard a speech he had to make about 'stealing' and Avon and I were to report each and every Saturday (until our detention was over) to the Police. About 2 months had gone by and just like clockwork Avon and I would report to the police station and would sit and talk about our studies, church activities, and etc. We were staying out of trouble that's for sure.

One particular Saturday Avon and I reported to the station and while we were sitting around cutting up with the officers, (by now they called us by our names and oh yes, we knew theirs too) now we were all good "buddies" right? Wrong. One of the officers sat down right next to me, after pulling up his chair, so we could see eye-to-eye, nose to nose. I smiled, thinking he really liked me, and he couldn't seem to get close enough to me. Silly girl I was, and this is what he says looking at me the whole time. "Miss Linda can you guess what I found in the back seat of my patrol car, tucked down real far between the back seat?" Oh crap, I was caught, thinking to myself, I am really dead now, off to prison I go, I am too young to die, not this way. I almost peed my pants and the officer continues to describe what it was he found. And I quote, "a pretty make-up case of Angle Face, face powder, you know how it got there Miss Linda?" I never ever stole a thing after that, it just was not worth it and I was so mad, here I am going through this hell and never even got to use the item I stole, what a lesson learned.

Wanda Harjo and I roomed together; later on I roomed with Donna Willeford around 1966 or so.

Well Wanda did something that made me mad but I didn't let her know. She was always ticking me off. But one day she wanted someone to cut her hair. I jumped on this one really fast and said I would and I would make her look so beautiful, she knew that I could cut hair, had done it for years, so Wanda agreed. Bad idea on her part, I took those scissors and I started chopping, and chopping and more chopping. I gave her the haircut of a lifetime, one she would never forget and probably hasn't forgotten it to this day. She looked awful for a very long time and that was before WIGS. I smiled for days.

Oh yes, that was one scary incident...

I was in Jr. High and my boyfriend Warren Marler's big brother had a car. I met Warren and his brother at the park and I decided I was going to drive his car and he let me. Ya see just how dumb some guys are? Anyway, here we go. I am in the driver's seat and coming up and around the bend going west... passed the

Legion Home sign, still going west at about 30 miles a hour, laughing, having lots of fun, showing off, and all of a sudden, being the blonde that I am, I made a quick left hand turn onto a residential street, houses on both side. I lost control and away the car went. There were people outside in their yard picking up leaves, etc.... I crashed the car into the brick house...I got out of the car and saw this really big box on the lawn... and away I go to hide, oh yeah, in the box. Here come the police and found me hiding under the box...

Linda Stewart Dundee ('69)

BARBRA (MAHORNEY) ALUSI ('66)

As I've said all along these stories validate our time living at the Home. Sandy has been writing her life story and she realized as I have, that writing stirs up lots of memories, some good, and some not so much. It may take you some time to go to the closet where you keep your memories, drag them all out and then work through them.

For me, I found all my memories exactly as I left them, and when I took them out and re-examined them, I was quite surprised that I felt the same feelings that I had felt when I put them away. Those things that made me feel sad when I put them away, still made me sad, the memories that made me laugh still made me laugh. It was those memories that I hadn't dealt with from years ago or never really got over that still hurt when I took them out and re-examined them again.

If I had any feelings of shame about something that I had done, the shame was still as fresh as it was the day I put them away. In order to get through this difficult process I had to realize that I did things as a child, and understand that children do childish things. I had to face the things that I did wrong and forgive myself and realize that it wasn't as bad as I made it out to be. I found that by keeping a deep dark secret or a painful experience locked in the closet of my mind that somehow the hurt grew and was much harder to deal with in the end. I realized the only way to get through this was to bring all the hurt and pain out into the light (Christ Light) and when I did it no longer held the power that it once held over me.

My suggestion to you while trying to write is to find the painful memories or any regrets that you have. Face them and work them out in your mind, realizing you did the best you could when you could. Forgive those people who wronged you, not because they asked to be forgiven, or that they deserve to be forgiven. But forgive them for yourself, because any un-forgiveness that you have only builds up a wall between you and God's relationship. Which keeps you from receiving God's best for your life.

I found that by concentrating on my life at the Home it was easier to write about, than writing about living with mama and daddy. It also helped to remember all the girls I grew up with. Those memories were the most important part of living in the Home. I embraced the good that came from sharing my life with all of you. I validate your life as a young girl and you validate mine. A life given to us by God Himself, and I am grateful for His gift. It's not everyone who was lucky enough to have such a large family as ours.

As I told Sandy every one of us has a story to tell, even though we all experienced the same days, weeks, years, hearing the same lessons, but we each took those lessons and responded individually to those circumstances. By writing down your own personal story you're giving the greatest gift you can give to your kids, by telling them how you grew up during those difficult times and showing them how you survived and how you became stronger for it.

I love you, Sandy and Sherry Brissel, Nancy Curnutte, Grace and Darlene and Charlene Wilson, Linda and Carol Stewart, Donna and Diann Cowling, Avon Appleman, Beverly Wheeler, Susan Summers, Judya Mingus, Verda Evans, Rita and Mary Childers, Lavonne and Yvonne Lanter, etc. Because you all became my sisters, I was honored to have spent my formative years with you. We all validate each other's lives, I was there and I saw each of you struggling to become the strong women that you are today. After all we were Legion Girls.... Remember the song we use to sing with words like "no matter where we go, you'll recognize her smile, and say she's a girl I'd like to meet, she's a Home School girl."

I remember when our cook had open heart surgery and the lady who replaced her didn't make sweets, so Mrs. Mayhue gave me the recipe to make a chocolate cake for all of us which served over 100 kids...now that was a challenge for me. Remember how I am always saying that I am cute but a little bit challenged, well you'll understand when I tell you I lost track so many times while I was counting the cups of ingredients. Hey I had every reason, I was counting what seemed like a hundred cups of flower, sugar, etc.... When I lost track I would have to start all over. In the end I had a nice cake from scratch, which I would keep making for the rest of the summer. That first cake I made got me a standing ovation because we hadn't had anything sweet in forever and everyone was starving for sweets...it was fun.

Remember, the measuring cups for institutions like we used at the Home were huge, so when it calls for 15 cups of flour....that's a lot of flour. The mixer was a hummer, a big gigantic mixing bowl with a huge blade. Now that wasn't easy to lift to clean!

Barbra (Mahorney) Alusi ('66)

160

DARLENE WILSON TANNER

Lord, I wish Charlene was still alive, between her, Avon Appleman, Star Lowe and Yvonne Lanter, there has to be tons of trouble they got into and could write about. With me being in the senior girls' dorm and not living alongside my twin Charlene, thanks to Mrs. Dacus, I only remember her being in trouble all the time. You might want to get a hold of Yvonne and learn a few to print in the book.

As for me, I was the quiet shy one over in the corner. I remember once getting blamed for changing a price tag on a swimsuit. I did not do it but got grounded for it and Grace came to my rescue, she always had to do that for Charlene. Charlene would get so mad at Grace because she couldn't get her out of the messes she got herself into.

We, Charlene, Grace and myself, left in August of 1965 and I returned in March 1966 by myself. I think I can name the girls who would have graduated with me. I may be wrong about a few.

Although the second time after I returned to the Home, I sneaked out late at night and got caught. Mr. Summers asked me if I was trying to be like Charlene. Then he said, "I don't know if I should whip you or ground you." I said I would prefer the whipping. He yelled at me, "I didn't ask you which one you wanted." That's funny today but wasn't at all funny at the time. I got stuck grounded, cleaning out the walk-in freezer. Oh, I hated that.

Then I ran away with Linda Coburn for the last time at the end of May 1966. Charlene and her boyfriend came and picked us up from school. I never went back. I do not know what happened to Linda after that.

I remember the girls I grew up with and who were close to me in age and grade were Linda Stewart, Gloria Stewart, Linda Rowe, Becky Long, Diana Cass, Sue Cassleberry, Belinda Tucker, Eleanor Breedlove, Kay Champlain, Star Lowe, and of course my twin Charlene Wilson.

Darlene (Wilson) Tanner

FRANK SMITH

Eddie Turner and I were going to graduate in 1967 and we needed new suits. We went into town to the Sam Lee Store and the owner measured both Eddie and me. He made the comment that Eddie was the perfect size, 28 x 28. Eddie bragged for about a month that he was a perfect size.

Eddie and I were below the hill cleaning the chicken coup and Bill Bailey was there overseeing us. Eddie was mouthy and acting real cocky towards Bill so he picked him up and turned him upside down and put his face in the poop, telling him that should cure him of his cockiness.

There were lots of pecan trees below the hill and the pecans were used at Thanksgiving and Christmas. The pecans had to be picked up and Mrs. Flower assigned the task to me, John Walton and James Hamilton. Of course we turned a chore into having a great time.

One time James Hamilton and I got a Texas cigar which was a foot long and 1 1/4 diameter. Mr. Summers caught James smoking it and made him smoke the whole thing. By the time he was finished his eyes looked like road maps.

Every year all of us kids were required to go up to the office and stuff envelopes with fund raising material. The letters were then mailed out to solicit donations. There was a system we had to follow, a certain pile for the envelopes that were ready for mailing. We were all busy stuffing, and James Willeford and I were talking about all the fun we were having. Mr. Summers came in to see how we were progressing, and he found some unfinished envelopes in the finished pile to be mailed. He asked who put them there and James told him that I had told him to. Mr. Summers got really angry with me and I got into big trouble, even though I hadn't told James to put them in the pile.

Frank Smith ('67)

ALICE GRISSO COFFMAN

I am sure if I think about it there are other stories. Did I tell you about the time we stole dry red (pinto) beans by the handful and cooked them in tin cans that we got out of the trash? It was a cool Saturday morning so you know we were having beans for lunch. First just one, then another group of girls would start another "pot" of beans to cook. We just built little fires in the backyard behind the little girls dorm and we had a ball. Must not have been any rules about stealing from the pantry under the laundry and nothing about setting fires. But, I do remember the first batch did not have any salt in them. Nothing went wrong like setting the hill on fire but it is an interesting memory.

We were always sliding down the banisters and would swing on the bell rope just for fun. The big bell was only rung three times a day to announce breakfast, lunch and dinner. We weren't supposed to ring it at any other time. But we had to go past the rope hanging over our heads every time we walked on the stairs. Sometimes we just couldn't resist the urge and we'd swing on the bell rope and then when it rang we'd run away. We were always doing back bends down the stairs. Dangerous? Yeah, but we did it anyway.

Had lots of interesting characters that came to work at the Home. One that comes to mind is a lady by the name of Mrs. Harvey; she was a relief matron with permanent quarters upstairs in the (middle size girls building). She taught us how to groom our nails with buffers and cuticle sticks and how to tat. It was fun but I never learned past the first step in tatting. You'd have to hold the thread just right and pull the knot just so; it does make very pretty lace. Anyone who accomplishes this craft can do some fantastic things with knots, unfortunately, not me.

Looking back on growing up in the Home I picture most of our crazy antics as "little rascals type escapades" which made growing up with a bunch of kids our age just perfect. Just as with conventional families, what one kid did not think of the other ones did. Oh, did I mention taking rides on the trolley that carried the slop buckets down the hill to the hogs? We did that too. Again it was just for fun. It wasn't like we didn't have a playground with swings, slides and teeter totters, a two legged pole and trapeze to play on. But kids just like to make up things to get into. We all spent hours working on jigsaw puzzles. A couple of girls would start working on one in the living room and any and all worked on them as they felt like it.

Never a dull moment, except mandatory naptime in the summer, which was a safeguard against the dreaded Polio, for which there was no vaccine yet. It worked, as there was only one confirmed case in all the kids in all those years. That is from Mrs. Summers. Don't remember if the child survived or not as it was early thirties or forties. Glenda got sick one summer and it was rumored even at the hospital that she had a light case of polio. But she doesn't remember it.

Oh yeah, one summer we (big girls) all made squaw dresses. Yards and yards of material used for the 3 tiered skirts and oodles of decorative braid and rick-rack. They were a big fad at the time we made them without a pattern just using measurements, which was quite a chore. The top was not fitted, sort of blousy with elastic; the waist was covered with a concho belt, which were made out of silver. They would rub black at the waistline (it was proof that they were real silver but they weren't very expensive, there were stones that appeared to be real turquoise). I was in the 8th grade when we made the squaw dresses, mine was turquoise, and some were blue. Imogene Pruett made hers pink with a fitted bodice. We also wore big can cans called Alice Lon petticoats from the singer dancer on Lawrence Welk TV show. We made the can cans the same way as the squaw dress skirts, by using yards and yards of net. We wore them under all full skirts, like the squaw dresses and under the full circle felt poodle skirts, which were also home made by us; at the time they were all the fashion rage. Barb we had the best there was for that sort of home. I have to say I loved it then and still cherish the memories.

Among those memories are the trips we took as a group. We made 2 trips to Woolaroc Museum up near Bartlesville; the first with all the kids to the Museum by bus and the second several years later in a Phillips Petroleum Airplane, which was just girls in Junior High through High school. Pauline Hodson got airsick and had to use the little bag for that purpose that was on board. Mrs. Hollowell bought flight insurance in a little vending machine in the Airport Lobby; we all made fun of her.

We had a trip to Robbers Cave State park down near Wilburton, Oklahoma, where we spent the day swimming and picnicking. I don't remember if it was a sack lunch occasion or if they cooked out hamburgers or hot dogs for us. But we all looked forward to the treat of a soda with our meal. Don't know who provided for us, maybe the American Legion Post in the Area, but it may have just been an outing arranged by the Home School. There were several outings similar to this through the years. I don't remember ever being told where we were going or more than a day ahead; we had to get up early to get ready to leave on the bus.

We went to Tonkawa every summer for a watermelon feast and fireworks show. Mr. Summers started the tradition, took us by bus and served hot dogs and homemade ice cream as well. The park had a large raised concrete stage that we danced on all evening -- doing everything from the polka, schottische, waltz and square dance when there was a caller. But the highlight was the watermelon (all we could hold) and the fabulous fireworks show that lasted until at least midnight which added some color to our young lives... there was never a dull moment.

To the best of my memory no one ever got hurt or in trouble on any of these trips. We knew good manners and how to behave. We were a super generation.

We went to a farm over somewhere by Tulsa and picked cucumbers one summer. We were provided with a lunch and paid a few dollars for picking them. We also went to a pecan grove a couple of years and picked up pecans. It was cold and we had a cook out and got paid a little for doing it. It was not free slave labor and we played more than we picked... either at trying to beat one another or just goofing off and not doing our job...

About 6 of us girls would sell poppies on Poppy Day for the Ponca City Legion Post. This was a labor of love but I do believe they may have given us a dollar or so as a thank you. Many people who bought the poppies gave us tips, which we turned in with the money. I liked doing it and went every year; it was strictly on a Volunteer basis on one of our Saturdays.

Several of us also served as waitresses at some of the Legion banquets and big dinners throughout the year. We just got to have a good time and sometimes we danced afterward if they had a dance. Mainly it was so we could do our part to help out and we could always look forward to a nice meal, usually a pot luck, where we served the coffee and tea. We were always treated by the local Legion Posts like special guests at most of these events but they did not treat us like kids they pitied. We were happy kids and kept very busy.

I understand the hesitation of my good friend, although when we were growing up he expressed a desire to know about the lives of the rest of us before and how we came to be at the home... But later as an adult he has expressed regret that even though we bonded together as we did, no one ever shared their family histories of why they had to live in the Home. We all seemed to take for granted each other's past figuring it was similar to our own; we just picked up from when we got to the Home. He now asks, "Why didn't we ask and talk about our past with one another? Talking about our past was almost treated as taboo." I guess we didn't ask for fear of embarrassing the others or having them ask us for answers that would embarrass us. Kids have such resilience and great instincts. They have the ability to put horrors and grief behind them and go on with their lives, much easier than the adults around them can understand. We didn't have what was considered normal family lives by most standards, but we were normal and had each other... We all knew who we were and knew that our peers were in the same boat with us, it made survival and even obtaining excellence so much easier.

Alice Grisso Coffman ('58)

LAWRENCE GREGORY

The other day I was reminiscing about some of the activities that we, as kids, living at the Home School experienced on a regular basis. Most of the time we (the older boys), were kept busy doing some kind of worthy project. If my memory serves me well, we also had some "good times." Mr. Summers seemed to know that not only did we need to work and be busy but that we also needed to be kids and experience some fun activities along the way.

After we finally got our irrigation well drilled down on the "south-forty" there was plenty of available water for irrigation of the fields and now we could harvest multiple alfalfa hay crops. Cutting and bailing the hay crop was a breeze compared to hauling the hay to the barn and stacking it in there for future use, especially on a hot summer day. Once the hay was cleared from the fields we immediately went to work setting the aluminum tubes (pipe irrigation) system in place. This was usually accomplished about sundown. Once we turned on the irrigation water you can just guess the next sequence of events. We all got out in the field in front of the big sprinklers to cool down. Then came the mud wrestling. You would think we would be so tired by the end of the day that we would just want to crash. Not so, we rolled around in the field wrestling in the mud like a bunch of little pigs in a mud bog. Believe it or not, this was a lot of fun. We somehow found a way to have fun under even the most difficult circumstances.

There were also times at the end of a long hot day when Mr. Summers would load all of us into the Home School van and someone would transport us over to the Lou Wentz swimming pool for an evening of swimming and cool down time.

I can also remember on several occasions, during the summer, when we packed a sack lunch and boarded our school buses and we were off for the day to some place that I had never heard of, like the Roman Nose State Park for swimming and a picnic, or a visit to Watonga to a museum. These outings were not only educational as well as a rare treat but they were also very enjoyable, especially for a kid like me that came from down in the sticks, hill country, in southeast Oklahoma.

Then on a more personal note, my Sponsors, (Fairview, Oklahoma American Legion Post), would invite me to visit their fair city each summer. The Post Commander, Mr. Harold Lee Carrier, and his family would invite me to stay as a guest in their home. They had children my age and they did their best to make me feel like part of their family. Mr. Carrier would always have special activities planned and this was a vacation for me. We went horseback riding, boating, picnicking, etc. One summer during the Fourth of July, Mr. Carrier took me along with his family to Lake Carlton to the boat races. He arranged for me to ride in the "pick-up-boat." That was the rescue boat that went out and picked up the drivers that crashed or turned over during the race. It was my job to throw a towrope to the guys in the water. Then we would tow them to the dock.

There was a beverage/food tent set up to serve the guests and that afternoon I was helping serve the beverages. They had large square tubs filled with ice to cool the bottles of beverage (In those days most beverage bottles had bottle caps that required a special bottle opener.). I was serving the beverages and using the bottle opener when the neck of one of the bottles broke off and the broken bottle cut my thumb (severe cut). I wrapped my thumb with a napkin, discarded the broken bottle and went to get first aid. It was a holiday and Mr. Carrier took me to town where he called a doctor and he came down and opened his office and proceeded to tend my wound. He had to put several metal clamps in my thumb to close the wound, I survived and we went back to the party.

While in Fairview, (which was a small town), one of the favorite things to do on a hot Summer afternoon was to go down town to a place called the Ice House, (a storage facility where they kept large quantities of ice). There we could buy a bottle of cold soda and sit out under the shade trees and visit. Even though I was the outsider, everyone made me feel welcome.

Then there was the time that I was invited to the Carriers' home prior to Christmas. One of the men from the local Legion post came to visit me. He wanted to know what I would like to have for Christmas and I told him that I really wanted a 22-caliber rifle for hunting. Before I returned to the Home I was presented with this beautiful 22-caliber Marland rifle, in a metal carrying case, a cleaning kit and a brick (a case) of ammunition. It was a rare thing for anyone at the Home to own a firearm. Mr. Summers knew I was a responsible individual and I was allowed to have the rifle. It was kept in the House Parent's apartment and when I needed it I could get it and go hunting. That rifle is still in my family. I passed it on to my son and he in turn passed it on to his son.

Then there was a time when I was a junior in High School. I saw a pair of western (cowboy style) boots at a local tack & saddle shop there in Ponca. I really wanted those boots and I had earned and saved enough money while working for a local farmer in the wheat harvest to purchase them. I talked to Mr. Summers about this purchase and I decided that the boots were a luxury item that I could live without. I found the following information about a year ago when I received my old personal record folder from the Home School... Mr. Summers always sent out newsletters highlighting the achievements of various kids. These letters were sent to certain American Legion Posts all around the state. I had received several awards and was doing very well in athletics that year so Mr. Summers sent the McAlister Post (that's the area of Oklahoma where I had come from) a summary of my accomplishments. The local Commander of that Post wanted Mr. Summers to bring me and attend the State Convention. Unfortunately Mr. Summers had a time conflict and I didn't get to go. But, I found out that during a conversation between Mr. Summers and the Post Commander that the Post wanted to do something nice for me, being I was one of their local boys. Mr. Summers mentioned the boots. Mr. Summers never told me about this, but suddenly there were sufficient funds available for me to be able to purchase the boots. I loved those boots and I took special care to wear them only on special occasions. I have a pair of boots just like then today. I would never have known the full story of where the money had come from had I not gotten my Home School records, all these many years later.

My senior year there was a designated, "senior skip school day." I can remember that most of the seniors planned to go to Lake Ponca for a picnic. Our alfalfa hay field bordered the road that went out to the lake. That morning instead of skipping school I was on a tractor working in our field. I could see the seniors in their cars going along the road to the lake. At first I thought this is not fair, but I soon realized that what I was doing was beneficial to the Home and I really didn't mind not being able to go to the lake.

As I said before, we always seemed to find some way to make our laborious task into a fun and an enjoyable event. One example: when we were helping build our new office/gymnasium it was our job to mix the cement mortar and carry cinder blocks for the skilled workmen. This was hard dirty work; the workman would call out, "more mud," when they were running low on mortar. We boys picked up on this phrase and as the day went by we were chanting, "more mud" as we mixed the cement. This sounds silly now, but at the time, it seemed to take the edge off the difficulty of the project.

A little something to think about was at that time of the year football season was beginning and all team members were required to attend two-a-day practices, one in the morning and another one in the late afternoon. Since I played football I had to attend these workouts. I would go to the morning practice, come home to help mix the cement and carry blocks until it was time to go back to the late practice. Then when I got home I still had my regular assigned chores to do there at home. I have often wondered how many kids today would be willing to make this kind of commitment in order to play sports, just something to think about.

A FUNNY STORY -- Of course it all depends on which side of the boulder you were setting on. Remember that our facilities were built on the top of a hill and almost all our property and fields were behind the buildings and the landscape dropped off very sharply - consisting of large boulders for about fifty yards to the bottom of the hill. One day the plumbing in our building got plugged and required a professional plumber to solve our problem. This older fellow and his helper, a kid like ourselves, showed up to service the system. It was determined that the blockage was located over the hill and down in the boulders. The old man and his helper got some tools and went to work moving boulders so they could dig out the sewer line. The old man ordered the young man around like his slave. He had the kid digging and doing all the heavy hard work. We really didn't appreciate his attitude and the way in which he order the kid around. We all took up positions on the upper high boulders like a bunch of vultures, watching every move. When the kid uncovered the sewer line the old man pushed the kid aside and proceeded to take over the operation. He took his hammer and proceeded to knock a hole in the clay sewer pipe. Little did he realize that that pipe was full of water and sewage that was backed up in the line halfway to the top of the hill, NOW THE GOOD PART - Justice is served - At that moment this old man earned his keep. When he opened the clay pipe the sewage came spewing out of that hole like "Old Faithful." It gave him a bath in sewage that I am sure he will never forget. All of us kids sitting on the boulders started laughing like a pack of hyenas. We laughed so hard that we fell off our perches and we were rolling on the ground in laughter. I know our actions were not very nice but I think one can see the humor in the situation.

Lawrence Gregory ('56)

ALICE GRISSO COFFMAN

I was a friend and lower classmate of Lawrence's and I remember when he won an award as "Outstanding Wrestler" at the Geary Tournament his senior year. At the time of the tournament he had boils on one of his arms that caused him a great deal of pain. For those who don't know there were frequent outbreaks of boils as they are normally a staph infection and spread with close body contact and are picked up from the mats that the boys wrestled on.

He had beaten every man in his weight of 158 and I don't think he had lost any match to anyone all year and when it came time for the state-wrestling tournament he was wrestling a young man for first place in his weight in the final round of the tournament. Lawrence had gone to the tournament so sick (according to his coach) that he should have been home in bed. He was running a high fever and his coach was not sure he would hold up long enough to finish his match, but he did and for the first time he lost by one point. It was a heartbreaking loss but the fact that he had managed to even go to the tournament was a victory in itself.

I asked him once what he might have done had he gotten the chance to go to the Olympics instead of being hurt. He said he had often wondered from time to time, he felt that he would have certainly been a contender. Being hurt in the oil field accident kept him from ever finding out how he would have done.

He deserves a big cheer and everyone needs to know how hard he worked against what seemed to be insurmountable odds. Not just more or less all alone when the rest of the guys from high school had much more enviable moral support from their dads and extended families. He has expressed to me that was one of the things he missed most. That was of course a problem for many of us living at the Home School. I had Jack Newman, Homer Tanner and Bill Atkinson, all members of the board who helped me out by standing in as my father for the father daughter banquets and other places where a dad was needed. Also my wonderful friend in grade school Linda Crawford's dad whom she shared for Girls Patrol (we monitored the doors during recess and lunch hours as well as before and after school. And he stood in as my dad at the Campfire father and daughter banquet.

So, I believe Lawrence deserves far more recognition and praise than he can give himself. I know that he understands how much I value his friendship today. I still have the same respect and admiration for him.

I know there seemed to be a lot of kids at one time when I first arrived in 1949; it was a little over 3 years since the end of WWII. We had as many as 10 in an age group and we had wall-to-wall bunk beds. After Mr. and Mrs. Summers came he reduced the number of beds by sawing the metal bunks in two and making two beds out of each. This reduced the number of kids they could accommodate to 100; I know this was what the Summers called max occupancy.

Yep we were a lot of kids and seemed to have more time together and make lasting friendships. The Legion and Auxiliary was more active but still during that time we didn't all go off for Christmas and all the holidays. When I first arrived we had terrible house parents for the most part, to me they were just live in babysitters who did not interact with us, and that was ok. We did not want them to replace or try to replace our parents no matter how bad our parents were. However, at that time I don't think many were there because of abuse, but just had absent parents or parents that could not take care of their kids. Many kids did leave the Home and go back to their natural homes, some after a few months, others after spending 2 or 3 years there. Mr. Summers didn't like to lose the kids. He wanted us all there and I know in some cases he actually put up barriers against adoptions. I believe the worst thing that happened was when families were broken up by adoption.

The cruelest thing I remember ever happening was how the house parents waited until an adoption was final to tell their older sister that they were never coming back. In most cases those kids who had been adopted seemed to just disappear. Their siblings that were left behind were left to figure out their brother or sister was not coming back. Eventually they were told that the child had been adopted. I saw how this devastating news affected the older sisters. I remember Linda Turner for an example, she had a younger brother and sister that were adopted then finally Mrs. Mayhue gave her the sad news. She was only about 8 or 9 herself, she was very sad and felt all alone. It's the kind of loss that you never ever get over. I have seen some of the girls today that had their little sisters adopted and they still feel the horrible loss but it has been replaced with anger and pain. The special bond they had as children was forever broken and even though it's been 50 years they still feel the sadness.

I remember Mr. Tanner who was an active board member at the Home, he and his wife were always inviting me to their home. They had 2 grown children a son who was a schoolteacher and a daughter who was an attorney who had gone to the home in hopes of adopting a child or two. Mr. Summers who had no idea at the time that she was Mr. Tanner's daughter told her that there were no kids up for adoption at the home. Of course with Mr. Tanner being an active board member he knew there were kids eligible for adoption. But they did not fight him over it.

I never got to keep half of my money nor did I have any in my account when I left... A lot of kids had this problem. I got a check for about $100 for books the first year of college. Glenda and Luther got nothing. Glenda and I worked every summer we were there; we rarely got to go swimming.

So there is a lot of anger, or was at the last meeting I attended, one of your first reunions you held... Lots of grumbling about the money found in Mr. Summers' desk and given to Mrs. Summers.

May be his intentions were good but it worked a hardship on us who worked and I was forced to turn all my money in to Mr. Summers. I could have saved it better myself and would have.

I worked for $20 a week and Mr. Summers would be there with his hand out to take our money as we got off the bus.

I only earned enough money to pay my room and board at school. I would have been better off with the college scholarship offered by the school -- mine only paid for tuition. Therefore after the second semester I no longer could afford to buy books and supplies. Some classes required blue books for test (a dime apiece) and I remember one semester exam when I could barely afford the blue book (cheap little notebooks with blue paper covers), I bought the have-to's and it was hard, sometimes I was able to borrow a text from another student for some classes I had no text book for. I have to say it was not easy. So I can see why some of the kids have some built-up angst about the past. My brother Luther went to Boys State but had barely any clothes when he left after graduation. Just the way it was. Thanks for the super story. I knew Bill was smart… just didn't realize he was such a super kid. He did tell me Mr. Summers and Mr. Buck insisted on him going to medical school and he didn't want to and think he dropped out because of it. Later went back to OSU on his own and got a degree.

Love you, Alice Grisso Coffman ('58)

VAUGHN LANTER

I remember when Beatle-mania hit our little community and Jack Walton and I were sitting on a top bunk with our hair combed down and singing "Yeah yeah yeah." Mr. Goats walked in, ripped his belt from his pants (you all know that sound) and began wailing on us and yelling "We're not gonna have it. Get your hair combed right!" Bad move on his part. We were definitely Beatles then. This was about the time that Johnny Brissel formed his "heist" club. You could only be a member if you brought back "the goods" from a Saturday on the town going to the movies and going through stores on the way back to the bus at the Junior High School. English Leather was popular along with some great albums that I would love to have today. Of course we got caught. We had a trip to the county seat (Newkirk) to see the Judge. We also had a get-together with Mr. Summers in the gym where about 20 of us were lined up against the wall and Bucky gave his little speech. There was the individual get-together in his office that included "swats." Then, there was the embarrassing item in the newspaper. I've tried to tell this story to my three sons as a lesson. I don't think I told it very well -- they went through the same experience. I thought I had such an abnormal childhood and reasons for being so dumb for so long, but as it turns out, it was closer to normal than I thought (with a few exceptions).

Love to all, Vaughn Lanter

BARBRA (MAHORNEY) ALUSI

Vaughn talked about the stealing... I remember the story about the stealing very vividly. One Saturday, after we came back from town Mr. Summers called all the buildings' house parents and gave strict instructions to tell everyone who had stolen something from the stores in town to bring the said stolen merchandise to his office, "Now!!!" If you didn't and later it is found out that you were involved, the punishment would be much worse. Mrs. Mayhue told all the girls in our building what he'd said and to take the stolen articles up to his office. I remember looking out the window seeing all the kids coming out of their buildings making their way to his office. I remember thinking the next Saturday when I got on the bus to go into town to the movies that everyone was grounded, because the bus was real quiet, almost empty, and was for quite a long time. Thankfully out of the many things that I had done wrong stealing wasn't one of them and that is one office visit I didn't have to make.

Barbra (Mahorney) Alusi ('66)

JANICE FRANKLIN NEELY

Carolyn Alford and I were in the kitchen... Carolyn was at the sink and we must have been cleaning up when we noticed a box of oranges in the pantry. The fruit was there for the grade school lunches, and we decided we could take a few and hide them for later. Carolyn stood there at the sink and I took oranges out and put them into a small tree. We decided what I took wasn't enough, so I just kept adding more and then I looked out the window and could not believe how many I had put into the tree! I did think maybe I had better put some back, because it was starting to look very decorated. It actually reminded me of a Christmas tree because we had so many.

While we were looking at the decorated tree, we got to laughing and I went out the back door to take some out and there was Mr. Summers...he said he'd been sitting in his office watching me the whole time. I am sure I wasn't laughing anymore when I saw him. I don't remember getting into trouble but the next week when I had to go to the dentist Mr. Summers said it was punishment for taking the oranges, and he had the biggest grin. I didn't grin, I was in too much pain!!! Ha!

Rose Appleman, Ann Curnutte and Mary Thurston and I climbed out the upstairs window and down the tree for a few minutes time to play in the gym. Back then we sure took a lot of chances. It was fun times we had. I thought I was going to fall when one of the girls stepped on my hand while climbing down…

Another time when Glenda Grisso and I were living in the little girls' dorm, we decided to hide up above the closets. Back then the closets were up real close to the ceilings, they were high ceilings. We were hiding from Elsie Harris; we were trying to keep quiet and Glenda kept saying ouch! And each time she said it she was a bit louder. She was being stung by a bee! You know I don't even remember how we got up there…

When Louise Wright and I were in grade school we had some sparklers, I don't remember where we'd gotten them. But we sat on a top bunk and lit them, not knowing we were burning small holes in the bed spread. When we did realize what we'd done, we hid the spread in the space above the same closets where we'd hidden before…

Janice Franklin Neely ('61)

BARBRA (MAHORNEY) ALUSI

When Mrs. Mayhue got sick she became the head housemother and they hired Mrs. Andrew to be our main housemother. Then Mrs. Mayhue would relieve both her and the little girl's housemother. I think Sandy was telling me that she sold them cigarettes and then told Mr. Summers that they were stealing them from her. I remember when Mrs. Andrew first came she wanted us all to do her hair all the time. I ended up in a fight with her when she caught me talking on the phone. I had asked Mrs. Mayhue's permission because she wasn't there. When she came into the building she walked past me to go to her room as I was talking and said that I was grounded for 6 months for using the phone. I told her that I had permission, which she ignored and told me that I was grounded again. By that time I was finished and I said "Mrs. Andrews you can go to hell." I knew that Mrs. Mayhue was standing back by the sunroom door but I still said it. All Mrs. Mayhue had to do was to give me a look and I would shut up but she didn't say anything either. Mrs. Andrews came up real close to me and took off her glasses and told me to hit her. By this time Mrs. Mayhue told all the girls in the living room to go to the sunroom, to me she was saying that she condoned my actions. I told Mrs. Andrews that I had more respect for myself than to hit an old hag (or bitch) like herself. She screamed and hollered and said she was taking a note up to

174

Mr. Summers' office and slip it under his door, informing him that I was grounded for six months.

I was fed up and got back on the phone and called a girlfriend and told her to come pick me up. I climbed out the window and met her at the front of the building. She took me to the bus station and I bought a ticket to Tulsa to go to Sallie's. When I got there I called Mrs. Mayhue and told her that I was with Sallie, she said, "she was glad I called and she'd pick me up at the bus station, and by the way Mrs. Andrews is no longer with us." The signal I got from this was I was spoiled rotten and Mrs. Mayhue was always fair with me. She knew from my actions that I had always respected her and she was treating me the same.

Barbra Mahorney Alusi ~ '66

GRACE (WILSON) STROUD

I remember this well! We - Sandy, Donna, myself and I think Nancy - were the ones who helped get your suitcase out the windows with bed sheets. Later on we felt bad and we told Mrs. Mayhue what we had done, she just looked at us and said, "I am disappointed in you girls," (all the time she was kind of smiling at us) but she knew what was going on with that woman.

I thought Mrs. Andrews was a BITCH. She was always trying to get me to tell her everything that was going on in the building. I too, came close to hitting her over my little sister Darlene was accused of switching a tag while she was in town shopping. We got into a huge screaming match, it was awful and it was the only time I was ever sent to the office. When I got up there Mrs. Mayhue was there. She took me into the library and talked to me until I calmed down and then sent me back to the building. It was right after that that you left and then they got rid of Mrs. Andrew, which was a blessing.

Grace (Wilson) Stroud ('69)

BARBRA (MAHORNEY) ALUSI

I want to thank Alice Grisso Coffman, Glenda Grisso Barber, Sallie Mahorney Bush, Sandy Brissel Jackson, Nancy Curnutte Butler, Donna Willeford Haffner, Grace Wilson Stroud, Darlene Wilson Tanner, Linda Stewart Dundee, Rita Childers Hartzog, Verda Evans Sisney, Michael Ruth McAdams Jones, Lawrence Gregory, Bill Bailey, Johnny Brissel, Vaughn Lanter and Janice Franklin Neely for all taking the time to write down your memories of growing up in the Home. Sharing our stories enables the reader to get a small glimpse of our everyday life. Looking back like this we see those days were some of the best days of our lives. And I keep saying everything that we write in this book will be here a long time after we're gone.

"Our Book" will enable our kids and our grandkids to see how we lived and played. But more importantly they see how we became a unique Family, made up of so many different children. I have found while writing this book, if I were to meet an alumnus who lived in the Home before or even after me, I would feel an immediate connection with them, knowing that we came from the same family even if we lived in the Home at different times. I think that this section of this book is so important because in writing down our different memories of living and growing up in the Home, we will enable the kids who are living in the Home now to see that even though life was tough we still found loads of things to entertain ourselves.

The great bond that we had as children has helped when one of our own passes away. When we lost our sister Avon we girls were able to put together a collage of memories for her three children. Our stories gave them a chance to see and get to know their mom through us. Her daughter Joy said she was touched by how much we all loved her. She said that it actually helped in the healing process of losing her mom, helping her find comfort in our thoughts and our wonderful memories and getting to know her mom through us.

She noticed all of us legion kids who grew up with her mom called her Avon while her siblings called her by her first name, Linda. And when she asked them, none of them knew why we called her Avon instead of her first name. So I told her the story of how when I first arrived in 1957 there were so many Lindas. Mrs. Mayhue called a meeting sometime after I first arrived and told Avon that there were too many Linda's. So from then on she would go by her middle name, telling all of us girls to call her Avon.

When Sallie I went to the home in September 1957 so did a lot of other families. Mary and Rita Childers, Lavonne and Yvonne Lanter, Linda, Gloria, Carol Stewart, Ann and Nancy Curnutte, Diann and Donna Cowling, Sherry and

Sandy Brissel, all came shortly after me but Beverly Wheeler had been there for several years. All these come to mind as I remember living in the little girls building when I first arrived. Then I moved to the senior girls building when Mrs. Mayhue moved over to take charge of it.

I loved Avon and in turn love Joy because she is her daughter. I wanted to give Joy some peace and happiness by sharing with her our memories of her mom when she was a young girl. Giving her the gift of honoring the innocent girl of Avon's youth. Giving Joy a gift she can cherish the rest of her life at the same time giving respect to Avon's memory, which is something you do in families.

Barbra Mahorney Alusi ~ '66

BIG SISTERS

I asked all the girls I grew up with to write about the first day they arrived at the American Legion Home School. We each describe how we held onto our older sister's hands as we walked through the front doors. Holding their hands brought us comfort and the courage to face living in this new environment. We each described that first day as a memory of a sea of young faces that were just as interested in us as we were in them.

My sister, Sallie, was only 14 when she made a life changing decision that would not only change her life, but also the lives of her three youngest siblings. She had faced the fact that life with her natural parents was unstable and getting worse. In September 1957, fearing for her life, Sallie ran to the neighbor's house for help when her mother chased her with a baseball bat and threatened to kill her. The neighbor was the local Judge, and knowing the family circumstances first hand he had the mother taken into custody by the Sheriff and took all parental rights away from both parents. Sallie had heard of the American Legion Children's Home and she asked the Judge to send her there. The Judge agreed and decreed that she would be picked up on Sunday, September 22, 1957 by Mr. Earl Summers, the Superintendent of the Home.

The big day arrived and Sallie had her younger sister, age 9, and two brothers, ages 11 and 6, all bathed and dressed in their Sunday best. She told Mr. Summers that she wanted to take her brothers and sister with her because she was afraid they would not survive if left behind. He told her that he only had the Court's permission to take her. She was so determined in her purpose that she told him that she was sorry for his trouble, but she would not go and leave them behind.

Mr. Summers had a keen sense of judging circumstances and he realized that he had to make a quick decision regarding these children. He had a court order to follow. He also knew he had limited space with a large number of new students arriving during the next couple of months. Mr. Summers discussed it with daddy who agreed that he would allow him to take all of us. I have the legal documents from our records from the American Legion Home School showing that it took a whole year to gain full legal custody of all four of us.

At the time of our arrival in 1957 the Home was dedicated to taking care of children of Veterans. In order to be considered to live in the American Legion Children's Home a parent, usually the father, had to have served in the military and been discharged with an honorable discharge. Like most of the other fathers of children who were living in the Home at the time of our arrival, our father had injuries from service in the war and was unable to care for his children. We all were simply children of parents who were, for one reason or another, unable to care for us. We were not delinquent or problem children, we simply were destitute and needing a home.

Sandy (Brissel) Jackson describes how she held onto her big sister Sherry (Brissel) Bean's hand. Sandy describes the night of their arrival at the Home. The night we finally made it out to the home school, I was scared as I could be. Not of what would happen to us out there, but of all the madness that had led us to be at the home school. I was in the end of my 4th grade year when we arrived. I was crying and very scared. I just knew that whoever had been chasing us all over the United States was going to find us "out there"! The housemother, Mrs. Mayhue, was fussing at me and telling me to hush up and get upstairs. Sherry was just a little bitty thing, 3 years older than me, and had been wearing the "Mother" shoes for quite some time. She got up on a chair so that she could be face to face with Mrs. Mayhue, and shook her finger at her and said, "You leave my little sister alone, and quit yelling at her. You have no idea what we have been through!" Needless to say, she is my hero. I was and am lucky enough to have three heroes in my life: Sherry, my brother Johnny, and my little brother, Terry.

I used to go over and sleep with Diann. She was the sweetest "big sis." I was so terrified for so many years, that I would beg her to let me sleep with her, I told her I would sleep in the crack against the wall, and she wouldn't even know I was there. She would just laugh, and talk to me until I fell asleep. What an awesome thing to do. Another "big sis" was Susan Summers. She and I became best buds; she introduced me to all of Ian Fleming's books (James Bond, of course). I got to go visit her for a weekend when she was at college. She always made me feel good about myself. She believed in me and most of all she shared her mom and dad with me, with all of us. Mr. Summers and I had a great bond. He liked my spunky attitude, and I liked the way he reacted to it! Haha!

Nancy (Curnutte) Butler describes how she would sneak over to the older girls building to sleep with her big sister Ann. Diann Cowling held older sister Donna (Cowling) Elis' hand, gaining strength from each other.

Linda (Stewart) Dundee and her younger sister Gloria held onto Carol (Stewart) Free even though she was only a year older than Linda. Twins Darlene (Wilson) Tanner and Charlene (Wilson) Knight had their big sister Grace (Wilson) Stroud looking after them and holding their hands. Lavonne (Lanter) MacDonald held the hand of little sister Yvonne. Rita (Childers) Hartzog held onto big sister Mary (Childers) Bolding. Rita writes,

I have shared the story of how we lived at the Home with several family members to read so they could maybe understand certain things and maybe moods I go through. Sharing what you send out Barb lets me realize that sometimes my quiet moods are nothing more than still soaking in what has happened in life for us all. Just remembering some of the kids that have passed on made such an impact in my life and the memories still swirl in my mind. Even though I try to say they don't matter doesn't make it so. Sometimes I still feel like a "little girl lost." Each and every time I lose someone through death, love, or whatever my emotions kick into overdrive. Because the rejection or someone being taken again and again is something that I never got over but sometimes hide it pretty well. I am crying as I type this. Damn the mascara it runs and burns my eyes. Just some thoughts to share with you let you know I will never feel real secure in life I trust no one except my Children for love. How lost is that. I Love Ya sis.

Sandy (Brissel) Jackson writes, What Rita said about trust… I think all of us felt the same way. My wonderful, beautiful Jim taught me to trust again. It's hard to trust when your own mother promises you that she will come see you, yet never does. I know now that she was so very sick and most times was in a mental hospital, but for a little girl of 9 or 10, it was all about the promise. Rita used a phrase that I have often used when describing myself (even at 61) "little girl lost." I think most all of us were.

Judya (Mingus) Garrison was the big sister to Thelma, whom she had mothered all her young life. Then one day she had to face the fact that Thelma was adopted and she lost her little sister. Mary Thurston also had to face having her little sister Wilma adopted. She, like Linda Turner and Judya, never really got over the loss of their younger siblings to adoption. Alice (Grisso) Coffman felt like the mother of all her siblings. Going to the Home helped take the parental responsibilities off the shoulders of a 10-year-old child.

We younger kids could never have faced the huge change in our lives had it not been for our big sisters who had become our substitute mothers. So my heart goes out to Sallie for bravely standing in front of a Judge at age 14 and telling him she wanted to go live in the American Legion Home School in Ponca City, Oklahoma. She ultimately convinced Mr. Earl Summers to take my brothers and me, which in the end saved our lives, even though for them it would only last a short time.

Even though Sallie is only five years older than me, she has taken her role as mother to me very seriously for the past sixty-two years. She visited me many times while I lived in Paris, Malta, Ireland and England, bringing my sons care packages from the states filled with food, candy, the latest shoes and clothing. She is foremost in our family, serving as aunt and grandmother all wrapped up in one person. She taught me how to love and be generous of spirit. I can't even imagine my life without my big sister. SALLIE

SALLIE AND BARBRA MAHORNEY

ALICE GRISSO COFFMAN'S MEMORIES OF
PHYLLIS ORCUTT'S DEATH

Mr. Baker was the Superintendent of the Home the summer of 1950, he was a slightly round man (looked like the Monopoly man with Mr. Moneybags build). He was a jolly man, with a good singing voice. He wrote little jingles and sang them to us kids while playing a guitar. I do remember one of the songs he'd sing was "Ole Shep" another song he sang a lot, was "Ghost Riders in the Sky."

My sister Glenda and I went into the Home School on November 1, 1949. I had just turned 10 in October 1949 and three months after we arrived, Glenda turned 9 in February 1950.

In early June of 1950 Glenda and I shared a room with Phyllis Orcutt. The room had three bunk beds and I had the only single bed in the room. Phyllis and Glenda were both 9-years-old and Phyllis was a beautiful, feisty little redhead. Phyllis was part of a group of girls that had their tonsils taken out when school was out. Phyllis had two sisters; Fronnie was 10 and Wanda was probably 14 or 15 and in junior high.

I remember when I first went to live at the Home there were a lot of kids our age and younger who had recently been moved to the home from the VA hospital at Sulphur, Oklahoma. They were always complaining about having to do "duties" at the Home, because they had been waited on hand and foot and did not even have to make their own beds while at the hospital. I think coming to the Home and having to do so many chores was a shock to them all.

The Orcutts were among those children, if I remember correctly, who came from Sulphur. Glenda and I think that the kids that were in the VA hospital were from families with a history of TB and they were being quarantined before being moved to the Home in Ponca City. They were actually being treated like they were in a hospital. According to the kids who came from there, the only clothes they wore were little shorts outfits and had very little else to wear. They only slept under sheets and weren't use to having blankets on their beds; they were acclimated to the cold even during winter. This is the reason we thought possibly they had been exposed to TB. The VA hospital had constructed a special tuberculosis sanatorium for veterans in 1921 in Sulphur, Oklahoma.

Phyllis Orcutt and both her sisters were redheads, but Phyllis was more of a strawberry blonde. All three of the girls were very bright and talented. The two older girls could draw very well. Fronnie and I were fairly close as we were about the same age and had similar interests. We both had little sisters we felt responsible for. They had moved Fronnie and several others our age out of the room and put them upstairs (in the middle size girl's dorm) with mostly Junior High girls.

Everyone loved Phyllis, she was a tiny, very cute, sweet little girl, and she was very active and healthy. I don't remember her ever having a problem with anyone her age or older or younger. She'd just had her tonsils out along with several other girls, and had only been home for several days.

During that summer we were shown movies outside. At first they projected the movies onto the wall of the Senior Girls' dorm, then moved them to the garage wall. We would sit on the sloping driveway in the early evening with both boys and girls from all the dorms. They usually showed comedies first then a serial and then the regular movie. At that time most movies were in black and white. Color was out then but was usually only shown at the theaters in town. Back then we did not have TV's yet, and when we got them of course we watched everything even the soaps.

On this one particular evening we had a movie where all the kids started screaming and kept it up (for fun) all evening. Phyllis's had just recently had her tonsils out and she had been screaming along with the other kids watching the movie. She started bleeding about the end of the movie and it was not too bad at first, but it kept getting worse when we got back to the dorm. Several of us went to tell Mrs. Willard, the matron. She was a very large heavyset woman, so large in fact she could hardly walk, she would just sit in a chair and smoke. Her breath really stunk so I hated to get very near her. She also had Palsy, and being kids, cruel little dickens that we were, we all called her "Shakespeare." We didn't call her that to her face, but she knew because we talked about her within her hearing. Relief matrons did not have a lot of authority, a lot like substitute teachers. She was the relief and the one on duty at that time. She also was of the Christian Science faith and she believed everything (all illness) was in your head.

When we told Mrs. Willard that Phyllis needed attention she just sent us back to bed. I watched Phyllis needing to keep going to the bathroom to spit out the blood and as she was up on the top bunk it kept us all awake. My bed was the only single bed in the room and it was next to the bathroom, so I traded beds with her, so she could go back and forth to the bathroom easier. The next morning the bathtub and sink were both stopped up with blood clots and there was blood standing in it. She may have run some water trying to wash it away but there was blood everywhere, including all over the floor and ceramic tile walls.

Early the next morning her sisters came to see about her because they too had told Mrs. Willard that Phyllis needed attention. But they found out that it was too late to do her any good. Mr. Baker was the superintendent and his office was in the room next door. We normally didn't see him that early, but he was there that morning before breakfast. So he heard the commotion as some other adults had and finally tried to get some help, but it was too late. Mr. Baker had some of the older boys pick the mattress that Phyllis was lying on and carried her out to the van on it. I believe she was already dead and he had them carry her that way so they wouldn't have to have to touch the body.

After breakfast Mr. Baker called all of us together in the living room and he sat in his overstuffed arm chair, with some of the younger ones sat on his lap and the rest of us sat on the floor at his feet as he very somberly said "little Phyllis is no longer with us." Those were his exact words. We were all stunned, and of course we all cried. Some of the girls really bawled loud, not only from a sense of loss but also from fear. He cried along with us. It was just very traumatic and especially hard on her sisters. They just went wild, which was understandable, and no one tried to stop them.

At Phyllis's funeral we all sat in the front of the church as family members. She was so pretty, dressed in a beautiful little sheer orchid colored dress. I do recall how beautiful the dress was and so appropriate for Phyllis with her strawberry blond hair. Phyllis was such a cute, smart, well-liked little girl and was missed by everyone.

Even though I was only 10 years old and the oldest in the room. I always felt like I should have done something more, even though we all told the housemother more than once that Phyllis was bleeding, she did not do a thing, she didn't want to be bothered. What else could we have done we were just little kids ourselves? I did the best thing I could do by giving Phyllis my bed next to the bathroom door and taking her top bunk. All the adults on campus lost their jobs within a day or two of the funeral.

They had taken Pat Hoffman's and my tonsils out earlier during the school year. We were in the hospital together and our friend Juanita Simmons was in the hospital recuperating from rheumatic fever when we got there. Pat went to Washington school and I went to Garfield. Pat got to the hospital before me so she got to be in Juanita's room and got the only pair of Pajamas left. We managed to have fun racing up and down the hospital halls in Juanita's wheel chair that first evening before our surgery. The next day they gave me ether and oh my, what a headache! Glenda was scheduled to have her tonsils out with the next group coming up after Phyllis died, but they didn't do any more tonsillectomies after her death.

Phyllis had an older married sister who lived in El Reno, OK and her sister Fronnie ran away a short time later to be with her.

After Phyllis died we girls who shared the room with her refused to clean up the bathroom or even go back into the room, so when a new housemother came she had to clean it up in order to move in.

Another very sad story was about Johnny Alford he was 6 or 7 when he first came to the Home. I think he was terminally ill when he arrived because he was sick when he first came. He had yellow jaundice caused by a liver disease. Johnny was an adorable little black haired boy with big brown eyes.

He spent a while in the same hospital room as my brother Al who got a severe burn and spent all summer in the Hospital. Johnny later died from a congenital kidney or liver disease.

Back in the 50's Mrs. Summers told me that there had only been 3 deaths at the home since it opened and one happened during the 20's or 30's when a little boy died from polio. The other two of the three were Phyllis and Johnny and they died within days of each other. For some reason we didn't go to Johnny's funeral that I know of, seems like maybe his service was in Oklahoma City where his mother was. I just don't remember why we didn't go.

Carolyn Alford, little Johnny's sister was the same age as Louise Wright and they were best friends all their years they lived in the home. They were about the same size as well and ran away together on several occasions. They finally were sent to their mother's for good. Louise went to Guyman, OK and Carolyn to Oklahoma City. Carolyn wrote Mrs. Mayhue and some of her friends from time to time. One time she said she was not going to have any children because she had had surgery to keep her from getting pregnant. She died from cancer around the same time as Carolyn Dodd and Ann Curnutte. I believe her obituary was in the Oklahoma City paper in the late winter (Feb or March) 1965. She had married and her obituary with her picture said she had died after a long bout with cancer. I suspect she was diagnosed with uterine or ovarian cancer as a teenager when she had the surgery. Her brother David was in the Air Force. I was twenty-three at the time and I believe Carolyn was 3 or 4 years younger than I. Also, her maiden name was included in the obituary so there was no mistaking who it was.

Right after Phyllis and Johnny died our Superintendent, Mr. Baker, was fired along with all the other adults on campus. Then they brought in another wild bunch, a Mr. McCauley became superintendent and some nasty people came with him. I can't remember all their names, but one man I do remember was Mr. Shanahan, we kids called him "Shagnasty" he was the house parent in the senior boys dorm. He was a big blond man and always carried a baseball bat around with him; he would use it to beat the boys up.

I just remember on a whole how nasty and dirty all these new people were and for some reason I can remember thinking that they had come from a carnival. The woman, who became the housemother for the senior girls, was a good example, she was either a former stripper or carnival dancer, she looked nasty and well used up. I have only vague memories about this group. Thankfully they were only there a short time, but unfortunately, long enough to loot the Home School's coffers. When they left the Home for good, all the operating funds including money that belonged to the kids was gone. We kids had bank accounts and all we had to do was go to the office to see how much money we had. The money was on deposit at the Ponca City Savings and Loan. These accounts included all money sent to the individual kids by relatives, friends and sponsors and they kept a ledger and account for each kid.

Mr. and Mrs. Summers were the last to be hired to run the Home while I was there. I was 10 in 1949 and that was nearly 60 years ago so these are my memories of that time.

I hated milk and never voluntarily drank milk or ate an egg. One day the housemother insisted I drink my glass of milk. I gulped it down as fast as I possibly could to get it down, then without warning, I had projectile vomiting, I cleared the entire dining room. The rest of the time I lived at the home school I was never forced to eat or drink anything I didn't want to ever again. Someone besides me had to clean the dining room after my incident and I can't remember who the housemother was or anything else about it.

I also remember when a little blond girl was trying to clean the bathroom and she could not get a mark off of something. Mrs. Mayhue would check on her from time to time and kept having her do it over and over until she did it right, and she was whining because the mark wouldn't come off. Mrs. Mayhue told her to use a little elbow grease. After a bit she looked up at Mrs. Mayhue and asked, "Where's the elbow grease?"

For entertainment along with the movies every Friday night, Mr. and Mrs. Ramsey would come out and practice with the square dance team and before they practiced we all danced. We did learn square dances, the polka, schottische and ballroom dancing. We waltzed with the best of them. All the boys danced too from the tiny ones to the grown ones. No one had to force any boy to ask the girls to dance. They taught us social etiquette along with dancing. We really loved it and we had fun.

Mr. Abbott, who was the Commander of the Ponca Military Academy (PMA) when I went to the Home, had been the superintendent at the ALCH before we came. It had not been long since he had gone to the PMA as all the little girls still remembered him. I remember seeing how close he was to all the Legion kids and would help them and play with them and was always teaching them. During the summer after I arrived he took the PMA boys swimming on the same days, as we ALHS kids would go. He would spend all afternoon teaching the little PMA boys to swim, and that is how many of the kids at the home had learned to swim after he left the home. We would all line up on the side of the pool and follow his instructions to his charges and we (Glenda and I both) learned to swim that summer along with the PMA boys.

Glenda and I were members at the First Christian Church and during the summer they changed the services around so that church service was early and the Sunday school was afterwards. For some reason our Sunday school class let out late one Sunday and the bus was gone when we got outside. Mr. Abbott was also the PMA bus driver and they would park their bus alongside our ALHS bus. When we got out to where the buses park and saw that we had missed our bus Mr. Abbott gave Glenda and I a ride home on the PMA bus. He drove the PMA bus right down the road and let us out in front of our building. It was a wonder that we were not restricted for life; because we weren't suppose to have anything to do with the PMA boys. But no one ever mentioned a thing about it. Glenda was in the 9th and I was in the 10th grade. Fraternization? Oh My! And that was about the time of all the PMA trouble.

Another interesting PMA story: Farina King (Fudgie) was dating a PMA boy named Johnny Isaacs who somehow took the stripes off his pants, and walked down across the gully between the PMA and Legion Home, and came in the front door and sat in the living room all evening with Fudgie as her date. Mrs. Hollowell, our housemother at the time, never suspected a thing.

The trouble really started after some of the PMA boys started climbing through the girl's windows. Back then there were several girls in each of the three big dorms. Patsy Shaffner, Fudgie King, Juanita Sammons, and Helen Geno were all dating boys who attended the Ponca Military Academy (PMA), across the gully west of the Home. The PMA boys were off limits so the girls saw them on Saturdays by meeting them at the movies and Sundays I believe they met at church.

Those boys thought it would be fun to come across in the middle of the night to see their girlfriends. It was one of those super dark moonless nights when I was awakened by a light flashing in my eyes. I only got a glimpse of a boy whose haircut and size looked like one of our boys. As I was trying to figure out what was going on and realized it was not the person I knew, I started to open my mouth to scream. Suddenly, a hand clamped on my mouth and a young man began to talk to me, telling me everything was all right, etc, he took his hand off my mouth when I promised not to scream.

I shared a room with Fudgie, Patsy and Juanita. The boys had climbed the cedar tree outside our kitchen and come over the kitchen roof into our 2nd floor bathroom window. There was not any hanky panky going on, after all there were 7 or 8 girls in the room they were in. They were mainly just visiting. They may have been kissing but no other out of the line behavior. The main thing was it was an adventure for the boys; none of which were so hard up they needed to break in to see their girlfriend. The one who talked to me was named Ivan; he was nobody's guy. The reason I didn't yell immediately was I thought he was my friend Delain and I wondered what he had been into now. The thought that he was hiding from cops or Mr. Summers crossed my mind and I wasn't about to give him away. I cared too much for him even though he had not been my boyfriend since the 6th grade.

The boys left without incident, but since they got by so easy and hadn't gotten caught, they decided to come back again at a later date. I had moved out of the room and someone else who was seeing them moved into the room, so they returned I don't know how many times. One of the boys who had been seeing Fudgie found a new girlfriend. Fudgie learned that they were going to come back and she turned them in to the housemother. I wasn't there that night, but found out the next day that there had been a welcoming party of Mr. Summers and some of our older boys waiting to greet them.

All the girls still in that room were restricted and given extra chores to do instead of being allowed to go to the movies on Saturdays. Mr. Summers had blocks of wood nailed in each of the windows including the ones that there was no access to from the outside, so we could only raise the windows about 4 inches. That was during late spring I think the last foray for the boys before they graduated, and since our cooling system was a large attic fan, when summer set in shortly after we were sweltering in the heat. No one said anything about the blocks being put in and no one said don't remove them, but all the girls were afraid to take them out, even though we were burning up. One day during a really hot day I decided that I had had enough, so got a claw hammer and removed all the blocks in every window in every room. During the day we always made sure that all the windows were lowered back to their original 4 inches that the blocks kept them at. Or they were back in place if we were out of the rooms or if Mrs. Hollowell, the housemother at the time, headed up the stairs.

But one day, over a year later in the fall, someone accidentally left the window up in one of the rooms and Mrs. Hollowell saw it. On a full inspection they discovered that all the blocks had been removed. Living up to our special code of honor, no one would tell who took the blocks out, but to keep everyone from being punished for what I had done I admitted that I had done it. When Mr. Summers came down to our building for dinner that evening, Mrs. Hollowell took me to him, telling him that I had something to tell him. Mr. Summers looked at me very sternly and said, "What have you been up to now you little trouble maker?" and started laughing. She on the other hand was so angry and was so stern she almost couldn't talk. So I started laughing and told him I had taken the blocks out of all the windows, I told him that no one else helped me and I had done it all by myself. Telling him that I had done it a week after he had put them all in. He asked me why I did it. The only answer I had was it was too hot with the windows down. He laughed and patted me on the shoulder and we went into the dining room and ate.

In the entire 8 years I was in the home, I was never once in trouble, except for the paddling I got for fighting with the girls that jumped on my little sister. I was never restricted not even in a group disciplinary action, for some reason I was never in a group that got caught doing anything wrong. Didn't mean I didn't do anything wrong, just means I never got caught.

Much to Mrs. Hollowell's chagrin I was never punished, and she did not like me. I think it was because everyone else did and she had a daughter who just graduated from college named Margaret Ann. She acted like the girl was perfect and I was in competition for Margaret Ann's attention. Not so. Both she and her husband were weird. She was the one Mrs. Mayhue had to take over for and make her take me to the hospital when the doctor would not come and insisted that we meet him at the hospital.

As far as the blocks went they were never nailed back in the windows. I guess at the time he had the blocks put in he wondered how long it was going to take for us to take them out. But what surprised him most was how long it took for me to get caught for taking them out in the first place. He was also surprised that we had all stuck together and the girls wouldn't tell on me for doing it. Since I was not a part of the group seeing the boys, everyone appreciated that I had let in the air, so they chose to protect me, even though no favor was asked and no promises were made at any time.

Glenda still has the bible Mrs. Mayhue gave her for her fourteenth birthday in 1955; it was white with her name in gold on the cover.

Glenda and I have been reminiscing about the good ole days; we had lots of fun and treasure the memories. Some very funny things happened while we were there and some very sad. One time Mrs. Mayhue took the older girls on a fishing trip. We went to Bucky Summers' and his brother's cabin on the Chikaskia River. She told us it was okay to take off our clothes as long as we kept our panties on. We did and I will never forget how badly the redheads burned. Shirley Mason and Patsy Shafner were both miserable from sunburn. Mrs. Mayhue cooked for us and showed us how to do lots of outdoor things. I caught a Gar and Glenda caught a turtle, both of them tore up our borrowed rod and reels. There was a picture taken of the girls in the mud.

There were several run a-ways at the Home. One time a group of little girls ran away and went down the hill across the alfalfa field then down Lake Road toward town. Jack and Bertie Newman lived down the road near the Pioneer Woman statue and they picked the girls up and gave them a ride back home in their station wagon. Louise Wright stayed in trouble, she got a spanking almost every day when we were little. We had a very large woman, Mrs. Willard, as a housemother, we called them matrons then. She would try to paddle Louise and Louise would run around her as she tried to paddle her and she couldn't keep up with Louise. Naturally we all stood and laughed and put Louise up to doing ornery things so we could watch. We always had fun.

My brother Al got gasoline on his jeans cleaning bicycle parts and they caught fire when he put trash in the incinerator and Delain Geno got a whopper of a case of poison ivy. Both boys were in the hospital for several weeks. I would go visit my brother when someone would take us and visit with Delain as well. For a while Delain could not even talk as his mouth scabbed over and he could not open it.

One of the older girls got married in the living room of the senior girl's building and it was a large wedding. She wanted it to be a very special occasion and was concerned that the little girls would cause a disruption. Whoever the house mother was at the time, put us all out on the sun porch and we attended the wedding from the opposite side of the room. The guests were seated so they were facing us as we peered through the doors. Bet she wished many times that we were in the back of the room instead of behind the preacher gawking through the French doors.

There are many, many stories like these that took place. We came home one day from going somewhere and there were no adults on the place. They were all fired after that incident with Phyllis. Two of the board members assigned all the cooking, laundry and care of little ones to the senior girls. Mertylene Lebow and Lois Owens did the cooking and laundry I was a volunteer helper as I hung out in the kitchen and laundry and knew the recipes and routine. They called me that "little girl," I knew how many potatoes to peel and how much soap for laundry and how to make the starch. In those days everything washable was cotton and needed starch. They also put Dulin Snyder, in charge of the little girls, and life went on without a hitch until they were able to find new staff.. That was a great summer; you might say it was an "Idyllic kids world."

Mr. Summers did catch my boyfriend Lawrence and I out one night after hours (10:00 p.m.). Lawrence had walked me back to my building after study hall. Mr. Summers had been somewhere and as he drove past our building we were in the little entryway, smooching. He yelled, "Alice it's lights out, time to go upstairs and Lawrence time to go home." He knew who we were without even being able to see us clearly. But we did not get in any trouble for being outside at 11:00 pm when the rule was to be in by 10:00 pm. Mr. Summers was partial to Lawrence and I knew he liked me too; the fact that he didn't get onto us proved that he liked and trusted us both.

You know, I noticed there is a big difference in the Home today than what it was like in the 1945 newspaper article that I read, saying there were 200 hundred kids then. Today the Home has 62 children and 84 employees looking after them. To me there is something wrong with that picture. No wonder there is such a financial problem at the Home. Back in 1945, like it was when I was living there during the 50's, we had a Bus Driver, three cooks and a laundress and only five house parents at the most a relief Matron and the superintendent and his secretary…count them 11 or 12 adults taking care of 200 kids at one time. And the kids that grew up there were the best that came from those overcrowded times. Not saying the ones there now are not good kids but they are being treated different than when I was growing up. It even looks like they no longer are sent to public school, which is a shame. We did and were able to interact with kids from normal families and learned social skills that way. Like I said it is no longer the home we grew up in.

Doesn't sound to me that they are doing much… I am glad that they are teaching Americanism and letting them participate in various Veteran celebrations. We were not in a special class we just learned it. We learned patriotism, love, respect and loyalty from the adults and kids we were associated with. I don't ever remember any special classes except study hall and Mr. Summers would give us a long series of lectures on "How To Win Friends and Influence People" by Dale Carnegie. He did a good job and it did teach us a lot. We learned good manners from a very strong disciplinarian who was the housemother in the big girls' dorm. When I first arrived at the home we used cloth napkins and all the tables had cloth tablecloths for every meal. We had a formal dining room that included being seated all at the same time and asking to please be excused when everyone at each table had finished eating. One hand had to be in our lap and the other used to eat with, Keep your elbows off the table and chew with your mouth closed. We were taught to break a slice of bread into four pieces before eating. "Thank you" and "Please" were used all the time between our peers and ourselves at the table when we asked for something to be passed. Our housemother was a tough taskmaster but she was right. Never forgot those etiquette lessons, how could you we as we were required to use them every day.

While I was growing up in the home in the 50's there was a very large plaque called the Honor Roll that hung on the wall. I was told that it was a list of all the kids from the Home who had served during WWII. I remember there were at least 5 of our kids killed in action. The plaque was made entirely of wood and all the names were heavy brass letters with stars noting those killed in action. I also think the branch of the service each one served in followed his or her names. There were at least five women listed on the bottom right hand side. One and maybe two were listed as killed in action. I don't think there were any except WAC's and Waves during WWII and they were nurses who served.

You have to admit the Home School boys who served during WWII and ultimately gave their lives for their country, were the cream of the crop. They were kids that grew up with the mettle and conviction to make the supreme sacrifice to give back to their country. It has to make you proud, and kids who were progeny of WWII vets were just coming of age in my age group...and the Home was only taking school age kids by the time I arrived in 1949. The war had only ended a little more than 3 years before in 1946, so we were the beginning of the baby boomers. We were the continuation of a group of kids that took pride and respect for their home.

I loved the place and the kids I grew up with. I felt back then and still feel a great deal of respect for those who served in WWII and I think they were awesome. It's amazing so many actually survived the ordeal. I think our young men had learned to lead and follow their leaders and get along in a group situation, skills they learned while growing up in the Home School.

Alice Grisso Coffman ('58)

MR. SUMMERS' BONFIRE ~ WRITTEN BY BILL BAILEY

One day when I was about 16 or 17, Bucky and O.C. Fowler told us high school boys, Jim Wheeler, Darrell Bean, and Clifford Overturf and myself to drive down and empty the trash barrels and afterwards set the trash in the dump on fire as it was full and needed to be burned. Well, it had been raining that spring and everything in the dump was wet and no matter what we four Boy Scouts tried, the fire would burn for a few minutes and then would go out.

So we took the pickup, back up the hill and told Bucky and O.C. that we couldn't get the dump to burn due to the rain, to which Bucky said as he looked down at the four of us through his bifocals, kind of frowned and said impatiently something like "Bullshit, I will show you how to take care of the trash and get it to burn." He dispatched two of us to the cafeteria to find an empty two-gallon pickle jar, which I believe Mrs. Jackie Laird, the cook at the time got it for us. Bucky took this jar got in the pickup with O.C. and told all of us to get in the back. He drove over to the gas pump near his house on the east side of the circle. We pumped enough into the top cylinder so Bucky could fill the two-gallon jar with red tractor gas full to the brim. Then he screwed the lid on tightly and put the jar in the pickup bed.

Bucky then said jumping back in the truck "Let's go get that dump started on fire." Great, I thought why didn't we think about setting the dump on fire with gasoline ourselves? What dumb kids we were and all four of us hunkered down in the back of the truck silent and feeling guilty on the way back down to the dump. When we drove up to the dump, Bucky quickly got out, found a rag that he wrapped around an old broomstick, doused it with gas and then set it on fire. He then threw this smoldering torch into the dump expecting it to quickly catch fire. Well, the dump didn't catch fire. After several minutes we four boys looked at each other and smirked, and all must have said quietly to ourselves in unison. "Didn't work did it?" and "We told you so. It is too wet to burn, Ha Ha, uh, Ha Ha." Well Bucky looked at us smirking, must have read our minds, and you could see him grit his teeth, and I knew from past experience this dump was going to burn that day.

I had great respect for Mr. Summers, and still do. But you had to know Mr. Summers real well, he was a doer: a great builder, could fix any piece of equipment, take care of any farm animal, knew farm crops and also had great knowledge of many other things, but when he got irritated and/or mad at something or someone his patience would vanish, his face slowly would turn red from the neck upward, and pretty soon his forehead would turn bright red like a "bad sunburn." Then everyone knew it was time to either look the other way, or slink off slowly, or just stand quietly there and wait for Mt. Vesuvius to erupt. "Oh damn," I used to say to myself when I saw Bucky get like that as you knew someone was in for an "ass kicking or an ass chewing" or worse. I could only imagine what was about to happen next with this fire!!

Well sir, when Bucky saw our smirks and as his forehead slowly turned sunburned ochre. I looked over at Mr. Fowler, and from his expression he too knew Bucky was about to "erupt." All five of us stood there waiting for our supreme commander-in-chief to make his first big move. We were all lined up on the edge of the dump like six innocent bystanders watching the torch fire burn slowly down and down and down until the flame was about to go out, and waiting for something to happen.

Then Bucky narrowed his eyes, and said confidently something to the effect "By God, I will take care of this fire right now." He turned around, looked directly at that jar full of gasoline that was sitting nearby. He strode over, picked up the jar and without a second look heaved the jar with almost two gallons of gasoline into that miserable excuse of a little fire. The jar sailed up and out like a slow big balloon full of a slushy, red liquid and then it descended like a dead rock onto that wet dump dropping straight toward that dwindling little flame. We all leaned forward in anticipation as we said under our breath that this dump was really going to burn now, burn baby burn!!

And then all I remember was the faint sound of glass tinkling, followed immediately by a tremendously loud BOOM. The heat that slammed into our faces was like a hot Sahara windstorm, bending us backwards with gale force. And a glass shard grazed the left side of my face just below my eye and whizzed on past like a bullet and I actually heard it "Zip" on off past my left ear and then the smell of my eyebrows and hair being singed, and the hot breath of hot fire on my skin as the fire flashed outward and engulfed all six of us in a huge wall of flame. And because we all were frozen to that spot it seemed almost in slow motion as the entire dump whooshed upward in a wall of red angry flame, a full ten feet into the air, and snaking out 20 feet in each direction, like a Viet Nam napalm bomb bent on its path of deadly, rolling destruction. All of us were dumb struck and shaken, no one could move or say a word or even swallow. We just stood there. I remember my reflexes causing me to about pee my pants, my stomach sinking in fear, wondering if I were bleeding from glass, and slowly becoming aware that all six lives had just been spared from some terrible fate. And suddenly I was thankful that God with a miracle had spared these six fools from their fate. As my full senses came back to me, I slowly turned right and look at Bucky and O.C. and there was no color in their faces, their resolution gone from their frightened eyes, and knowing that the lesson they hoped to teach these four young men about fire had completely fizzled and backfired on them. I know all of us welcomed the damp cool air on our skin and were so glad we were unhurt.

"Damn it!!!" Bucky said with embarrassed anger at his monumental mistake, and after pausing turned around and motioned for us to get in the pickup. We silently drove away toward the house with the dump blazing angrily upward behind us, with four frightened kids, and two men who knew that all of us had damn near been killed that day or seriously hurt.

Later that night the four of us over and over had a great laugh recalling Bucky's actions to the other boys, his "take charge attitude," his big explosion, and the lucky fact that somehow all of us were miraculously unhurt. Then all four of us would realize that this poorly planned event had almost killed us all and the entire room would quietly hush, each of us just thankful to be there. I believe that when Bucky described that same incident that evening over dinner to his wife Lolabelle, I can only imagine what she said to him. Lolabelle was always his chief council confidant and leveling force but she probably chastised him for his actions that day.

Forty-three years later, when I recall this incident and touch that same spot below my eye where the glass left a red, streaked whelp that day, I wince. Then I remember the surprised look on Bucky's face that instant after he "lit that big fire" and a smile comes to my face with the absurd, almost comical actions of that incident long ago, I am still so very thankful that all six of us were unhurt and spared by the good Lord because He had other plans for each of us at some future date, as tomorrow promised to be better.

Bill Bailey

JACKIE LAIRD'S PERSONAL OBIT READ AT HER FUNERAL

Mary Ellen Legy (Leesel) McFarlin Laird, better known as "Jackie" lived almost a century. Born in Oklahoma Territory to Jess and Martha Mellvina McFarlin April 16, 1896 at Dale Oklahoma, she grew up on the famous 101 Ranch where her father was in charge of the dairy industry. She, together with two sisters, Mamie and Susie, and two brothers, Dan and Jess, attended school at the 101 Ranch Schoolhouse. She longed to travel with the 101 Wild West Show and at a young age, managed to stowaway with the show. When her father discovered she was missing he wired Joe Miller in New York. Joe wired back "yes, Jackie was there and he personally would oversee her." Jackie rode in the opening parade at Madison Square Garden and trick riding and roping and a love of the show forever flowed in her veins. She was with them while giving a command performance before royalty in England - a bugler rode into the ring, stopped the performance and announced that England had entered World War I. Spurs, saddles and heavy stock horses were commandeered and men of German descent were detained. The 101 show came back home.

When the show wasn't on the road, Jackie cooked at the Arcade Hotel, the local 'watering hole' for the great and small. Stories galore she told of Joe, George, and Zach Miller and Lew Wentz.

She became the companion of Mary Virginia Marland, when E. W. traveled: and in time cooked the wedding dinner for E. W. and Lydie at the mansion.

On 1944 she married Dewitt Laird and they settled near Morrison. During this time she met Margie Lou Wood who continued to send her a card every week for a number of years!

She married Johnny Robedeaux March 18, 1919 and they lived on a farm near Morrison, they had no children. Jackie eventually was a chef at the Jens Marie and in later life cooked for the American Legion Home School, where she became part of the family and the kids called her grandma. There she met Melvin Eckert who was to help her off and on the rest of her life. Jack and Roberta Newman were close friends and when Jackie was older, Roberta saw after her needs. In talking to visitors about Jackie at the Pioneer Woman Museum, Roberta has said on numerous occasions, "I never was with Jackie but what she made me feel better," and I would have to concur with that. After she became confined to a wheelchair and I would lift her into bed at her home, she would never complain, no matter how much it hurt. She was always very appreciative. My son, Scott, came home from law school on weekends to stay the night with her so she could continue to stay in the home she loved with her cats and dog, after his marriage, Jonathan stayed.

A second Governor, George Nigh, touched her life when he named her "Pioneer woman of the Year in 1983."

Even after she was confined to a wheelchair she lived for three things: Talking to Harold and Allwida on the telephone at least once a day: The 101 old timers Parade every August and Louise's articles about her prior to the parade. I had aluminum ramps made so we could roll Jackie's wheelchair into our van and my wife, Jan, took her every place, the Ponca Pow Wow, parades, out to eat, you name it.

Red shirt and bandanna and her cowboy hat (in later years mine) were a must for the 101 parades. She loved Johnny Heinz calling to make sure she would be there and then waving her and Mike Sokoll into place to lead the parade, 76 trombones couldn't have made it more special. "Wave" she'd yell to everyone in the car. "You've got to make a parade happen." She loved to vote, one year Larry Stevenson, a close friend, came and lifted her from her wheelchair to his car to take her to vote.

It became difficult to find enough help to be able to keep her at home, so John Warren conservator. Arranged for Shawn Manor to become her home and Evelyn Swope saw after her person needs. Many at the Nursing Home took her "under wing." She had a sweet, sweet spirit that made you love her. Perhaps the biggest blessing was her final roommate, Juanita Mackey, who was of tremendous comfort to Jackie until the end.

She is survived by one stepson, Harold Laird of Pawnee and several nieces and nephews. Her parents, two husbands, two brothers and two sisters preceded her in death.

She was a member of E.H.C. C.

FAMILY REUNION WAS WORTH RISK

San Jose Mercury News ~ Wednesday ~ June 8, 1988

Isaleen Nadalet and David Walker sat across the kitchen table from each other Monday in Nadalet's pleasant Santa Clara home. Although Nadalet's husband, Al, and Walker's wife, Jo, were also in the room, Isaleen and David couldn't take their eyes off of each other. They hung on each other's words. They smiled. They laughed. They cried.

They are brother and sister, reunited after 57 years. Walker had long assumed that Nadalet was dead. Nadalet, after years of looking, had given up her search for Walker more than two decades ago. And yet, as improbable as it seemed, here they were. Over cups of coffee the words tumbled out, words that spoke of faded memories, lost years and full lives spent apart.

"It's just happiness," said Nadalet. "I didn't know until a month ago that I had a family," said Walker, who lives in Everett, Wash.

Their natural father had died the same day David Walker was born. It was during the Depression, in Dust Bowl-era Oklahoma. "Our mother was young, in ill health just a farm girl really and unable to take care of us," said Nadalet. "She took us to the American Legion Home in Ponca City, Okla. There were three of us. I was the oldest. I was 6. The baby, David was 2. The other brother, Don, who died 16 years ago, was 4."

"She couldn't read or write at the time, and she told me later that she wasn't sure what she had signed. But she had signed us over for adoption." Walker, the youngest child, wasn't in the orphanage long. He was adopted by a family from Tulsa. Nadalet and the other brother stayed at the home for three years before being adopted together. "When I became an adult I started trying to find the baby brother," she said. "I was told that the family who adopted him didn't want him to know that he was adopted and that the records had been closed. But I did find my natural mother. And I kept in touch with her, and I took care of her the last few years of her life."

Walker was told when he was 15 that he had been adopted. When he went into the service he received a copy of his birth certificate, which gave his original name and the fact that there had been two other live births in his family.

"I considered the people who adopted me to be my mom and dad," he said. "I knew if I ever wanted to look for my family it would be after they died. I didn't want to hurt them. I had a very good life. I had a contented life, and I guess that's one reason I didn't pursue it.

"I always had the assumption that my family had two other kids and they couldn't afford me. It was during the Depression. I thought I was the only one that was given up for adoption. I had another thought during those years. We lived in what was called tornado alley, and somewhere along the line I got the idea that everybody was lost in a tornado, except me."

Tears glistened on Nadalet's face. "That breaks my heart to think that you always thought you weren't wanted, that you were the only one given up. That's one good thing about this. David knows that our mother had to give us up, that she didn't want to."

It was Walker's daughter, Patricia Ewin, who found Nadalet. Through extensive searching she found a family cousin in Oklahoma who knew of David Walker's older sister. That discovery set in motion events that led to the family reunion in Santa Clara.

Many people, of course, are separated by time and circumstance. Some people never stop hunting for each other. Some never look at all. How does it feel to find someone after 57 years? Is it what you thought it would be?

Nadalet went first. "It was hard for me to find out who my natural mother was, and it was very hard the last few years, taking care of her. She had a terrible illness. I was a little anxious when I heard about David. I didn't know what kind of life David had less, how I would feel about having him for a brother. I can't say it's the thing for everybody to do. You are taking a chance."

Walker said he felt the same way. "I was a little leery," he said, "describing the unsettling feeling of comparing your life to that of a complete stranger, who nonetheless had the same mother and father."

The Walkers and Nadalets are planning additional reunions. "I don't know if I'd recommend this or not," Walker said, breaking slowly into a grin. "But I probably would say what the hell? Give it a try." Everyone at the table laughed. The brother and sister, after 57 years, looked into each other's eyes.

I READ THIS QUOTE BY IRIS BLUE AND FOUND IT TO BE TRUE

"If you keep stuff in the dark, it's ammunition for the Enemy. If you keep it in light, it's testimony. There are only two choices for power in the universe. You either walk in darkness, concealment, and lies, or you walk in the light."

While in Paris all those many years ago a friend of mine from Oklahoma was moving back home. She had bought Charles Stanley's tapes and when she left she gave them to me. The monetary value of the tapes was great, but the value I found to heal my soul was unbelievable. That is when I was first able to start healing; it's been as though each lesson was directed at me. Each feeling that I had was brought up in one of the lessons. I carried those tapes to each country and have gone over them time and time again. I got to the point of taking notes. (I'm sure Mrs. Mayhue would have been proud) I took every word to heart. Thankfully I can now go to In Touch website and listen to his weekly lessons.

He was the one that said that when God gives you a project to do, he gives you the vision of the beginning, the middle and the end, saying only to listen to God's voice. Saying not to listen to the nay slayers, telling you that you can't do what God's given you to do. It's clear they can't see what God has given you to see? When I was putting together the first book He did this for me. I clearly was able to see the beginning, the middle and then the final book before I even started.

I have been working a manuscript for at least twenty years. I call it a healing in process. While living in my first marriage I had been beaten down, not only physically but also verbally. My spirit was crushed by those constant attacks, but God would come to me in my dreams. I was taken back to when I was once again in the senior girls dorm, safe with Mrs. Mayhue and all of the girls I grew up with. During those awful days my dream to write was pushed down underneath all the pain that I was going through at the time. But the dream was never totally forgotten and when I was able to find love and respect. I was given the strength to do what it was that He wanted me to that was to do the first book.

Right now I know that I have been going through more healing as more subjects have been brought to my attention that I have to deal with. I have to face the fear that I have kept hidden in the darkness. I know from past experience that He's there to help me through each and every thing I dig up from the past. He gives me the knowledge to come face to face with the ugly and the ability with His love to learn, to heal, to move forward, and to do what it is that He has planned for me.

For example I have always frozen when it came time to write anything. Writing the simplest thing I have a huge mental block. Simply writing a note on a postcard has been difficult for me. I had this problem even as a child, I found it difficult to even write to my sponsors to tell them what I wanted for Christmas.

When writing my life story I have always had the fear of rejection. I have always been scared people will think badly of me? Will they condemn me the child victim and make me feel as if it's my fault. All of these feelings I believe comes from a darker source, something that is trying to keep me locked up. Unfortunately I allowed this to keep me from moving forward in my writing. I have witnessed when I have allowed the Holy Spirit to flow through me. The words flow freely and my words come straight from my heart onto the page.

I can see in my writing when I stand in God's way, it comes out in my bad punctuation and bad grammar. But when I am writing something important that God has directed me to write, he then steps in and while the reader is reading He allows them to see with their hearts rather than the naked eye. He allows them to understand what I was trying to say by allowing the reader to see straight into my heart. I am not saying the fear I have with writing has completely gone, nor am I saying that I don't still freeze up. I am saying that God has intervened on my behalf and is allowing me to really understand that He loves me. Simple words and you think anyone gets that, no question. But I have to say mouthing the words is easy, but taking them to heart, in all things has been difficult. Each day, each week, each month, each year I have grown stronger. My writing has improved one 100 percent and still not good, but from where I have come from, it's fantastic. I don't feel as cold and distant as I have before when writing about a difficult subject. I have tried to show the reader what's inside my heart, rather than worry about the correct way of structuring a sentence.

Slowly but surely I am forging ahead with my story telling even though at first it was difficult to write about the hurt and pain from the past. In order to write about a particular hurtful subject, I would first have to acknowledge there was pain, re-experience it as an adult, and then use the tools I was given to heal. In some instances I would hide until I was ready to let God heal me. His timing was involved, I learned it was up to me to either let the pain get the best of me, or to face the demons. This is the reason why it's taken me all these years to write. Some of my hiding lasted a long time; other times only I only hid for a short while. Either way here I am trying to put down on paper a little at a time.

Was any of this process that I have gone through to write our life story been easy? No. Was it necessary? Yes most definitely, but it wasn't fun. The good thing was that God never once left me hanging out there by myself. He stayed with me through it all, while uncovering the ugly, the hurt and pain from the past.

At times I felt like I was doing a test, and you ask, did I learn anything during this test? Yes absolutely, more than you can ever imagine. One of the major issues I faced was fear of rejection that I told you about. I felt they were judging me when I told my story. Making me worry how they would respond to me after hearing my story?

A huge question that I had to face and it was an important one to my healing. Could I break the bad habit of putting on and wearing the labels that some people labeled me with? The strange thing was when I was in the abusive marriage. He would call me nasty, nasty names saying horrible things to me. I knew what he was saying was wrong. I knew that I would go against my own self, if I let him convince me those terrible things he was saying was right. It was like there were two teams, him and me on opposing teams. He was against me and would say the horrible things, as if believing him I went on his team side, against myself. So God has had to teach me that everyone has their own opinion and which he or she is entitled to. It might differ from my own but I don't have to believe what they are saying if it is said just to hurt me or to belittle me. So remember the saying putting on the armor of God has come in handy.

It's like when we were kids and one of us young girls would run to Mrs. Mayhue, saying, so and so called us this or that. Her pat answer would be in the form of a question, "is it true? Then she'd say, "if it's not, don't worry about it. If it is, then do something about changing it." It's like a lot of other things it sounds so simple but to put into practice is really difficult. I don't know why I am so hard headed, that it takes so long to learn my lesson. At times I have taken more time than allotted, just to get the simplest of lessons.

The thing that has kept me trying to write our story was the thought that by some off chance that by sharing my heartaches, my pain, of how I have managed to let God heal me. Thinking that perhaps this would help someone else move ahead in their own lives, giving them the ability to win over all the ugly of their past. I felt it wouldn't be a waste of my time or to the reader.

The statement "keeping things in the dark" triggered me to write about some things that have been locked inside for a long time. I had no plan to write about them, it just came out.

I don't think that any of us can ever be told enough that we are loved. And I want each alumnus to know that they are truly a blessing to me. I value them as sisters and brothers. They validate my childhood being a witness to my struggle to mature into a woman. All the girls that I grew up with are the ones that come to mind when I remember playing games, or working in the kitchen or the ones that I was grounded with.

We were children together; we spent what seemed like a lifetime trying to grow up. In writing our story I am not trying to live in the past nor harp on the bad that happened. I think the reader will think what we had as children was a good thing. Others who read our story will quickly realize we had a unique bond forged as children that would last all these many years. The girls I grew up with have always been the most fascinating group of women that I know.

By telling our story, the good the bad, the indifferent, the ugly, shedding a light on the similar redeeming qualities that we all managed to acquire while living together. All of these things are unique unto us; after all it's an experience living with over 100 other kids. My memories of living at the Home are different than others, but it doesn't make mine right, nor does it make them wrong, they are just different. Each one of us has our own spin on our life together, each one, is entitled to their life story, without judgment or criticism for those memories.

I find that facing the truth is one thing and re-telling the story in truth is something else. I in no way want to inflict pain or ugliness on anyone, by how I tell my story of our life together.

Chapter Fourteen

Girls State

LEGION AUXILIARY UNIT 14 ANNOUNCES DELEGATES TO GIRLS STATE AT OCW

Ponca City News ~ April 6, 1965

DIANN COWLING AND BARBRA MAHORNEY

Selection of the seven Ponca City delegates to the 1965 Girls State has been announced by the American Legion Auxiliary, Unit 14. Two of the delegates are residents of the American Legion Home School, and are sponsored by the Department of Oklahoma American Legion Auxiliary. They are Diann Cowling and Barbara Mahorney.

Miss Cowling is a member of the National Honor Society and Dynamiters, secretary of the American Field Service Club and was nominated as a candidate to represent the AFS Club here as a student abroad. As a member of Tri-Hi-Y, she attended the pre-legislative meeting at Oklahoma State University and the youth and government convention at Oklahoma City.

Miss Barbara Mahorney has been homeroom president and a member of Paramedic Club and girl's glee club. The 1965 Girls State will be May 29 to June 5 with 420 girls participating in the citizenship training on the Oklahoma College for Women campus at Chickasha.

Girls State was first held in Oklahoma in 1940 at the University of Oklahoma and was moved to the OCW campus in 1945. "The entire program is a non-partisan, non-political attempt to teach and inculcate in the youth of our nation a love of God and country. Through actual participation as citizens of a mythical state, selected girls are trained to assume the duties and responsibilities of voting citizens," explained Mrs. Ted Quilling, Chairman of the local Auxiliary's Girls State Committee.

During the week of activities at Girls State, Barbara Mahorney was elected Mayor of one of the 14 mythical cities and received a medal from Mrs. T. J. Hobbs, Midwest City, and state auxiliary president. Diann Cowling was elected floor leader, and became one of the two Girls Staters to be a delegate to Girls Nation in Washington, D.C.

GIRLS STATE GETTING OFF TO QUICK START
OFFICERS ELECTED TODAY

The Sunday Oklahoma ~ May 30, 1965

CHICKASHA ~ The 420 high school junior girls who are citizens of 1965 Girls State have been on Oklahoma College for Women campus a short time but they already are moving in high gear to cover the outlined program in Americanism, citizenship and practical government. Girls State is sponsored and directed by Oklahoma Department American Legion Auxiliary.

City meetings are scheduled for 8:45 a.m. Sunday, prior to the departure of the young women for services in Chickasha churches. This marks the first time the young women will have visited Chickasha churches. A joint service is usually held on OCW campus.

On Sunday afternoon Girls Stater will elect officers in each of the 14 "mythical" cities and will attend a class on city government taught by Dr. Samuel W. Evans chairman of OCW's history department, serving his 19th year as educational director the program.

Both county and district mixers are scheduled for afternoon and evening. Cars packed with young women and clothes pulled into the campus Saturday afternoon. Some "citizens" used public transportation and some special buses brought groups.

Upon arriving on OCW campus, the young women registered with their previously assigned cities. They will live in these units throughout the eight-day period. All five of the college dormitories house the young women.

At the time of registration, each Girls Stater drew for membership in either the Boomer or Sooner party.

Mrs. Joe E. Brown, Dustin, director of the 1965 Girls State, presided at the opening general assembly Saturday night.

Mrs. Brown and Dr. Charles Grady, OCW president welcomed the students. Mrs. T. J. Hobbs, Midwest City, president of the sponsoring American Legion auxiliary of Oklahoma, extended greetings.

"Americanism" was the title of a talk by Mrs. W.A. Biggert, El Reno, past state president of the auxiliary and a past director of Girls State; Mrs. Biggert's talk is traditional on the opening night program.

During the week, Girls Staters will progress from party precinct organization through the election of state officials. Precinct elections were Saturday night.

The Girls State Committee, which has set up the program for the week include Mrs. Hobbs, Mrs. Brown, Mrs. E. L. Crawford, Shawnee, and Mrs. Clevel Smith, Tahlequah, recent directors of Girls State, and Mrs. George Demke of Oklahoma City, secretary-treasurer.

Other members of the staff, in addition to Mrs. Brown and Dr. Evans, are Mrs. Kay Klein, Oklahoma City, newspaper editor; Mrs. Leslie Swim, Stillwater, music; Mrs. J. Sam Johnson, Edmond, dining room supervisor; Mary Gilmour, OCW, nurse and Sarah Ellis, OCW, publicity director, assisted by Virginia Embree, OCW.

Each of the 14 "mythical" cities has a senior and junior counselor. Serving as senior counselors are Mrs. R.O. Brannon, Dustin; Mrs. James Catron, Tulsa; Mrs. Harold Champlin, Oklahoma City; Mrs. John de Steiguer, Tahlequah; Mrs. Earl Evans, Kingfisher; Mrs. Louis Garber, Vinita; Mrs. Tom Heidebrecht, Altus; Mrs. Chester Hendrix, Fort Gibson; Mrs. Odie Humphry, Mineo; Mrs. Norville Johnson, Alva; Mrs. Albert Karr, Altus; Mrs. Gen Reeder, Chandler; Mrs. George Roberts, Heavener; and Mrs. DeRoy Skinner, Ponca City.

Mayors- The mayors of the 14 mythical cities at Girls State are shown shortly after they were elected Sunday afternoon during the "city" phase of their concentrated study of government sponsored by the Oklahoma Department of the American Legion Auxiliary.

The new mayors, their home towns and "city" are left to right

Miss Pam McCroy ~ Sapulpa ~ Scudder City
Miss Kay Howard ~ Ringling ~ Lillard City
Miss Cathy Purcell ~ Cheyenne ~ Rice City
Miss Cynthia Trussel ~ Perry ~ Akin City
Miss Brenda Robinson ~ Hollis ~ Gilmore City
Miss Sharon Wooley ~ Sapulpa ~ McAlister City
Miss Kathy Hieronymus ~ Woodward ~ Parker City
Miss Barbra Mahorney ~ Ponca City ~ Crawford City
Miss Bana Burkett ~ Woodward ~ Demke City
Miss Susan Prater ~ Tulsa ~ Brown City;
Miss Judy Janie Henshaw ~ Tulsa ~ Buck City
Miss Judy Austin, ~ Mill Creek ~ Phillips City
Miss Linda Armstrong ~ Clinton ~ Reed City
Miss Mimi Dye ~ Oklahoma City ~ Ballard City

Chapter Fifteen

Norval Bryson ~ "Butch"

NORVAL BRYSON TO GIVE RECITAL MAY 16, 1962

NOJC FOUNDATION ESTABLISHES
NORVAL BRYSON MUSIC SCHOLARSHIP
NORTHERN OKLAHOMA JUNIOR COLLEGE

Sunday ~ January 5, 1964 ~ Ponca City News

Tonkawa- A Norval Bryson Music Scholarship was established at Northern Oklahoma Junior College by trustees of the NOJC Foundation, Inc, at the January meeting of the group Thursday evening in the Library-Administration building.

The scholarship of $100 will be given annually to a worthy area student who is majoring in the field of music. Applicants will be screened by the college music department and approved by the foundation scholarship committee headed by J. Morgan Bush, Tonkawa. The scholarship will be effective with the fall term September 1964 and applications will be taken this spring.

The scholarship is in memory of the late Norval Louis Bryson, former outstanding NOJC music student who died unexpectedly December 18. While on the Tonkawa campus, Bryson was accompanist for various musical groups and ensembles, as well as the Tonkawa Lions Club, and had leading roles in school stage plays and operettas.

The Bryson Scholarship is the first specific grant to be named by the foundation, a non-profit organization designed last spring to act as a coordinating and cooperating agency between the many area communities served by the college and to provide scholarships, student loans and campus improvements.

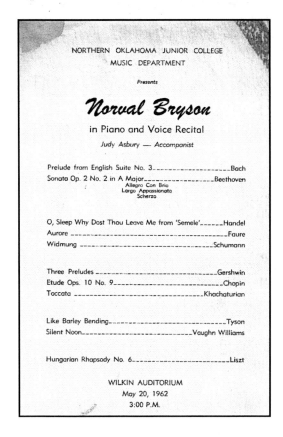

The foundation has a minimum $5 annual membership fee and all membership received from this date will extend through June 1, 1965.

Special gifts will be accepted for the Bryson Scholarship. All former students of NOJC and UPS, as well as friends and boosters of the college, are invited to participate in this "investment in youth," said Lin Trueblood, foundation chairman.

Memberships and contributions may be mailed to the President's Office, NOJC, or to A. R. Smith, 413 North Sixth or Mrs. J. S. Gilber, 1404 East Grand, Tonkawa.

In other business Thursday night, R. R. Brining, Tonkawa banker, was named treasurer for the remainder of the fiscal year which ends June 1.

A. R. Smith, chairman of the membership committee, gave an annual report and Mrs. Merle Paynter, Ponca City, chairman of the NOJC Former Student Banquet, announced that the event will be held May 30 in Memorial Union and will honor the class of 1914.

Announcement was made that the second issue this year of the foundation publication "Crimson Rambler" will be mailed in mid-February. Mrs. Kenneth Bradley Blackwell is editor of the publication.

Dr. V. R. Easterling, college president, spoke briefly to the group. Present were Trueblood, Mrs. R. W. Gearheard, Mrs. Gilbert, Smith, Ben Robison, Dr. Easterling A. R. Gregory, John Blubaugh, Merritt Witter, Brining, Clem Ogg, Rep. Brian Conaghan, Mrs. R. S. Asbury, Mrs. Paynter, and Harold Weigle, Blackwell.

Butch had come home from college for Christmas break. He became ill and was taken to the hospital. I stopped during my classes to use the pay phone to call Mrs. Mayhue. I asked her how Butch was, "he's dead." My mind just couldn't get around what she had just said. I couldn't comprehend that she actually meant that he was really dead. But she finally got through to me that he was dead. I hung up the phone returning to class where I sat in shock the remainder of the class. It was when I ran into others that I was able to share the awful news.

Chapter Sixteen

The 1940's

HOME SCHOOL ONLY ONE IN UNITED STATES
BROAD TRAINING IS GIVEN CHILDREN IN LEGION PROJECT

Ponca City News ~ June 14, 1942

GEORGE ABBOTT

The American Legion Home School built northeast of Ponca City in June 1928, is the only one its kind in the United States.

A total of 117 children are now at the home school, each sponsored by the auxiliary unit, legion post district or by the 40 and 8 or the 8 and 40.

The children at the school attend the Ponca public schools, with the transportation of two buses. They are maintained at the school until they graduate from high school or reach the age of 18.

THREE GOLD STARS ON SERVICE FLAG AT LEGION HOME

Ponca City News ~ February 16, 1944

The placing of stars, three of them gold ones, on the American Legion Home School service flag has been completed, George Abbott, superintendent, reported. The stars represent sixty-nine men and women who formerly lived at the home school, all of whom volunteered for service in the war. The flag now hangs in the Home School office. The names are as follows:
Killed In Action: Alvia Minor ~ Navy and Carl Reynolds ~ Army Air Corps.
Missing in action: William Peterson ~ Navy
Navy: Donald Port, Alvin Cassingham, Ira Smith, Buster Bond, L. B. Conrad,

Gene Gustin, Charles Chastain, Paul Shannon, J. R. Tabor, Bufford Justice, Walter McCoy, Robert Wilson, Jesse Bingham, Clifford Bingham, Arliss Reynolds, Lavel Gardenshire, Muriel Denton, Charles L. Braxton, Harry Chambers, Doyle Dailey, Oleta Tiner-Waves

Army: Elvis Reynolds, Bill Greenwood, Gordon Cavner, Duane Moore, Wendell McCoy, Warren McCoy, Bob Reynolds, Rubin Gooch, paratrooper, Douglas McNew, Charles Ray Hill, Arthur Titus, Payton Leon Rider, Delbert Adair, Clifford Penrod, William L. Dover, Kellan Adams, Harrison Beattie, Lloyd Hill, John Wayne Humphries, Sidney Marks ~ Paratrooper, Bill A. Cash, James L. Parks, Clifford Parks, Elmer Gattis, Ruth Prestage ~ Cadet Nurse

Army Air Corps: Paul Masters, Joe Bond, Earl Hooker, Stanley Cavner, Neal Cavner, Jimmie Jameson, William Porter Masters, T. L. Rider, Elmer Dunlap, Claude Bray, Lester Gattis, Cornelius Hobbs, Johnny Marks, Jimmy Rigsby, Eugene Rigsby

Marine Corps: Raymond Coffins, Arthur Warren, Kirby Rider, Kenneth Gunning
Merchant Marine: Bobby Jo Cooley

WAR BABY FAMILY

The Daily Oklahoman ~ September 23, 1945 ~ by Mark Sarchet

There's a big family living east of Ponca City in a home overlooking the Arkansas River Valley in the Western Osage Hills that can tell you more about the results of World Wars, two of them than any other group in Oklahoma.

The children in the family number 200 and they live there because their father served the United States on land and sea, paying the total price for being Americans. Many of the Children have seen their brothers and sisters follow their father's path.

Hanging inside the front door is the World War II service flag with 77 stars, five of them gold and two for women. Every star on the flag represents a volunteer.

George "Dude" Abbott, World War I veteran, who with Mrs. Abbott act as mother and father to the children for the Oklahoma Department of the American Legion, says the typical answer to why the youths were volunteering was: "Well I think Dad would want me to."

Since the American Legion Home School was opened in 1928 a total of 293 sons and daughters of Oklahoma veterans from both World wars have lived there as residents. The 200 now living in the home range in age from three to 18 years. Eight of them are children of Sooners killed during World War II.

Basic rule of the Abbott's and of the Legion is to give the children the same feeling and the same food, shelter, clothing, education and childhood pleasures that make the average American home the best in the world.

Many of the boys and girls represented on the service flag of the school can remember no other home. Others came to the school after their family fortunes were shattered in later years.

Every child at the school works, the girls in the buildings and kitchens and the boys on the yards and the farm plots of the 110-acre site. They have saved more than $1,000 in war stamps during the past year.

Legion Posts and Auxiliary units over the state sponsor the children, each one being responsible for clothing, summer vacations and the little extras that make childhood a pleasure.

First casualty from the home in the second war came on Dec 7, 1941 where Alva Minor was killed aboard a battle ship.

Other gold stars at the school are for Lieut. Ruben Gooch a paratrooper lost in a jump in the south Pacific: received the Purple Heart and paratrooper's wings. Lieutenant Porter Masters, air force pilot lost on Atlantic patrol: Sgt. Carl Reynolds, gunner on a Flying fortress lost in North Africa and his brother, Sgt. Elvis Reynolds, paratrooper lost in the battle for Germany.

Two other brothers of the Reynolds, Bob and Arlis, are serving with the Navy in the Pacific.

Abbott and the Legion are busy trying to make plans for the future. They know the demands on the school will increase now that World War II is over, as far as the fighting is concerned.

Many leaders in the organization believe that a second home school should be built rather than add to the one in Ponca City. They think that a larger group would lose the "home" touch of the present setup.

The eight "new" children who are the sons and daughter of the two men killed in the European campaigns. Betty Lou Veal 13, and Bobby Joe Hardy, 10 are the children of Coy O. Hardy, killed in the European theater on July 9, 1943. Their mother died at Durant last year. Betty Braxton, 16, Clarence Braxton Jr. 14, John C. Braxton, 12, Rose Marie Braxton, 11, and Beatrice, 7 are the children of Clarence Braxton, killed on Sept 7,1944, in Europe.

THE LEGION KNOWS THERE ARE MORE TO COME

But, in the meantime, Abbott, who holds the Distinguished Service Cross, won near Feyen-Haye, France, Sept 12, 1918, when he saved the life of a comrade by charging a machine-gun nest alone, is keeping busy.

The former Norman High School and University of Oklahoma end and halfback, and former Ponca City High School coach, finds his time well spent delivering his children to school in Ponca City and going after them at night. On Sundays the school bus makes the rounds of Ponca City's churches so the children may attend the service of their choice.

ROLL OF HONOR

That our Country might continue in its pathway of freedom. These from the American Legion and Auxiliary Home School served in the Armed Forces of the United States during World War II.

HOME SCHOOL ONLY ONE IN UNITED STATES

The Ponca City News ~ June 14, 1942 ~ George Abbott

BROAD TRAINING IS GIVEN CHILDREN IN LEGION PROJECT

The American Legion Home School built northeast of Ponca City in June 1928, is the only one of its kind in the United States.

A total of 117 children are now at the home school, each sponsored by the auxiliary unit, legion post district or by the 40 and 8 or the 8 and 40.

The children at the school attend the Ponca public schools, with the transportation of two buses. They are maintained at the school until they graduate from high school or reach the age of 18.

VOCATIONAL TRAINING

Vocational training is provided for the students in the schools. Boys can take machine shop welding, electricity, cabinet making, architectural drafting or blue print reading. Commercial courses are offered in typing, bookkeeping and shorthand. Girls may select home making courses in cooking, sewing or mean planning.

The home school provides typewriters and sewing machines so students may practice at the home. Summer instruction is given in typewriting, shorthand, beauty culture, sewing and cooking. The school recently installed a permanent wave machine and hair dryer and a Hoffman press, so students can take instructions in beauty culture or in the cleaning and pressing trade.

HAS BARBER SHOP

Some of the boys and girls are employed regularly during the school year. During the last year three girls and a boy worked in the high school office. Several of the girls work in stores, and several boys work at various trades during the summer, including jobs at the sheet metal shop refinery or Western Union.

The children in the school take part in such activities as the De Moley, Rainbow Girls, Boy Scouts, Camp Fire Girls, Junior Aids or Sons of the Legion and Juniorettes. Boys participate in sports including football, basketball, track, wrestling, baseball and golf. Some are member of the student council of the high school or officers of the home rooms or clubs.

LURA-MAE CASSINGHAM
INTERESTING NOTES AND NEWS FROM THE LEGION HOME SCHOOL

Oklahoma Legionnaire ~ April, 1944

Students making the Honor Roll for the second nine week period of school were entertained Sunday afternoon, March 4, with the picture show, "Tonight and Every Night." After enjoying the picture show, the students left in the school bus for Lake Ponca Park, where the afternoon was finished off with plenty of hot dogs and pop. The following were Honor Roll students: Betty Jo Earl, Mary Ann Owens, Dulian Mae Snider, George McClevinus, William Finney, Howard Titus, Warren Haithcock, Juanita Baker, B. I. Vanloon, Lois Ledford, Burl Gustin, Nancy

Port, Edith Plott, Pauline Owens, Twyla Titus, Nell Hancock, G:enda Rae Ball, Joyce Ledford, Bernice Denton, Georgia Owens, Henrietta Lebow, Roy Ball, Dora Cowger, Buddy Snider, Nadine Wimpee, Wanda Johnson, Ramona Kelton, Patsy Gooch, Evelyn Snider, Susan Abbott, Johnny Webb, Geneva Cassingham, Lura Mae Cassingham.

Richard Mote, member of the FFA Chapter of the Senior High School, won first prize on his senior Duroc hog at the County Junior Stock Fair held at Newkirk March 8 and 9. Richard also won a fourth place ribbon on his junior pig. This is Richard's second showing of his stock at the County Junior Stock Fair. He has made plans to purchase two Hereford calves from the L. D. Edginton herd for the Fair next year.

Sgt. Earl Hooker was a visitor at the Home School, March 15. The Home School kiddies were sure happy to see Earl as this is his first visit to the Home School since he enlisted in July, 1942. Sgt. Hooker was an outstanding student member of the FFA Chapter of the Ponca City High School.

Jo Earl, Mary Row, Joan Watson, Alpha Johnson, and Susanne Abbott attended the father d daughter Camp Fire banquet held at the Continental Associates Building, Friday evening, March 16. Mary Row, a holder of the Woodgather rank, took part in the entertainment program given by the Camp Fire Girls for the dads.

Danny Owens, Roy Ball, Clarence Braxton, Clinton Braxton, Billy Gustin, Craigdon Vesper, Joe Sanders, and Walter Hume, members of the Seahawk Patrol took part in the paper drive Saturday, March 17. Each scout will receive a General Eisenhower gift if his troop picks up an average of 1000 pounds per scout member.

The following new children have recently been admitted to the Home School: Betty Lois Br. ton, Clarence Braxton, Clinton Braxton, Rosemary Br ton, Beatrice Br ton, Maxine Crow, Alfred Wilson, Alvin Wilson, Charles Wilson, and Dorothy Mae Wilson. Only four of the children have a sponsor at this time.

ATOKA MAN GIVES INSURANCE MONEY TO HOME SCHOOL

Ponca City News ~ February 21, 1947

Because a deceased World War veteran was interested in the welfare of children, the local American Legion Home School is being enabled to purchase new furniture, Ralph Burglund, chairman of the Home School Committee, announced today.

When Tom Norwood died January 3, 1946, at Atoka, he left insurance policy amounting to $4,858 to the American Legion Home School. Proceeds of the policy are being used as a beginning of a movement to re-furnish the school. .

'DOUGHBOY' RECALLS WWI
GEORGE ABBOTT~ HOME SUPERINTENDENT

By Sarah Livermore of the Transcript Staff
(I believe this was taken from an Oklahoma City paper)

World War I, the first global conflict in modern history, was "the war to end all wars." Thousands of young men were drafted for an army that fought its battles in the trenches of Europe.

One of the your doughboys recalls his part in the war, George Abbott, who was born and raised in Norman and who now lives outside of the city on Rt. 4, brought home the Distinguished Service Cross when he returned from Europe in 1919.

Abbott, an OU student, was drafted Sept, 5, 1917, and became a "line sergeant" in the 10th Division, 357th Infantry in France. He saw action in the bloody battles of St. Mihiel and at Meuse Argonne and was with the occupation forces at Coblenz, Germany.

He earned the second highest medal the U.W. bestows for saving a soldier's life near Feyin-Haye, France. The citation says Abbott "saved the life of a soldier who was directly under the fire of an enemy machine gun by rushing the gun, killing gunner and capturing the gun, its gallant conduct inspired the men of his platoon to continue the advance."

The actual awarding of the medal was done in France without telling Abbott. The Army officials arrived, the men in his company were called together and Abbott "thought they were going to hang me." Instead they gave him the Distinguished Service Cross for his bravery.

Later in 1924, the French government awarded him the Croix de Guerre, a grandiose citation and a "picture of Joan of Arc or somebody."

Abbott saw plenty of action, but he was never hurt, although he "was scratched a few times," he said. "But you had to be careful or the Germans shot at them or any heads that truck up."

Poison gases were employed against the doughboys. But contrary to popular belief, the gas was no wafted across the no-man's land between the Allied and central powers trenches. Instead it was shot across in artillery shells.

Horns sounded warnings was near. The uncomfortable gas masks were donned and the fighting continued, he says.

Later as the tide of the war turned for the Allies, and advances were made, the doughboys "went over the top" of their trenches. "We usually advanced to the German trenches and took over those." Then the U.S. units behind theirs "leap-frogged" over them to the German trenches or positions on the front.

After the peace came and he served a stint in Germany with the occupation forces, Abbott returned to Norman to finish his schooling at OU. While at OU, he coached football at Norman High School from 1919 to 1922.

The GI bill was yet to be passed and the doughboys were "given only $60 when we left the Army," he said. "We were the ones who started it all and got the GI bill passed for others later," Abbott said.

He was graduated in 1922 and went to Ponca City to coach "everything" in the school system. Later he became superintendent of the American Legion Home School, a coeducational orphanage, there.

In 1954, he returned to his hometown to work as a recreational therapist at the Central Hospital veterans' domiciliary.

Abbott has always been active in the American Legion. He was a charter member of Post 88 and served as commander in 1922. He is also a member of the First Presbyterian Church of Norman.

There was a picture of Abbott proudly showing the campaign service medal, the Distinguished Service Cross and the Croix de Guerre, which he won while serving in France During World War I.

Chapter Seventeen

The 1950's

CALVES FROLICKING ON HOME SCHOOL PASTURELANDS

Ponca City News ~ December 21, 1950

Calves were donated to stock the American Legion Home School pasturelands. There were enough for nearly every one of the twenty-four older boys to have a calf to care for. Eleven were white face, from good blood lines, and some were Hereford. They came from all over, but mostly from Osage County ranches, and some from Kay and Noble counties.

The gifts of calves fit into the expanding agricultural program which has a herd of fine hogs that took top prizes at the Kay County Junior Livestock Show, and the state fairs in Tulsa and Oklahoma City.

The home has 100 acres of land. Sixty- five acres of it is cultivatable, twenty acres in pasture and fifteen acres in garden. Seventeen acres of maize were grown this year, and more will be grown next year to feed the calves.

Tom Grizzelle, general supervisor and in charge of agricultural work, said a plan is being made to credit each boy with the results of his work with his calf.

There were lots of girls who wanted calves and H. B. Roper donated a fine three weeks old calf to the girls. Bobby Webb and Stanley Neeley still need calves.

The donors and the boys in charge of the calves are: Bob Donelson to James Owens; (anonymous) to Edward Hodson; Clarence Schultz to Bobby Hardy; Ralph Barton to John Weston; A. R. Kerns to Lynn Trostle; Okla and Kay Vanselous to

K. D. Calvert; Ralph Graham to Raymond McCallon; Oscar Hadden to Harold Watson; Jay G. Paris to Barney Calvert; Crane and Nuckols to Neal Trostle; Alfred Hall to Carl Porter; Jim Braden to James Adams; Allen Wilson to Frank Wright; Bert Colby to Bruce Trostle; Mr. and Mrs. Jim Bowen to John Hoffman; Frank Midgley to Raymon Eliot; C. A. Marchesoni to Johnny Webb; Angus Poole to Buddy Snyder; Sid Dellaplain to Jere Blaney; Gene Mullendore to Ed Sherzer; George Smith to Fred Reynolds; Clyde Glasgow to Carl Means.

T. J. Cuzalina was responsible for getting this program started.

L-R SITTING AGAINST THE CAB: JERRY GLOVER ~ JAMES HAMILTON ~ JOHN MICHON ~ JOHNNY WALTON ~ BOY HANGING OVER EDGE IS JIMMY LOWE ~ SITTING ON HAY IS MELVIN ECKERT ~ KENNETH COLE ~ BEHIND HIM IS RICHARD SCHARNHORST ~ JOHN GENTRY

**THE EARL FAMILY: BOBBIE ~ MARJORIE ~
JOAN ~ NORMA ~ BUGGER ~ BETTY**

**HAZEL MAYBERRY AND
TROYLA TITUS**

**NADINE WIMPEE ~ JEFFIE WESTMORELAND ~ LOSIE WILSON ~
PATSY GOOCH ~ LURA MAE CUNNINGHAM**

**HAZEL MAYBERRY AND ETHEL
GREENWOOD**

ALICE AND GLENDA GRISSON

JAMES OWENS ~ JO WATSON ~ BARNEY CALVERT

DONNA COWLING ~DIANNA BEGGS ~ WILLIAMS ~ LINDA TURNER ~ LAVONNE LANTER ~ DIANN COWLING ~ JANICE OVERTUF ~ WILLIAMS

DIANN COWLING ~ LINDA TURNER ~ EMMA THOMPSON ~ MOLLY BICKLE ~ JANICE OVERTURF ~ AVON APPLEMAN ~ 1959

**L-R: ROBERT HOYT ~ RICHARD HOYT ~ GENE WYATT ~ B. DODD ~
DON BAILEY ~ LUTHER GRISSO ~ JOHN MICHON ~ DONNIE RIVERS ~
MARCH 1959**

**L-R: JOE LEE THOMPSON ~ LUTHER GRISSO ~ CLIFFORD OVERTURF ~
GENE WYATT ~ DON BAILEY ~ ROBERT HOYT ~ UNKNOWN ~
JIMMY CHOKER, MARCH 1959**

MARCH 1959, BOYS AT EASTER L-R: SAMMY COWLING ~ CARL BEVENUE ~ SAMMY SCHORNHORST ~ JOE RIVERS ~ DONNIE RIVERS ~ JIM LOWE ~ MELVIN THOMPSON

MORE BOYS MARCH 1959, L-R: JOHN GENTRY ~ UNKNOWN ~ JOHN MICHON ~ JERRY EVANS ~ MIKE BEVENUE ~ JAMES BEVENUE ~ RICHARD SCHARNHORST

DAVE CALVERT HOME SCHOOL

**1956 BOYS STATE: LAWRENCE GREGORY ~ MIDDLE
~ 3RD FROM LEFT**

STAR LOWE ~ AVON APPLEMAN ~ UNKNOWN ~ CAROL STEWART

GIRLS ON BACK PORCH OF LITTLE GIRLS BUILDING

Chapter Eighteen

1960's

LEGION HONORS RALPH BERGLUND

In mid-November, 1962, Ralph Berglund, popular Ponca City Legionnaire and architect for The American Legion Home School was honored at a dinner in the Ponca City Legion building.

Berglund, a former member of the American Legion Home School Committee has been active in working with the children and the Hoe School committee in providing better living facilities at the home.

In early 1950, Berglund served as architect for the Administration and Recreational building that now occupies an important place in the Home operation.

The administrative offices, library, hobby shop and a recreational area are used daily by the staff and children.

In 1958, Berglund again served as architect for the centralized dining room that seat 200 children. The modern facility was completed in 1959 and now occupies a beautiful spot on the Home School grounds.

The dining room consists of a stainless steel kitchen, large dining room area; kitchen quarters for the cooks and contains air conditioning and central heat. Meals can be served cafeteria or family style to the children.

In 1961, Berglund served as architect in renovation and remodeling the girls building. The building was completed in November 1962 at a cost of $95,000 and is a popular building on the campus.

Berglund is now engaged in drawing plans and specifications for renovation and remodeling of the older boys building that is scheduled for completion in 1963.

Following completion of the older boys building, Berglund will start plans for the young boys building to be complete a renovation project of all buildings at the Home School.

BERGLUND HONORED

At the November dinner in Ponca City, Department Adjutant A.R. Tyner, Jr. presented Berglund with a plaque, citing Berglund for service beyond the call of duty to The American Legion Home School. Tyner briefed the audience on Berglund's faithful and devoted service to the Home School and his love for the children.

Berglund contributed his architect talents to The American Legion as a devoted legionnaire. He is chief architect of the Continental Oil Company, Ponca City.

The American Legion salutes Berglund for his outstanding contribution to the organization.

101 RANCH STAR JACKIE LAIRD DIES

By Louise Abercrombie ~ Ponca City News Staff Writer

Jackie McFarlin Laird will ride and rope no more. The 101 Ranch Wild West Show and Great Far East Show trick rider and roper died Tuesday in Shawn Manor Nursing Center at the age of 94.

The western showgirl had performed on the same bill with Hoot Gibson, Jess Willard, Buck Jones, Tom Mix, Will Rogers and Pawnee Bill. Jackie rode with the famed Miller Brothers show working with a quartet of horses trained by the late Wes Rogers. Her horses were named Alice, Major, Zack and Colonel. Her favorite was Alice, who would knee, pray or lie down at Jackie's direction.

The most dangerous trick she performed was known as "tail back." This difficult trick involved sliding off the backside of the horse and hanging onto its tail and being dragged around the arena. She was with the show from 1914 to 1926.

Her costume was a buckskin skirt with deep fringe and shirtwaist silk blouse. A wide-brimmed Stetson, wide-cuffed leather riding gloves and expensive boots completed the costume. She was the lead rider for the "Oklahoma Cowgirls." The cowgirls were to appear wholesome and were not allowed to wear rouge or lipstick.

Jackie was her stage name. She was born Mary Ellen Laird and close friends called her "Leasey." But to the public she was "Jackie."

After the 101 Ranch Wild West Show folded she was chef for hotels in California and later returned to be chef of the Arcade Hotel for a number of years. She often told about Will Rogers' fondness for her special chili. Mexican Joe gave the recipe to her. In later years she was the chef for the American Legion Home School.

During her show business career she was married to Johnny Roubideaux, and Indian of the Missouri tribe. After she separated from Roubideaux she married Dewitt Laird, a cattleman who died a few years later.

In 1983 she was named by Governor George Nigh as the recipient of the Pioneer Woman Award given annually here at the Renaissance Ball at the Marland Mansion. Jackie joined the show business world at an early age running away with the circus at the age of 11. While she was performing in Madison Square Garden her father J. A. McFarlin wired her to come home at once, but she stayed on for 12 years. A trick rider, Jackie appeared in one of the most popular acts of the 101 Wild West Show. She sat in a covered wagon when the Indians set fire to it during the popular "Indian raid" act.

Although Laird was with the show just a dozen years of her nearly nine and half decades, she was always in her heart a young rider and roper riding with the best.

Another chapter of the 101 Ranch Rodeo Wild West Show enters the history books with the death of the cowgirl named "Jackie."

HOME SCHOOL GETS ESTATE OF KAW CITIAN

Ponca City News ~ June 10, 1960

The report that the American Legion Home School is recipient of the estate of the late Mrs. Carrie M. Holloway, Kaw City, was confirmed this week by Earl Summers, Home School superintendent.

The estate consists of $34,000 in cash, bonds and royalties, 60 acres of grass land and a five-room house and garage. It is located three miles east of Kaw City.

School officials are planning to use the farmland for livestock and training operations. No decision has been made regarding the house and surrounding buildings.

Cash funds will enable the school to plan renovations and remodeling of the girls' building.

HOME SCHOOL DAY PROGRAM

April 29, 1962

Place: American Legion Home School, Ponca City
Registration: 8:30 a.m. Home School Recreational Building
9:30 a.m. Meeting called to Order ~ Clinton D. Shag Allen, Dept. Child Welfare Chairman
Invocation ~ Home School Boy
Remarks ~ Jack Clayton, Department Commander
Louise Crawford ~ Department Auxiliary President
Mrs. O.W. Attaway ~ National Vice President, Auxiliary
Musical Program ~ Home School Students
Introductions ~ Mary Demke and Art Tyner
Remarks ~ Walter Bonham, Department Child Welfare Officer
J. Earl Simpson, American Legion Home School Liaison Representative
Homer Tanner, Chairman Home School Committee
Introduction of Graduates ~ Earl Summers, Superintendent
Contributions ~ Ike Crawford, Member Home School Committee
Presentation of Transistor Radio ~ Ike Crawford
Benediction
Lunch will be served by the Home School

HOME SCHOOL NOTES DECEMBER 1962

Luther Grisso, one of our Senior students, takes his wrestling as seriously as he does his school work, and as a result has become one of the top scorers on the Ponca City High School Wrestling team, winning several matches, and also having his picture in the Ponca City News.

Several of our girls are making great strides in their Camp Fire Work. Belinda Tucker has now earned 50 beads, Johnnie Hutchison has 89 beads and Grace Wilson has a total of 222 beads. These beads are sewn on the jackets of the girls, and are worn with their campfire uniforms at ceremonies and work functions.

Grace Wilson has been elected "Best Citizen" for the Sixth Grade at McKinley for the third time this year. Grace certainly deserves this recognition.

Michael Ruth McAdams was elected Student Rotarian for the month of November, and was privileged to attend the Rotary meetings. Along with the reward, Mr. Jack Bowker of the Bowker Motor Company offered Michael Ruth a convertible to drive on Christmas Day. Too bad that Michael Ruth will not be able to take advantage of the offer.

Those singing in the Choir for McKinley School Christmas program were: Billy Childers, Mike Heneha, Benny Howell, William Needham, George Walton, roger Walton, Jeff Rowe and Richard Lee.

The Ponca City Lions Club entertained our younger children at the production of "Red Shoes" given at the Ponca City Civic Center on Friday December 7. Everyone enjoyed this stage play, and each said that the dancing was outstanding.

On November 28, the children were entertained at the Knights of Pythias Christmas Circus. This was an all-animal entertainment, and was greatly enjoyed.

To all of the Members of the American Legion Posts and Auxiliaries and all other people who gave of their time and means to remodel our lovely new home, we wish to say "Thank you All." It is beautiful, modern, and convenient beyond our dreams, and it is difficult to find words to express our gratitude. We all assure you that we will work very hard to keep it nice for the future occupants after we are gone on to other quarters. We are sure this building, which provides us with such gracious living will forever, be an inspiration to become truly useful citizens and fine ladies as you would have us be. Thank you once more, Mrs. Vala Dacus, Matron and Girls.

The American Legion National Commander James E. Powers of Macon, Georgia was at the Home School on Saturday December 15, 1962, when he was honored at a reception and luncheon at the Home School. He visited with the local Legionnaires and inspected the recently remodeled girls living quarters.

He praised the work being done at the American Legion home School. While touring the grounds and buildings, Powers commented that the atmosphere at the Home School made it seem "more like a real Home" than he had imagined.

As he walked our ground he stopped frequently to chat with the boys and girls and soon had a loyal following of eager children who literally took over the tour and led the National Commander around their home.

On Sunday December 16, we had an "Open House" which was a huge success. The guests toured the entire grounds. The girls served cookies, punch and coffee, and they also took charge of the guest book. There were a large number of Northern Oklahoma people that came, and we also had guest from Guthrie, Oklahoma City, Chickasha and Bartlesville.

On Sunday December 9, 35 of our younger boys and girls journeyed to Alva for a Christmas party held by residents of Vinson Hall of Northwestern State College and their dates. Each child was assigned specifically to one of the dormitory residents.

WILDCATS' STRENGTH LIES IN TRACK DISTANCE EVENTS

March 16, 1965

In the field event, pole-vaulter Jerry Evans has reached 13 feet. He had to do so with very little practice in the high school field. Jerry lives at the American Legion Home School.

Another prospect is Rodney Anderson who lofted the discus 137 feet in the first meet of the year.

"I am real pleased about the team. We have never had such good times this early in the season."

Wildcat track coach Gordon Stangeland was the speaker following the kickoff of a busy season Saturday in the Norman Invitational Meet

The Cats have a dual meet at Enid Wednesday and then head for more tough competition in an open meet in Oklahoma City.

"The Wildcats have been picked to finish near the top in the stated this year -- mostly due to their strength in the distance events." The cross-country team won the state championship last fall.

Coach Stangeland fails to be that optimistic. He sees too many holes in the sprints and field events. However, he noted the Cats have a good chance in the conference for two reasons.

HOME SCHOOL NOTES ~ NOVEMBER 2, 1966

Mr. Summers wishes to express his appreciation to all posts and units and American Legion friends who remembered him during his recent illness with cards and letters.

Mrs. W. E. Gilmore, Past Dept. President from El Reno, and Mrs. William B. Cosgrove from El Reno visited the Home School and brought a birthday gift for Jeff Row, who is sponsored by the El Reno Post.

The Home School children attended a football game as guests of the After 5 Lions Club.

James Owens, a former Home School boy, visited the Home School recently. He presently lives in Oklahoma City.

Carl Finney and family from Farmington, New Mexico, visited the Home School. Carl and four brothers and sisters were former Home School students.

Mr. Francis E. Hyde, who was elected Mr. Legionnaire of Kansas, visited the Home School during September.

Twenty-nine boys attended the Father-Son Banquet at the First Christian Church as guests of the Men's Bible Class.

The grade school children participated in the school carnival at McKinley School. The Home School furnished six ponies and the boys to lead them.

Three of the Home School children are members of the American Field Service Club at Ponca City High School. They are John Walton, Robert Castleberry and Ruth Hamilton. Ruth and Robert recently attended a district field service meeting in Tulsa.

Birthdays for the month of November are: Jeannie Harjo, 3; Jimmy Stewart, 3; Ronald Heneha, 4; Carol Stewart 15; Lee Jones, 16; Hurley Duncan, 17; Guy Walton, 20; Joyce and Lois Rowe, 26; Jack Walton, 26.

OPEN HOUSE AT HOME SCHOOL SUNDAY STATE LEGION, AUXILIARY MEMBERS COMING FOR CHILD WELFARE PROGRAM

Dr. James L. Dennis will be the featured speaker at the Saturday dinner, which will open the annual American Legion and Auxiliary two-day child welfare program and American Legion Home School open house.

The dinner will be in the American Legion Hut beginning at 6:30 p.m. Dr. Dennis will discuss "The Abused Child." He is associate dean of medical affairs and professor of pediatrics at the University of Arkansas School of medicine, Little Rock.

Entertainment will be by the Ponca City Chapter of Sweet Adeline's, Inc., directed by Ted Cobb. Pat Cooper is assistant director.

The annual open house at the Legion Home School will be Sunday, beginning with registration at 9:30. Bill Sparks, department child welfare chairman, will preside, assisted by Mrs. T. J. Hobbs, department Legion Auxiliary child welfare chairman.

Plans for the Home School will be discussed and the children introduced followed by a 12-noon luncheon with the children and a tour of the Home School buildings.

The open house is expected to attract hundreds of Legionnaires and Auxiliary members, guests and visitors. Members and other interested person are especially urged to visit the Home School on this special day during April, which has been designated as Child Welfare Month.

Main attraction of the open house is the older boys' building, which was completed in January 1964 at a cost of $45,000. The $10,000 bank note that was necessary to complete the building is expected to be liquidated this weekend with funds contributed by posts, units and individuals, officials of the Home School committee state.

Floyd Throckmorton, Kingfisher, is chairman of the Home School committee. Upon liquidation of the current indebtedness, plans will be made to remodel and renovate the younger boys' building, which is the last building to be remodeled on the school campus.

Earl Summers is superintendent of the Home School and Mr. and Mrs. T. J. Le Flore are commander and president of the local American Legion Post and Auxiliary.

Among the Legion and Auxiliary officials scheduled to be present include members of the Home School committee, Jack Newman of Ponca City and Ike Crawford, Enid' Mrs. W. E. Gilmore, El Reno, department president; Mrs. George Demke, Oklahoma City, department secretary-treasurer; Walter Bonham, Oklahoma City, department child welfare officer; Monroe Darragh, Kingfisher, state Veterans Commission, and Dick Atkinson, Oklahoma City, Home School liaison member.

VOCATIONAL TRAINING

Vocational training is provided for the students in the schools. Boys can take machine shop welding, electricity, cabinet making, architectural drafting or blue print reading. Commercial courses are offered in typing, bookkeeping and shorthand. Girls may select home making courses in cooking, sewing or mean planning.

The home school provides typewriters and sewing machines so students may practice at the home. Summer instruction is given in typewriting, shorthand, beauty culture, sewing and cooking. The school recently installed a permanent wave machine and hair dryer and a Hoffman press, so students can take instructions in beauty culture or in the cleaning and pressing trade.

ALHS SCOUTS GIVING THANKS, 1951: BILLY DODD ~ ALFRED GRISSO ~ RICHIE FIELDS ~ UNKNOWN ~ TRUMAN KIETH

**OLDER SCOUTS LATE 50'S
L-R: JIM WHEELER ~ ROBERT HOYT ~ RICHARD HOYT ~ BILL BAILEY
BACK ROW: UNKNOWN ~ UNKNOWN ~ T.L. RIDER ~ MR SUMMERS**

1958 DESCRIPTION: TOM DONOVAN SCOUT MASTER

**BACK ROW: GENE WYATT ~ BILL HOYT ~ BOBBY DODD ~ BILLY DODD ~ JIM WHEELER
SITTING ROW: ROBERT HOYT ~ RICHARD HOYT ~ TOM DONOVAN ~
RICHARD GREGORY -NY GUIDE ~ CLIFFORD OVERTURF
SIGN: BILL BAILEY TO LEFT AND DARRELL BEAN**

1962 PHILMONT SCOUT RANCH

SCOUT MASTER TOM DONAVAN

**BACK ROW: JOHN BRISSELL ~ BOB APPLEMAN ~ DON BAILEY ~ JOHN MAHORNEY~
JERRY EVANS ~ EDWARD MCEQWIN
SEATED: JAMES HAMILTON ~ LUTHER GRISSO ~ TOM DONVAN ~ JIMMY LOWE~
KENNETH COE ~ EDDIE GLOVER**

**BARBRA MAHORNEY AND WILMA THURSTON
WITH BIKE DURING PLAYTIME**

DARLENE AND CHARLENE WILSON

**JANICE FRANKLIN ~ DONNIE BAILEY ~ BILL
BAILEY ~ JOHN MICHON ~ TRUMAN KIETH ~ MARY
COPLIN
1954**

**JANICE FRANKLIN ~ CAROLYN DODD
~VICKY STALINGS ~ LINDA FIELDS ~ SUSAN
SUMMERS
AUX DAY 1954**

L-R: BEVERLY WHEELER ~ SUSAN SUMMERS ~ MARY COPELAND (THE COOK'S DAUGHTER) ~ LOUISE WRIGHT ~ BACK ROW IS PAULINE HODSON ~ CAROLYN ALFORD ~ PENNY KEITH ~ VIRGINIA FINCH ~ CAROLYN DODD ~ ROBERTA BEATTY

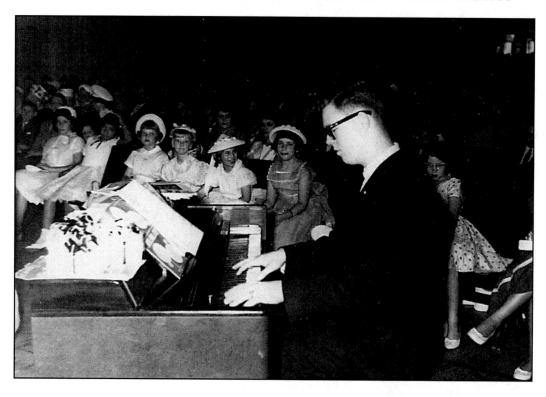

NORVAL 'BUTCH' BRYSON PLAYING ON AUXILLARY DAY, 1958 L-R BARBRA MAHORNEY ~ TROY (BROTHER) ~ SALLIE MAHORNEY, MY NIECE

Chapter Nineteen

Activities at the Home School

Stories about the Home School have appeared in many newspapers throughout the years, since 1928. These stories cover a variety of subjects, but help to explain the philosophy of life at the Home. They also tell about the many people who have contributed things, time, money and love to help enrich the lives of sons and daughters of American war veterans. Here are some of those stories:

HONOR STUDENTS VISIT WITH COMMANDER

Ponca City News ~ February 20, 1936

Honor students of American Legion Home School who brought in top grades for the first semester of school had the privilege of dining with the National Commander of the American Legion, Roy Murphy, and Wednesday evening. He visited the school immediately upon arrival in the city and stayed for dinner.

This group of 21 students includes one senior high school student, eight junior high school students and twelve in the grades.

The students are: Pauline Hill, senior high; Oma Conrad, Emma Fay Conrad, Porter Masters, Cornelius Hobbs, Bertha Justice, Alvia Minor, Oleta Tiner, Delbert Adair, all of the junior high; J. R. Tabor, Elvis Reynolds, Paul Masters, Ethel Greenwood, Arthur and Dorothy Warren, Marvin and Madeline Kinchen, Clifford Penrod, Dorothy Reynolds, Clifford Bingh, and Jessie Westmorland.

VOCATIONS TAUGHT AT LEGION HOME

Ponca City News ~ March 9, 1936

The development of a vocational program at the American Legion Home School is a new task that the school committee and the American Legion of Oklahoma has set itself, explained J. H. Crosby, superintendent of the school, in a talk before the Rotary Club Monday. Two boys are now 18 and most of them are in their teens. The Legion feels, stated Crosby, that definite training must be a part of its program, if capable, independent citizens are to be developed.

Already a start has been made. Two barber chairs have been installed. One boy is already a trained barber and a second is developing rapidly. The two cut hair for the 102 children in the Home.

Following Crosby's talk, he introduced the school's Hillbilly Band, composed for the occasion of T. L. Rider, Harrison Beatty, J. R. Tabor, Jiggy Rider and Elmer Dunlap. They wore appropriate costumes and gave five numbers in true hillbilly style.

BRADLEY, CARTER - THE SONS CARRY ON

Ponca City News ~ July 19, 1942

On a green bluff overlooking the valley of the Arkansas River, near Ponca City, is a home which boasts of 32 sons in the armed services of the United States.

These sons are with MacArthur in Australia, are "somewhere in the Middle East," and are scattered throughout the western hemisphere from Alaska to Puerto Rico. Though they call the same place home, the men are not blood brothers. But their fathers were buddies, and that counts.

The thirty-two are former residents at the American Legion Home School. All are sons of World War Veterans. They know that democracy is worth fighting for—it helped them to grow to manhood when their fathers, disabled or killed in another war, were unable to provide homes for them.

Until a week ago the group numbered thirty-three. Official word has now been received that one former student at the Home is missing in action.

He is Alvia Lee Minor, who joined the navy on December 7 - the day of Pearl Harbor . . . In Ponca City high school he was a good student and a popular football player.

240

Like many of the other thirty-two men, Alvia left the Home School with plans to work his way through college. Until volunteering he was a student at Capitol Hill Junior College. He had been sponsored at the Home School by the Ponca City Post.

LEGION HOME GIRLS GET DOLLS

Ponca City News ~ April 6, 1950

Sixty-five dolls were presented to the Legion Home girls. The dolls, all types and sizes, were purchased by an anonymous benefactor. Every girl at the Home received a doll and several extras were given to the superintendent, Leroy Baker, for the Home.

LEGION STAG PARTY

Ponca City News ~ June 28, 1950

A Home School fund dutch lunch and stag party was held by the Huff-Minor post 14 according to Carl B. Adams, post commander. The stag party was open to all men regardless of whether or not they were Legionnaires.

Admission was $1.00 for the party. All proceeds were put in the Home School fund.

Committee members in charge were: Harry McAnulty, general chairman; T. J. LeFlore, receptionist; Jack Newman, advanced ticket sales; De Roy Skinner, games and finance; C. O. Melberg, dutch lunch; H. P. Nelson, refreshments.

HOME SCHOOL GIRLS DISPLAY HANDIWORK IN OKLAHOMA CITY

Ponca City News ~ August 16, 1950

More than 150 pieces of work completed by a group of American Legion Home school girls here in textile painting sessions will be displayed at the state American Legion and Auxiliary convention September 24 in Oklahoma City . . .

Mrs. J. Frank Ramsey, 1408 S. Seventh Street, has taught the girls to do all types of textile painting and now is teaching them China painting. The Ramsey basement has been converted into a textile painting room...

So that Ponca Citians may see this work the American Legion Home School will have an open house Sunday from 3 to 5 p.m. at the home school . . .

The girls will have a booth in the lobby of the Municipal building where the convention is to be held . . .

HOME SCHOOL GIRLS CLEAR $325.00 ON PAINTING SALE

Ponca City News ~ September 4, 1950

Home School girls sold their textile paintings at the state Legion convention during the weekend.

The money was placed in the girl's vocational activity fund at the Home School for use by all the girls.

Edith Plott and Shirley Singleton from the Home and Mr. and Mrs. J. Frank Ramsey arranged the booth in the lobby of the Municipal auditorium in Oklahoma City. Mrs. Ramsey was the teacher of the class, which met in the basement of her home. Mr. and Mrs. Leroy Baker and Mr. and Mrs. Tom Grizzelle of the home attended the convention. The girls were dressed in stenciled costumes which they made, and were presented to the several thousand Legionnaires and auxiliary members present. They were Lois Owens, Carla Stevens, Lila Hammers, Sue Boss, Dulin Snider, and Betty Calvert.

Various Legion posts and auxiliary units contributed money to purchase materials and paints for this project.

LEGION HOME CHILDREN WILL ATTEND CARNIVAL

Ponca City News ~ June 5, 1952

Boys and girls of the American Legion Home School will be guests at the Don Franklin Shows this evening, starting at 6:30. The carnival is being sponsored by the Junior Chamber of Commerce.

TWO BOYS SELECTED FOR TRIP TO PHILMONT

Ponca City News ~ June 2, 1955

John Snyder and Bruce Wyatt were selected to represent the American Legion Home School on expedition to Philmont Scout Ranch in New Mexico June 23 to July 5, according to Earl Summers ~ School Superintendent, and Lee Askey ~ Chairman of the School's Committee.

The boys, both patrol leaders in the school troop, will join 10 other state Scouts on the trip to the famed Boy Scout Ranch. Both will serve as assistant Scout masters of their local troop on their return

IRRIGATION SYSTEM STARTED FOR HOME

Ponca City News ~ February 26, 1956

The first step in setting up a sprinkler irrigation system on the American Legion Home School's 60 acre farm east of town was completed Friday as workmen capped a 57-foot water supply well.

Home School Superintendent Earl Summers said the well will tap underground waters of the Arkansas River at expected 300-400 gallon-per-minute clip.

Present plans as outlined by M. L. Atkinson, home committee chairman, call for a motor and pump to be installed at the well later this week. Sprinkler heads and piping will be laid probably in March or April.

Summers says the irrigation project, financed by Ponca City businessmen and Home School backers over the state, has a multiple purpose.

Primarily, the watering system will allow Home School students to utilize their 60-acre farm to the fullest extent in truck farming vegetables for school consumption and alfalfa for the school's herd of cattle.

"We also plan for this project to provide training for Home School children in connection with their 4-H Club work and give them an outlet for their time during summer vacation months," the superintendent said.

Winters Drilling Company of Enid is handling drilling operations on a reduced cost basis.

There were many more newspaper stories about gifts to the Home School, but the following article that appeared in the Ponca City News on December 9, 1956 is a good example of how Legion Posts and Auxiliaries took care of the needs at the Home School.

HOME SCHOOL GIFTS RECEIVED

Contributions to the American Legion Home School received during November from posts and auxiliaries over the state totaled $2,084.51, according to department headquarters.

These gifts were in response to a call for items needed at the school, and included $300 from Vinita for the purchase of chests of drawers; $100 from Miami for study tables; $40 from Bartlesville $20 from Ramona for blankets; $400 from Oklahoma City for a laundry extractor $400 from Guthrie for a laundry dryer.

Of the total cash gifts, $114.11 was designated for the milk fund of the Home School.

It was also announced that a gift of $500 from the Claremore unit has boosted the student loan fund to $2,200. The goal for the fund is $5,000.

Gifts other than money received by the school during the past month includes twenty-nine blankets from the state units, and two picnic tables, two sliding boards and two sets of four swings from the Valley Steel Products Company of St. Louis, Missouri. These tables, slides and swings are now set up and being used by the children.

A kitchen range was given by Chickasha Post 54 and the Blackwell post has reported that they have ordered a new stove for the Home School. Three new washing machines have been pledged by the McAlester Post 79.

AMERICAN LEGION HOME SCHOOL DAY

Ponca City News ~ April 3, 1957

Legionnaires and Auxiliary members were guests of the children all during the day. The Home was open for inspection to everyone. A luncheon was served by the staff at noon.

District caravans were made. On each of these caravans, linen and towels, jellies and cash contributions are made by the Legionnaires and Auxiliary members.

VALLEY VIEW HOME DEMONSTRATION CLUB MAKES CURTAINS

Ponca City News ~ August 21, 1958

Women of the Club furnished one sleeping room in the senior girl's dormitory with new curtains for eight windows. The gift was part of the Club's co unity service project, and plans have been made to provide additional curtains for the other rooms in the dormitory.

SALE OF CORPORATION STOCK WILL FINANCE EGG FACTORY

Ponca City News ~ May 22, 1961

Share of stock in Ponca City's newest corporation is selling like hot- cakes in over-the-counter trading across the state.

Although the unique stock returns no monetary dividend, over 300 shares of a

500-share block have already been sold in the past few weeks.

The money at $5 per share will finance Chicken, Inc., a new project designed to put Ponca City's American Legion Home School in the chicken farming business.

Home School Superintendent Bucky Summers says the $2,500 obtained through the stock sale will buy a 500-unit egg factory to be constructed on home school grounds.

The program will provide Home School youngsters with educational d profitable job during spare hours. In addition to extra spending money, Chicken, Inc. will provide a dependable source of fresh eggs.

HOME SCHOOL NOTES

The Oklahoma Legionnaire ~ November, 1961

Several of the children participated in the Youth Choir Festival at the Oklahoma Baptist University in Shawnee. The Chapel Choir, of which they are members, received an A-rating. Those making the trip were: Nancy Curnutte, Dianne and Donna Cowling, Mary Childers, Rose Rusted, Luther Grisso and Don Bailey.

The East Junior High Ninth Grade Glee Club attended a showing of the opera 'Rigoletto' in Tulsa on Saturday. The management allowed time to show the children backstage where they were explained the procedure for color and sound effects, and various phases of production. They thoroughly enjoyed the opera and the trip. Those making the trip were: Lavonne Lanter, John Brissel, Beverly Wheeler and Susan Summers.

All of the fourth grade students at McKinley School took part in the Thanksgiving play presented at the school on November 22. Those from the Home School who took part in the program were: Eleanor Breedlove, Dianne Cass, Billy Champlain, Billy Childers, Becky Long, Linda and Gloria Stewart, Roger and George Walton, and Darlene and Charlene Wilson.

Seven members of the Pickens 4-H Club and their leaders, Mrs. Valla Dacus, attended the County meeting in Newkirk, and Mary Childers was elected County Vice-President.

SENATE PAGE

Ponca City News ~ May 16, 1965

Robert Castleberry of the American Legion Home School served as a page in the state senate last week. All during the time Robert was a page the Senate was sitting as a court of impeachment. Sen. Roy Grantham commended Castleberry.

JERRY EVANS WINS EAGLE

Ponca City News ~ June 6, 1965

Jerry Evans received scouting's highest award, the Eagle Scout Rank, in a Court of Honor held at the American Legion Home School June 1. He is Explorer leader of Explorer Post No. 7.

The Court of Honor was convened by Lee Askey, assisted by Tom Donovan, Explorer advisor. Presentation of the colors was followed by the oath of allegiance. Merit badge awards were made by Sam Lee, chairman of the post committee, to Explorers Jerry Evans, John Brissell and Richard Scharnhorst.

The Eagle Rank was presented to Evans by Joe Steichen. Tom Donovan discussed the heraldry and making of the scout emblem, and spoke of the founding of scouting in North America. An eagle feather was presented to Evans to be attached to the Post 7 Totem Pole, a land mark at the Legion Home School.

Members of the scout committee, Legion officials and the Home School student body were present to honor Evans, who is a 1965 graduate of Ponca City High School and a letterman in baseball and track.

CHILDREN'S HOME PRESENTED GAME

Ponca City News ~ December 15, 1976

A group of students at the American Legion Children's Home worked a long time to raise money to buy a Foosball game. After raising the money, they decided to spend it on material, and with the leadership of Barney Barnwell, built a carport, as a birthday present for Mrs. Lola-belle Summers, acting superintendent.

When members of the Chi Omega Alumnae learned about the project, they used money from their annual fund raiser, "Make It, Bake It, Sew It," to buy a Foosball game.

They provided cookies and pop for a party and presented the game to the Children's Home, December 8.

SENATORS AND LEGION LEADERS VISIT CHILDREN'S HOME

Ponca City News ~ August 22, 1977

State Senator Roy Grantham, Ponca City, along with many American Legion officials had lunch with the children at the American Legion Children's Home Saturday.

A ceremony was held at 11 a.m. at the flagpole circle and Sen. Grantham presented the children of the Home a flag that had flown over the nation's capital. The flag was provided by District One Congressman James R. Jones.

Senator Grantham also gave each child a copy of the Oklahoma Senate yearbook to be used in history and social studies classes.

This event was a follow-up of a visit to the state Senate last February by 46 boys and girls of the Home.

LEGION HOME KIDS HIT $100,000 MARK

Ponca City News ~ November 7, 1978

This election year has been a boon to the members of the American Legion Children's Home Student Council, who have walked thousands of steps since April to deliver 100,000 handbills.

Under the supervision of "Barney" Barnwell, the organizer, volunteer chairman, and activities coordinator for the council, the group beginning in the spring with one truck and 12 youths.

Due to the political campaigning the business has become so lucrative that in recent months the operation has expanded to a fleet of three trucks and a work force of 50 youths.

Barnwell says that the council can now hand out 2,500 handbills an hour. Although politicians have been the principal clients for several months, the youths do deliver for anyone who pays for their services.

The group is non-partisan, handing out advertisements for both Democrats and Republicans. .

In addition to Barnwell, other truck drivers are his wife, Vonda and Sharon Scwarnhorst.

Since August 7 the groups has been on most all of the streets 34 different times and have hit almost every house 17 or 18 times with everything from giveaways to political handbills and have walked about 3,785 miles.

The money the group raises goes to provide activities on a group level including skating parties, movies and trips to Frontier City and Six Flags over Texas.

Each year the council donates something for the Legion Home. This year the money will be used to buy plaques for the buildings on the grounds including one for the late director "Bucky" Summers.

ACTIVITIES AT THE HOME

Oklahoma Legionnaire ~ April, 1981

A trip to Bokoshe, Oklahoma to camp out was reported as being great fun and included hunting and fishing. Mr. Danley and Mr. Sisco accompanied the older boys for the weekend trip, taking tents, bedrolls and plenty to eat.

The younger boys made a trip to Kaw Lake for fishing and a picnic, accompanied by Mr. and Mrs. Daly.

In February the Ceramics Class had a regular instruction lesson and worked on painting rabbit and Easter figurines. The teachers were from the Prague Auxiliary Unit, Mrs. Iris Gragg, Mrs. Shirley Estes, Mrs. Alice and Miss Alice.

Lawton Post 29 funded a big Easter Party! There was a dance and concert in the gym, with a live band. Easter baskets were provided for each of the younger boys and girls, and they went to Lake Ponca for the annual big Easter Egg Hunt.

The small boys from Summers Hall, and Mr. and Mrs. Daly, made a trip to Oklahoma City to visit the Omniplex and the Planetarium. The boys enjoyed lunch at the home of Mr. Daly's parents, and then had a picnic supper in Lincoln Park before returning home.

All the girls from Holloway Hall enjoyed an outing at Great Salt Plains for a campout, and have also made a trip to Alabaster Caverns recently, accompanied by their House Mothers, Miss Taylor and Miss Breon, and Linda Reser. The girls pitched tents and cooked and had a good time exploring.

CHILDREN'S HOME NOTES

Oklahoma Legionnaire ~ January, 1982

John Dryden and his son presented to Superintendant Charles Danley the keys to a 1964 farm pickup which Stillwater American Legion Post 129 gave to the Children's Home. The truck has good tires and runs well, and the boys at the Home are very pleased to have it for farm chores and hauling.

The Future Home Makers Club and Dorothy Scott, Advisor, of Ponca City High School held their annual Christmas Party on December 1st for the grade school age children of the Home. This is always a fun affair with games and caroling, gifts for each child given out by Santa Claus, and lots of goodies for refreshments.

Fifteen boys are participating in basketball practice at the Home, with Leonard Williams as Coach. Games will be played in the local Church League.

Sylvia Pogue, 4th District Children and Youth Chairman, delivered a large linen shower from her district, in November. Also, Pawhuska Post and Unit 198 delivered both cash and linens.

MAX L. STOKESBERRY
LEGION KIDS TO OPEN NEW POPCORN ENTERPRISE

Ponca City News ~ May 23, 1984

With financial help and other encouragement from a Wichita, Kansas couple, the boys and girls of the American Legion Children's Home are preparing to open a popcorn business in Plaza 14 on North Fourteenth Street. Grand opening of the "Lil Kernels" is scheduled for Friday, June 1.

All 50 young people of the Home will have an active part in the operation, according to Larry Smith, the Home's executive director. Each will be paid for the hours he or she works. It has been set up as a non-profit venture with any income in excess of expenditures going into the Recreation Department at the Home, Smith said.

A gift of $10,000 from Ralph E. and Gertrude O'Conner Hartman is making the enterprise possible. The couple, who has been supportive of the Children's Home in several areas the past year, was interested in helping sponsor a project that would give the children hands-on training in operating a small business.

Mrs. Hartman , who grew up in Ponca City and continues to keep a home here, said the boys and girls will run the store, keep the books, learn how to wait on customers, operate the cash register, keep inventory record, buy supplies and make their own business decisions...

The young people will have adult supervision at the store. Kathy Jarvis, who graduated from Oklahoma State University, has been hired to head up the vocational training.

Mrs. Hartman said she and her husband, oil producer, were introduced to the youngsters and staff at the Home by Dr. Jim Thomas about a year ago. Apparently, they were favorably impressed.

"They are a super bunch of kids," Mrs. Hartman says enthusiastically.

The Hartman's, now frequent visitors at the Home, gave a barbecue for the children last July 4. Last Christmas they took them to dinner at a Country Club in Wichita, and afterward had each one fitted with a new pair of boots at a western store.

They have donated three horses and tack, a 26-foot boat, a barbecue with a trailer, as well as some pet pygmy goats, all for use of the children.

The former Gertrude Daack, Mrs. Hartman said while she was growing up some of her friends were from the Children's Home. She added that she and her husband were orphans who "were lucky to have been adopted by good parents. We both love kids."

A third member of the family; Mrs. Hartman's daughter Karen (Mrs. Steven Baker), has become part of the popcorn project by designing the logo for the new business.

Recently the Hartman's received a Certificate of Appreciation from the Department of Human Services for their efforts in behalf of youngsters in the Kay County DHS Child Welfare program.

There are 24 DHS children, as well as 26 private placement youngsters, at the Home and are all Veteran's children.

Chapter Twenty

Where Are They Today?

A reunion of the largest family in Oklahoma was held in Ponca City on August 21, 1983. It was the first get-together in 55 years for a family made up of children of Oklahoma war veterans. There were 120 present and it was a day of tears, laughter and memories for ex-residents of the American Legion Children's Home School in Ponca City.

When the Home was started in 1928, it met the need of that time (which was to care for the orphans of World War I veterans). None of the people who gathered in Ponca City on that Gala Day on June 17 to dedicate the Home School had the slightest idea that there would be children of veterans still needing help in 1984. But the American Legion was organized with a pledge to help their buddies, and that promise has never wavered.

By the time the first residents of the Home graduated from high school, they became involved in the service of their country during World War II. This was the time Governor Marland had predicted for converting the Children's Home to a home for old soldiers. But he couldn't have known that there would be a World War II, or conflicts in Korea or in Vietnam.

Before World War II was over the Legion Home again was needed as a refuge for veterans' children. Today, the need is still there with 14% of the residents being children of World War II veterans, 14% children of Korean veterans and children of Vietnam veterans.

There are only about 50 children at the Legion Home now but at one time there were as many as 200 children living there. Today most of the children stay at the Home short periods of time and there is a great turn-over in the enrollment. During the earlier times some children were completely orphaned and were adopted, but most children came with brothers and sisters and stayed ten to fifteen years until they graduated from high school. The Home School became the only home and family they could remember.

Each year the needs seem to change, but the American Legion Children's Home changes to meet the needs of the time. It is still unique, and the only one of its kind in the world.

Many hundreds have graduated from the Home and have said "good-bye" to their "parents" and have taken with them their diversified talents and abilities. They have established homes and are making individual contributions to society. Some have remained in Ponca City. Some have gone to other communities in Oklahoma and in other states.

One became a two-star general in the United States Army, and other served on the staff of General Douglas MacArthur. Still other served in the Bureau of Indian Affairs in Washington, D. C. There are doctors, lawyers, electrical contractors, ministers, teachers, real estate brokers, beauticians, mechanics, housewives, mothers and fathers.

Many of them met problems when they came face to face with the world without a houseparent or a sponsor to guide them, but they discovered that other young people had problems when they left the home nest, too.

The majority of the graduates are now active in school, civic affairs, going to the polls to vote, and taking their place among those who are the strength of America today.

An Alumni Association was organized and held a second meeting in Ponca City at the American Legion Hut of Post 14 on August 25th and 26th. The members voted to make it an annual event. Although they have been separated for years by miles, careers, new family ties, and even wide differences in age, there is a bond between them that only they can understand.

THE FIRST REUNION IN AUGUST 1983

OLDER ALUMNI AT THE REUNION
FRONT: JANICE NEELY ~ MADELAINE KINCHEN ~ ALICE APPEL ~ JOANNE
MONGER ~ JANICE CALVERT~
BACK: LORETTA HERNANDEZ ~ BILL BAILEY ~ REV. BRUCE WYATT ~ DR. FRED
REYNOLDS ~ FRANK WRIGHT ~ BARNEY CALVERT ~ HAROLD WATSON~

OLDER GROUP REUNION
FRONT: CARLA HAYDEN ~ MADLAINE KINCHEN ~
~ JOANNE MONGER ~ ALICE APPEL ~ JANICE CALVERT ~
BACK: FRANK WRIGHT ~ BILL BAILEY ~ FRED REYNOLDS ~
~ BRUCE WYATT ~ BARNEY CALVERT ~

50 YEAR REUNION
BACK ROW ARE THREE: VIRGINA EVANS ~ LAVONNE LANTER MACDONALD ~ SUSAN SUMMERS MARKS~
L-R FRONT ROW: RITA CHILDERS HARTZOG ~ DIANN COWLING ~ CAROL STEWART FREE ~ JUDYA
MINGUS GARRISON ~ VERDA EVANS SISNEY ~ SHERRY BRISSEL BEAN ~ BARBRA MAHORNEY ~ LINDA
STEWART DUNDEE

BARBRA (MAHORNEY) ALUSI ~ LINDA (STEWART) DUNDEE ~ RITA
(CHILDERS) HARTZOG ~ DIANN COWLING ~ MARY (CHILDERS) BOLDING ~
SHERRY (BRISSEL) BEAN

**BARBRA ALUSI AND LINDA (STEWART) DUNDEE
AT THE 50TH YEAR REUNION AT THE HOME**

**MY LIFE TIME FRIEND SINCE WE
WERE AGE TWELVE CONNIE
(ZEMP) DUNAGAN AND MY
ROOMMATE FROM AGE 9 NANCY
(CURNETTE) BUTLER**

50 YEAR REUNION 2007
IN FRONT: SANDY BRISSEL JACKSON ACTING CRAZY ~ L-R BARBRA MAHORNEY ALUSI ~ VERDA EVANS
SISNEY ~ YVONNE LANTER MCDONALD PEEKING OVER LINDA STEWART DUNDEE'S SHOULDER ~
CAROL STEWART FREE ~ JUDYA MINGUS GARRISON ~ RITA CHILDERS HARTZOG BETWEEN SHERRY
BRISSEL BEAN ~ DIANN COWLING LOOKING OVER ~ VIRGINIA EVANS ~ MARY CHILDERS BEHIND HER ~
SUSAN SUMMERS MARKS

From The Author

Mrs. Barbra Mahorney Alusi

BARBRA & MRS. MAYHUE ON HER 17TH BIRTHDAY

First of all this is the largest, most work intensified project that I have ever gotten myself into. I have realized quickly that it's not a job for the meek or certainly not for the lazy or one that I can take lightly.

I have said it many, many times to everyone who'll listen, that God is the one who planted the seed in me to do this book way back when I was arranging the first reunion. That was back in 1983 when I was first facing back surgery. At that time I had a young family, my youngest son Safie was a baby at 10 months old, his older brothers Demetrius and Lee were 4 and 10. The surgery was a new surgery that they no longer do because too many people died from complications of allergic reactions.

After the doctor visit where he told me that I needed the surgery and wanted to schedule it in the next coming days, he gave me a prescription to start taking for 48 hours before the surgery. The pharmacist asked me what was I having done. I told him and he said, "Don't let them do it, because this prescription is a strong anti-shock medication and this dose they've given you means they anticipate you dying."

I had been in so much pain before my delivery and it only had intensified since. Now it was so bad that I could hardly carry Safie. I started praying even harder asking God to spare my life, if not for my sake then for the sake of my babies. The procedure was a new surgery called kymo-pipain injection. They take the enzyme of the papaya and inject into my ruptured disc and it would act like a meat tenderizer and dissolve the disc. I had seen it talked about on a news program declaring it was less intrusive than normal back surgery where they cut. This one just consisted of one simple injection into the ruptured disc. They had found that women were highly allergic during their monthly cycle so the surgery would be scheduled away from my time of the month. They asked me if I would allow them to film the procedure since it such a new surgery, I said yes. It then would be used as a teaching tool for other doctors wanting to learn to perform the surgery. I was also happy when they told me that I would be awake during the surgery. I liked the idea, as I've had a problem waking up from anesthesia. The way I understood their explanation was, patients who were allergic to the medication would get a rash and go into shock and could die.

I had all my family and friends praying for me and I was wheeled into the operating room. I was lying on the table watching everyone set up for the surgery. I was praying and I heard God say to me, 'you're going to be allergic.' I told the nurse those exact words and added I didn't want to have the surgery because I didn't want to die. She went and got the doctor from the scrub room and he stood beside me and asked me what was wrong. I repeated what I told the nurse. He said "you're in a great deal of pain."

"Yes," I said, "but point is I am alive and I can feel the pain. If I am dead I can't feel anything." He said to let him just put in a small amount and that will be better than nothing and I agreed.

I realize that when I tell my story of things that happen to me like this, people look at me like I've grown another head. That's okay, I found things to be disconcerting at first and would question if it was Him or if I was trying to put words in His mouth. So during my talks with God, some might say I was trying to bargain with Him. Call it what you may but it sounded a lot like begging from my point of view. I did say to him I realized that I was not doing anything for others, and I was only taking care of my immediate family. I did ask Him if He would spare my life, I would do whatever He gave me to do.

The doctor came in and injected the medication, and I heard the nurse say "she was right." I don't remember feeling anything other than that I was alive and fine. I was taken into recovery and the Doctor was standing beside me using the phone beside my bed talking to my husband. He was telling him that he could have lost me had I not told him that I was going to be allergic, keeping him from giving me the full amount.

After the doctor left I must have fallen asleep and when I awoke I remember looking around the recovery room and thinking 'I've died, and oh my God I am in the morgue.' The reason I thought that was because all I could see were the outline of bodies covered with white sheets. Then God said to me 'go and do the first reunion of the American Legion Home School,' where I had grown up from ages 9 to 18. No, He didn't appear to me, he just came to me mentally, trust me I knew that it was Him.

When I got out of the hospital I started working on the reunion. The surgery took place in April and when I got home from the hospital I had to walk five miles a day. I would use my walking time to formulate my plans. First of all, believe me when I say that I believed with my whole heart that God had given me this to do. And I also believed that He would relay to me each step I took.

One of the first things I did was to contact Mrs. Summers; she was the wife of Mr. Earl Summers, who had been the Superintendent when I lived there. He had passed away but she was still working at the Home as an Assistant. I told her about how I was planning the reunion for that August. I know that she thought I had lost my mind and tried her best to tell me that I was really biting off more than I knew, saying it took as much as a full year for the kids at the local high school to plan and arrange their class reunions, and at least they had a list of students they were looking for. "Barbra you don't even know who you're looking for." I confirmed her thinking that I was nuts when I told her that God was going to do this through me and I was trusting that He would find everyone that was supposed to be there. This is the way I kept thinking throughout the whole planning process. If I ran into a problem I would pray and He would give me an answer while I was sleeping. I always say it was because sleeping was the only time that I wasn't talking.

Four months after my surgery we had the reunion, in August of 1983, and not surprisingly everything did run smoothly. All alumni joined together as one family, the older generation mixed together with the younger generation. It was a wonderful experience for all who attended.

It was at that time He came to me again, this time He told me that He was giving me a book. I could see clearly exactly what the book looked like. I later heard a sermon by Charles Stanley that when God gives you something like the book to do, he gives you the beginning, the middle and the end. In other words I could literally visually see the completed book. It finally sunk in that He said He was giving me a book and I said, "God this is Barbra, you know the 'cute one'… but don't you remember I am the one that can't spell?" And of course spelling was least of my worries good heavens. "Don't get me wrong God; I am willing to do whatever it is you want me to do. And if you really want to give me the book and you really think I can do it…then I will take it."

He continued His conversation with me by saying there is just one catch Barbra; yes God, what is that? You are to give all the proceeds back to the Home as a way of saying thank you. Ok God I will… and that is exactly what I did.

I was living in Broken Arrow, Oklahoma at the time when I realized my mail carrier was none other than one of the girls that had lived in the junior girls building when I lived there. Her name was Verda Evans Sisney; I hadn't known her well because she was much younger than me. She and Linda Stewart Dundee helped me with the reunion. And now she agreed to help me on this new venture by driving to Ponca City, Oklahoma to the American Legion Children's Home. We were looking for photos to put into the book.

I was really hoping to find photos of Mrs. Mayhue who had been my housemother for the nine years that I lived in the Legion Home and I was disappointed that I didn't find any. She had died right after my senior year; I had left right before she died and I had not known when she died. Needless to say I was unable to attend her funeral. I went to a counselor and he told me that I had to say goodbye to Mrs. Mayhue, saying it wasn't healthy to not face her death. While in Ponca doing my search for photos for the book I had found Mrs. Mayhue's old scrapbooks. I can remember her sitting in the Sunroom putting the scrapbooks together.

After returning home I spent the whole next day in bed crying. My husband became concerned and told me that he didn't want me to do the book if it was going to affect me this much. He was worried that it would upset the boys seeing me like this. I told him no, that I had to face all these different emotions in order to do a good job with the book.

That night, after crying all day God gave me a dream of Mrs. Mayhue's funeral. In the dream I was standing in the front of the Baptist church where we went to church and the church was full. The people of the congregation seemed as real, as if I was actually standing there at the pulpit. I was giving her eulogy, telling everyone how much I loved her and how she had become a mother to me and hundreds of other girls who had been in her care. When I awoke I was still crying and had tears on my face. The dream made me want to continue the

connection that I felt. So wanting to feel close to her, I picked up one of the scrapbooks that I had watched her lovingly put together and started turning the pages. All of a sudden I decided to un-tape a photo, I don't remember what photo it was but the tape was yellowed and pages were crumbling in my hands. I was shocked when I pulled the picture back and found another photo, it was not just any photo it was a picture of Mrs. Mayhue and me taken on my 17th birthday. For some reason she had hidden that picture and it had lain hidden for over 20 years. Can you imagine the shock and

the joy of knowing that this was a clear gift from God? First He gave me the healing dream of her death, allowing me to face her death and heal so I could move on with my life, then gave me the hidden photo. Well it was amazing how He orchestrated the whole life changing experience. I simply followed His instructions in doing the book and He rewarded me, with everything I needed to do what He wanted me to do. I thought; had I not followed His directions to do the reunion or to do the book as He told me to, I would never have reached this awesome healing that I had just experienced. I realized quickly that to receive all His gifts and blessing I had to trust what He gave me to do. And that is exactly what I was going to do with the entire project.

When this happened it was Christmas time and my husband Thana had been laid off from his job and he was in his last days at Tulsa University. We didn't have money to even have the boys' pictures taken with Santa Claus, so we took them to the Legion Post 1 in Tulsa; they had a Santa and were giving out treats to the kids of the members. My youngest son Safie was now 4 years old and he told Santa that he wanted a shirt for Christmas. My husband had tears in his eyes and said what kind of father am I that I can't even afford to buy my son a shirt. I told him that God had given my sons the best father and me the best husband in the whole world, and that everything would work out according to His plan.

The next day, Thana was outside of our condo working with the two boys, when a huge long limo drove up. The driver got out and let a gentleman wearing a 3 piece suit out. He walked up to my husband, and asked if he could tell him where Thana Alusi lived? "I am Thana," said my husband.

"Well I am from the Kiplinger Foundation and we heard from the University that you're a wonderful man who is down on his luck and we want you to have Christmas," said the man.

The driver had taken out baskets of food and boxes of gift-wrapped packages turning to my husband saying "These are for you and your family, Merry Christmas."

The boys were so excited that when the man left they asked to open one gift and we agreed. I don't remember what Demetrius got but Safie; the youngest, who had asked Santa for a shirt had unwrapped a shirt. So you see how much God revealed himself to us, there was never a question in our minds that God had given us these gifts. I had done as He had instructed me to do in giving all my proceeds back to the Home. We didn't have money and any amount from the sale of the books would have been a great deal to us at that time. But you see it was a test of us to see if we would do what He told us to do. Did we have the faith to trust Him to supply us with all our needs, we did. Our reward was watching Him work in our lives supplying my husband with a new job. It was awesome watching Him work in our lives and having Him close.

It was God's timing that the reunion and book was given to me when it was. I believe that His timing is again in play with this new revised version of the book. Think about it, there is a chance that the Home might close and at the same time He gives me the opportunity to revise the first book. I take on the new project and once again I am following His complete instructions. I believe that the revised book, along with my personal story of living and growing up in the Home, will help bring an awareness of all the good that the Home did for us Legion kids. It can help in raising money so they can go back to the way it once was when they didn't take federal funding.

First of all I am doing this project because God has directed me to and as a gift to my sons and granddaughters, so they will know from me just how lucky I was to have grown up with over 100 other kids. Second, I did it for all my alumni sisters and brothers. Yes I have put in a great deal of time and money into these books, as well as taking time away from my own children while I was working on them, but the outcome has been well worth everything that I have put into to them.

I have told this story of why I am doing this book so many times before, in hopes that everyone sees just how much God has done in my life. After pouring my heart and soul into doing these books and following God's directions every step of the way, I truly believe that I was blessed for being able to work with Him.

Like Mrs. Mayhue used to always say, "Give to the world the best you have and the best will come back to you." Here is my best and I pray that you enjoy.

Thank you and God Bless,
Barbra Mahorney Alusi ~ Alumni 1957-1966